WRITE SOURCE

2OOO

A Guide to WRITING, THINKING, and LEARNING

Teacher's Guide
to the handbook

. . . a teacher's guide to accompany

WRITE SOURCE

2OOO

WRITE SOURCE®

GREAT SOURCE EDUCATION GROUP

a Houghton Mifflin Company
Wilmington, Massachusetts

www.greatsource.com

About the
Teacher's Guide

The Teacher's Guide will help you use the *Write Source 2000* handbook effectively in your classroom, and it will also give you many tips and techniques for working with young writers and learners. We have tried to address the "big questions" teachers are asking today in a way that will help you integrate your professional experience with current research.

If you have any questions, please call. (Use our toll-free number— 1-800-289-4490.) We are always ready to help or receive feedback.

The Write Source/Great Source Education Group

Written and compiled by
Patrick Sebranek, Dave Kemper, and Verne Meyer
contributors and consultants: Laura Bachman, Diane Barnhart, Carol Elsholz, Candyce Norvell, Lester Smith, Vicki Spandel, John Van Rys

Printed in the United States of America

International Standard Book Number: 0-669-46775-8

4 5 6 7 8 9 10 -POO- 04 03 02 01 00

Table of Contents

A Quick Tour of the Handbook

Write Source 2000 serves as the perfect language handbook for middle-school grades, one that will help your students improve their ability **to write** (prewriting through publishing), **to think** (creatively, logically, clearly), and **to learn** (in the classroom, in small groups, independently). This quick tour will highlight the five main sections of the handbook.

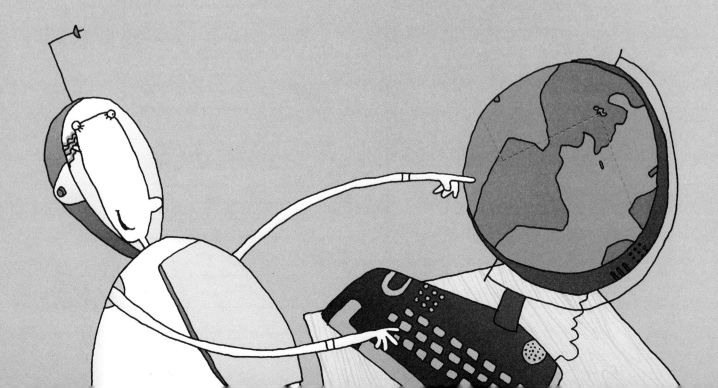

1 The Process of Writing

Students will use this part of the handbook to learn all about the writing process, from building good writing habits to learning about the traits of good writing, from writing with computers to developing persuasive essays.

Colorful illustrations and a personal tone make *Write Source 2000* very attractive to students.

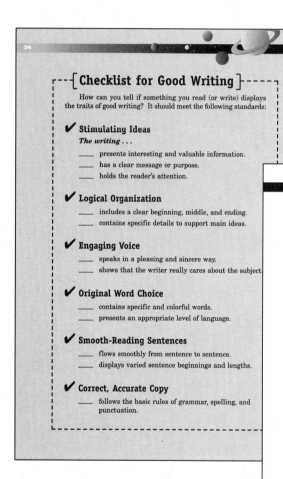

⌐[Checklist for Good Writing]¬

How can you tell if something you read (or write) displays the traits of good writing? It should meet the following standards:

✔ **Stimulating Ideas**
  The writing . . .
  ____ presents interesting and valuable information.
  ____ has a clear message or purpose.
  ____ holds the reader's attention.

✔ **Logical Organization**
  ____ includes a clear beginning, middle, and ending.
  ____ contains specific details to support main ideas.

✔ **Engaging Voice**
  ____ speaks in a pleasing and sincere way.
  ____ shows that the writer really cares about the subject.

✔ **Original Word Choice**
  ____ contains specific and colorful words.
  ____ presents an appropriate level of language.

✔ **Smooth-Reading Sentences**
  ____ flows smoothly from sentence to sentence.
  ____ displays varied sentence beginnings and lengths.

✔ **Correct, Accurate Copy**
  ____ follows the basic rules of grammar, spelling, and punctuation.

Helpful checklists, guidelines, and samples make information easy to use.

Writing with a Computer

What are the tools of the writer's trade? Notebooks, a good supply of favorite pens and pencils, file folders, a few reference books such as your handbook, and a personal computer—all of these might be used during a writing project. For many writers, however, the most important tool is the computer.

Those of you who have used a computer for writing already understand its value. Once you know how to use it, the computer can save you a lot of time. It also makes it easy to work with your writing, allowing you to rearrange information and add new ideas. And it helps you produce clear, readable copy to share with your readers.

WHAT'S AHEAD

Writers who are just getting into computers will find this chapter especially helpful. (Experienced "users" will learn some things as well.) It includes, among other things, a basic guide for writing with a computer and a special section on graphic design.

- ⊙ Understanding the Basics
- ⊙ Designing Your Writing
- ⊙ Effective Design in Action
- ⊙ Using a Word-Processing Program

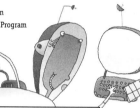

Revising in Action

Note the changes made in this sample to improve the quality of the ideas, organization, and voice. (See pages 14-15 for another example.)

> Ever since movies like <u>Jaws</u>, sharks have gotten a bad reputation. There are more than 300 kinds of sharks from the 19-inch cookie-cutter shark to the 50-foot whale shark. But only about 25 kinds of sharks have ever attacked people. Of the 100 attacks reported each year, few of them are ever fatal.
>
> Sharks are very beneficial to people. Sharks clean the seas of garbage and feed on sick and weak fish. They are also harvested for their luxurious hides for clothing and their flesh for eating.
>
> The great white shark, as seen in <u>Jaws</u>, has attacked people, but then the great white shark will attack just about anything. However, sharks are mostly scavengers and eat dead fish and garbage. Cans, jars, hats, tires, and even license plates have been found in the stomachs of great white sharks. Whatever gets dumped off a boat may end up inside of one of these sharks. ~~Their favorite food is really crab.~~

An interesting detail is added.

A paragraph is reordered.

More personal feeling (voice) is added.

An unnecessary detail is cut.

2 The Forms of Writing

In this part students will find guidelines and samples for personal narratives, book reviews, biographical stories, news stories, summaries, research papers, and much more.

Write Source 2000 addresses many forms of personal, subject, creative, workplace, and report writing.

Sample Personal Narrative

In the following sample, Jodi Klion shares a brief experience that started out as plain fun, but ended up to be much more.

Splash Mountain

BEGINNING
The writer starts right in the middle of the action.

This was it. There was no turning back. As the well-greased wheels pulled slowly up the track, my grip on the steel bar across my lap tightened. I heard shrill screams of excitement from the people in the front row. The train groaned to a halt, halfway up the hill, just far enough for me to see the water rushing down like a powerful natural waterfall.

My father glanced over at me from my right. He was wearing his favorite Mickey Mouse shirt, the one on which Mickey is golfing. His smile matched Mickey's. "Ready?"

MIDDLE
Dialogue helps make the story seem real.

"Even if I wasn't," I answered humorously, "do I have a choice now?"

"Don't forget to smile for the camera when we hit the drop," my father said, reminding me of the Disney tradition of photographing the screaming riders.

My thoughts were interrupted as the train jerked forward, racing us against the wind. It seemed to be only a few seconds. Then, SPLASH! The water at the bottom of the drop covered us like a blanket. When we had finally caught our breath, my father and I exclaimed together, "That was great! Let's go again!" We laughed, and it was then that I felt it. Sitting in drenched clothes, at 7:30 p.m., on a Disney World ride, with trees swaying in the breeze, I felt the strong bond between my father and me. I'm sure he felt it too, as we climbed out of the train.

ENDING
The writer notes the importance of the event.

As we walked to see how our pictures had turned out, Dad put his arm around me. We laughed at our facial expressions in the pictures, and I knew my father and I had done something special.

Writing Research Papers

When you are asked to write a research paper, you must do two things. First, you must learn facts and details about a specific subject. You will do this by reading, observing, and asking questions. Second, you must share this information in a clear, organized paper.

A research paper may include ideas from books, magazines, newspapers, interviews, or the Internet. All ideas borrowed from different sources must be credited to the original writer or speaker. Most research papers are at least three pages in length and may include a title page, an outline, the actual essay, and a works-cited page (bibliography).

WHAT'S AHEAD

This section will help you develop a research paper from start to finish, from selecting a subject to producing a neat final copy to share.

- Writing Guidelines
- Adding a Works-Cited Page
- Adding a Title Page and Outline
- Sample Works-Cited Entries
- Sample Internet Entries
- Sample Research Paper

Writing Guidelines

Prewriting --[Choosing a Subject]

Finding a subject for a biography should be easy. You should be able to think of many people to write about. Here are three ways to search for a subject:

1. Think of a person you know better than anyone else does.
2. Think of a person who has had a big influence in your life.
3. Think of an interesting person you have heard about in one of your classes or from a friend or family member.

Make sure to select a subject that truly interests you and would probably interest your readers, too.

[Gathering Details]

Gathering the best details for your writing may or may not be easy for you. It all depends on the subject you choose to write about. Here is a chart that can help you collect details. (Also see "Planning Tips" on page 165.)

KNOWLEDGE LEVEL	EXAMPLES	SOURCE OF INFORMATION
Well-known subject	mother, brother	Search your memory for ideas. Talk with your subject.
Somewhat-known subject	teacher, grandparent	Search your memory. Watch and take notes. Interview your subject.
Little-known subject	veterinarian, judge	Interview your subject. Watch and take notes. Read any related information.
Famous person	historical figure, author, athlete	Read magazines, library books, encyclopedias. Listen to radio/ TV interviews. Surf the Net.

3 The Tools of Learning

When students have a question about studying, reading, researching, or thinking, they should turn to this part of the handbook for help.

Study-Reading Skills

Study-reading is reading for understanding. It's all about reading efficiently and remembering what you read. It's the kind of reading you do when you read your textbooks, and it's also the kind of reading you do when you gather information for a report or research paper. By study-reading, you can find out . . .

- **who** is doing or has done significant things in this world,
- **what** natural and social changes have occurred,
- **why** certain events are important,
- **how** different things work, and
- much more.

WHAT'S AHEAD

The information in this chapter will help you improve your reading skills. You will learn about common patterns of nonfiction, such as description and comparison. You will also learn about two important study-reading strategies and some ideas for adjusting your reading rate. (Also see pages 361-365.)

Patterns of Nonfiction
Study-Reading Strategies
Adjusting Your Reading Rate

Write Source 2000 makes all aspects of language and learning active, enjoyable, and meaningful.

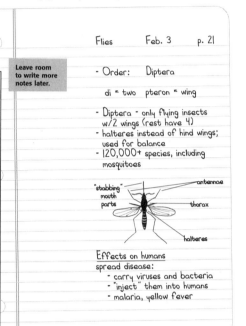

Setting Up Your Notes

Use a notebook or a three-ring binder for your notes and write on only one-half of each page. (A three-ring binder allows you to add and remove pages when you need to.)

Flies　　　Feb. 3　　　p. 21

Leave room to write more notes later.

- Order: Diptera

　di = two　pteron = wing

- Diptera = only flying insects w/2 wings (rest have 4)
- halteres instead of hind wings; used for balance
- 120,000+ species, including mosquitoes

"stabbing" mouth parts — antennae — thorax — halteres

Effects on humans
spread disease:
　- carry viruses and bacteria
　- "inject" them into humans
　- malaria, yellow fever

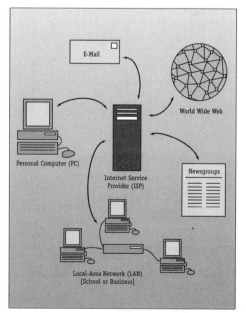

THE INTERNET AT A GLANCE

An Internet service provider (ISP) allows you to conduct research and communicate on-line. The provider gives you access, via a personal computer or a LAN, to the World Wide Web, e-mail, and newsgroups. (Study the chart below to see how the Net works.)

E-Mail

World Wide Web

Personal Computer (PC)

Internet Service Provider (ISP)

Newsgroups

Local-Area Network (LAN) [School or Business]

4 Proofreader's Guide

Whenever students have a question about punctuation, capitalization, usage, and the parts of speech, send them to this color-coded (yellow) part.

Marking Punctuation

Period

A period is used to end a sentence. It is also used after initials, after abbreviations, and as a decimal point.

387.1 — At the End of a Sentence

A period is used to end a sentence that makes a statement or a request, or that gives a command that is not used as an exclamation.

Homes in the future will have many high-tech features. [statement]

Check your video doorbell to see who stopped by while you were gone. [request]

Don't worry. [command]

Your household robot will not reveal your whereabouts unless programmed to do so. [statement]

Note: It is not necessary to place a period after a statement that has parentheses around it and is part of another sentence.

387.2 — After an Initial

A period should be placed after an initial.

E. L. Konigsburg [author]
Marie A. Smith [politician]

387.3 — After Abbreviations

A period is placed after each part of an abbreviation—unless the abbreviation is an acronym. An acronym is a word formed from the first (or first few) letters of words in a set phrase. (See 409.5.)

Abbreviations:

Mr. Mrs. Ms. Dr. B.C.E. C.E.

Acronyms:

AIDS NASA

Note: When an abbreviation is the last word in a sentence, only one period should be used at the end of the sentence.

In the twenty-first century, we'll get more of our energy from renewable sources, such as the sun, the wind, ocean water, etc.

387.4 — As a Decimal

Use a period as a decimal point and to separate dollars and cents.

For $2.99 on Tuesdays, I can rent three videos. But is it a bargain to spend 33.3 percent of my allowance on videos that I won't have time to watch anyway?

This easy-to-use guide answers all your students' editing and proofreading questions.

Editing for Mechanics

Capitalization

404.1 — Proper Nouns, Adjectives

Capitalize all proper nouns and all proper adjectives. A proper noun is the name of a particular person, place, thing, or idea. A proper adjective is an adjective formed from a proper noun.

Common Noun . . . . country, president, continent
Proper Noun . . . . Canada, Andrew Jackson, Asia
Proper Adjective . . . . . . Canadian, Jacksonian, Asian

404.2 — Names of People

Capitalize the names of people and also the initials or abbreviations that stand for those names.

Colin L. Powell, Frances McDormand, Aung San Suu Kyi, Mary Sanchez-Gomez

Note: If a woman uses both her maiden name and married name, the maiden name is listed first, and both are capitalized.

404.3 — Historical Events

Capitalize the names of historical events, documents, and periods of time.

World War I, the Bill of Rights, the Magna Carta, the Middle Ages, the Paleozoic Era

404.4 — Abbreviations

Capitalize abbreviations of titles and organizations.

U.S.A., FBI, M.D., B.C.E., C.E., NATO (North Atlantic Treaty Organization), M.A., Ph.D.

404.5 — Organizations

Capitalize the name of an organization, an association, or a team and its members.

New York State Historical Society, the Red Cross, General Motors Corporation, the Miami Dolphins, Republicans, the Democratic Party

404.6 — Names of Subjects

Capitalize the name of a specific course, but not the name of a general subject. (Exception—the names of all languages are proper nouns and are always capitalized: *French, Hindu, German, Latin.*)

Our summer recreation program offers an art course called Paint a Pet Dish.

Using the Right Word

419.1 — a, an

A is used before words that begin with a consonant sound; *an* is used before words that begin with a vowel sound.

a heap, *a* cat, *an* idol, *an* elephant, *an* honor, *a* historian

419.2 — accept, except

The verb *accept* means "to receive"; the preposition *except* means "other than."

Melissa graciously *accepted* defeat. [verb]

All the boys *except* Zach were here. [preposition]

419.3 — affect, effect

Affect is always a verb; it means "to influence." *Effect* can be a verb, but it is most often used as a noun that means "the result."

How does population growth *affect* us?

What are the *effects* of population growth?

419.4 — allowed, aloud

The verb *allowed* means "permitted" or "let happen"; *aloud* is an adverb that means "in a normal voice."

We weren't *allowed* to read *aloud* in the library.

419.5 — allusion, illusion

An *allusion* is a brief reference or mention of a famous person, place, thing, or idea. An *illusion* is a false impression or idea.

As he made an *allusion* to the great magicians of the past, Houdini created the *illusion* of having sawed his assistant in half.

419.6 — a lot

A lot is not one word, but two; it is a general descriptive phrase (meaning "plenty") that should be avoided in formal writing.

419.7 — already, all ready

Already is an adverb that tells when. *All ready* is a phrase meaning "completely ready."

We are *already* awake and *all ready* for breakfast.

419.8 — alright, all right

Alright is the incorrect spelling of *all right*, a phrase meaning "satisfactory" or "okay." (Please note, the following are spelled correctly: *always, altogether, already, almost.*)

5 Student Almanac

The last section contains a great deal of helpful information for students to use in all of their classes.

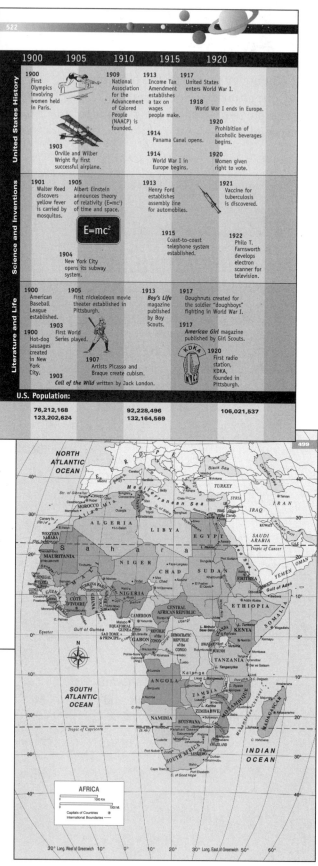

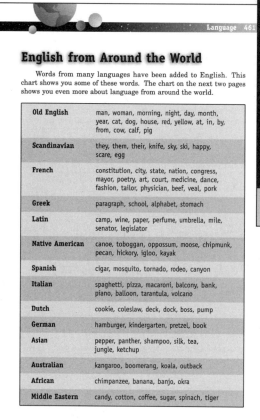

English from Around the World

Words from many languages have been added to English. This chart shows you some of these words. The chart on the next two pages shows you even more about language from around the world.

Old English	man, woman, morning, night, day, month, year, cat, dog, house, red, yellow, at, in, by, from, cow, calf, pig
Scandinavian	they, them, their, knife, sky, ski, happy, scare, egg
French	constitution, city, state, nation, congress, mayor, poetry, art, court, medicine, dance, fashion, tailor, physician, beef, veal, pork
Greek	paragraph, school, alphabet, stomach
Latin	camp, wine, paper, perfume, umbrella, mile, senator, legislator
Native American	canoe, toboggan, opossum, moose, chipmunk, pecan, hickory, igloo, kayak
Spanish	cigar, mosquito, tornado, rodeo, canyon
Italian	spaghetti, pizza, macaroni, balcony, bank, piano, balloon, tarantula, volcano
Dutch	cookie, coleslaw, deck, dock, boss, pump
German	hamburger, kindergarten, pretzel, book
Asian	pepper, panther, shampoo, silk, tea, jungle, ketchup
Australian	kangaroo, boomerang, koala, outback
African	chimpanzee, banana, banjo, okra
Middle Eastern	candy, cotton, coffee, sugar, spinach, tiger

Full-color maps, a historical time line, the metric system—*Write Source 2000* is truly an all-school handbook.

Introducing the Handbook

The pages in this section can be used to introduce *Write Source 2000* to your students and get them started on the road to becoming active, independent learners.

Getting-Started Activities

We created the *Write Source 2000* handbook with the goal of making it a handbook students would like and use every day. To make this a reality, students must first understand what's in the handbook and how they can use it. The activities that follow will introduce the handbook to your students and help them become proficient handbook users. (You will find the answer key for the getting-started activities on page 15.)

Scavenger Hunts

Students enjoy using scavenger hunts to become familiar with the handbook. The scavenger hunts we have provided can be done in small groups or as a class. They are designed for oral answers, but you may want to have your students write answers, especially for "Scavenger Hunt 2." (Have students say or write both the page number where the answer is found and the answer itself.) Also, you may want to vary the procedure, first having students take turns finding the items and then, on the next scavenger hunt, challenging students to "race" for the answers.

After your students have done each scavenger hunt, you can challenge them to create their own versions. For example, small groups can work together to create "Find the Fours" or "Search for Sixes" scavenger hunts and then exchange their "hunts" with other groups.

Special Challenge: Develop questions that teams of students try to answer using the handbook. Pattern this activity after a popular game show.

Other Activities

- Give students the following assignment: Across the top of a sheet of paper, write down three things you find difficult about school (remembering what you read, taking tests, doing math word problems, writing essays, spelling, using commas, etc.). Then explore your handbook to find chapters, sections, examples, and so on, that might help you with your problem area. Under each problem, write the titles or headings and the page numbers where you can find help. Keep this sheet to use throughout the year.

- A variation on the above activity is to have students write down all the subject areas they study and list under each heading the parts of the handbook that might help them in that subject.

- Have students write a thought-trap poem: After reviewing the handbook, close it. The first line of your poem will be the title of the handbook. Then list thoughts and feelings about the handbook, line by line. When you have listed everything you want to say, "trap" your thoughts by repeating the title.

- Have pairs of students create poster-size advertisements for the handbook. Each ad should have a headline, list important features (what is in the handbook) and benefits (whom it can help and how), show an example of illustrations (made by tracing or copying), and urge readers of the ad to get their handbooks now!

- Have students imagine that they are each going to send a copy of *Write Source 2000* to a pen pal in another state. Have each student write a letter to send along with it to tell the pen pal about the handbook.

Your First Week with the Handbook

Resources: *Write Source 2000 Handbook* (HB), iii
Write Source 2000 Teacher's Guide (TG), 7-16

DAY 1

1. Pass out individual copies of *Write Source 2000*. Give students, in pairs, a few minutes to explore the handbook and talk about it.
2. Duplicate and distribute "Getting to Know My Handbook" (TG 10). Have your students work with their partners to complete the activity.

DAY 2

1. Preview "Using the Handbook" (HB iii). Have students turn to the parts of the handbook that are mentioned on this page.
2. Then have students do "Scavenger Hunt 1: Find the Fives" (TG 11).

DAY 3

1. Continue with more getting-started activities (TG 8).
2. Have students work on "Scavenger Hunt 2: What Is It?" (TG 12).

DAY 4

1. Continue with more getting-started activities (TG 8) and "Scavenger Hunt 3: You Need to Know" (TG 13).
2. Give students a few minutes to prepare for a class discussion the next day. Have them take notes and be prepared to share what they like about the handbook, how they plan to use it, and questions they have about it.

DAY 5

1. Have a class discussion in which students share what they like about the handbook, how they plan to use it, and questions they have.
2. Give students "Write Source Word Find" (TG 14) and have them find as many of the 20 words as they can.

Note: Fill in, whenever you need to, with the "Other Activities" (TG 8) and the minilessons (TG 16).

Getting to Know My Handbook

Directions Find suitable words to complete the chart below. Be sure the words you select begin with the letters in the left-hand column. Use each answer only once. *Note:* You may not find answers that correspond to each letter for all of the categories.

	Commonly Misspelled Words	Thinking Terms	Computer Terms	Prepositions	Commonly Misused Words	Countries I Have Never Seen	Topics I Would Like to Write About
W	weird						
R		recalling					
I							
T							
E							
S							
O							
U							
R					red, read		
C							
E							

Scavenger Hunt 1: Find the Fives

Directions If you have not already learned how to use the handbook, read "Using the Handbook" at the front of *Write Source 2000*. Then, in a small group or with your whole class, find the following "fives" in your handbook. The first person to find each "five" should say the page number and then read the five items.

1. **Five** parts of a plot

   _____

2. **Five** steps in the writing process

   _____

3. **Five** types of primary sources

   _____

   _____

4. **Five** magazines that publish student writing

   _____

   _____

5. **Five** units of linear measure used in the metric system

   _____

6. **Five** tips for surfing the Internet

   _____

   _____

7. **Five** transitions that begin with "a" and show time

   _____

8. "**Five** Keys to Good Revision"

   _____

   _____

Scavenger Hunt 2: What Is It?

If you have not already learned how to use the handbook, read "Using the Handbook" at the front of *Write Source 2000*. Then, in a small group or with your whole class, find the answers to the following questions. The first person to find the answer should say the page number and then the answer.

1. What is an *oxymoron*? _____
   _____

2. What is the "Essentials of Life Checklist"? _____
   _____

3. What is a *paraphrase*? _____
   _____

4. What is a *phase biography*? _____
   _____

5. What is a *ballad*? _____
   _____

6. What kind of animal is a *cygnet*? _____
   _____

7. What is an *intensive pronoun*? _____
   _____

8. What is a *proposal*? _____
   _____

9. What is the "President's Cabinet"? _____
   _____

10. What is a "slice-of-life" commercial? _____
    _____

Scavenger Hunt 3:
You Need to Know

Directions	If you have not already learned how to use the handbook, read "Using the Handbook" at the front of *Write Source 2000*. Then, in a small group or with your whole class, find the page or pages where each answer can be found.

_____ **1.** Your best friend is spending the summer in Hawaii, and you want to send her a letter. You need to know the correct postal abbreviation for Hawaii.

_____ **2.** Uncle Fred wants everybody to write a limerick to recite at the big family party on New Year's Eve. You need to know what a limerick is.

_____ **3.** Your teacher assigns you to write a short story using the "omniscient point of view." You need to know what that means.

_____ **4.** It's your first week on the school newspaper staff, and the editor asks you to write an editorial about a proposal to require students to wear uniforms. You need to know how to write an editorial.

_____ **5.** To go with your social studies project, you want to make a line graph showing the numbers of tourists who visited your town over a five-year period. You need to know how to make a line graph.

_____ **6.** Your mom says you can call your grandmother in Alaska tomorrow. You know that Alaska is in a different time zone, and you don't want to call too early or too late. You need to know how Alaska's time compares to yours.

_____ **7.** Your teacher asks you to make a cause-and-effect organizer showing what you learned from your science reading. You need to know how to do this.

_____ **8.** You want to include some dialogue in a story you are writing, but you need to know how to punctuate it correctly.

_____ **9.** Your story is finished, and everybody who has read it says it is the best thing you've ever written. You would like to know how to enter it in a writing contest.

_____ **10.** You have been elected secretary of the ecology club. One of your jobs is to take minutes at all the club meetings. You need some guidelines.

Write Source Word Find

Directions Using the word hints below, circle the key words as shown. Answers read across, down, and diagonally. The first one has been done for you.

```
T A S E V I K U Q R A S T K U R E A D I N G I A W D
F U B J A R E Y I A B E I H N O I Q E K N A O X R E
A Q E S T A J O U R N A L Y I O R U A I E I R J I B
S R A C E K U Z E F I R A L O T W O S N I Y G I Z A
P A L R O F E B A K E Y O L G C E I F E R I J O S T
E F I S Y R D N S T A F X V A B V O C A B U L A R Y
A R O L M A P I R I T A U W F E O F U B G E L L E R
L A S H P U H O L R F A L A R Y Y R O B E K I X L I
S H F E S T A V O L E T O S U A R A S R O R E N R O
T O N U C O M P O U N D S E N T E N C E L A D E F L
I P E L A B E E G W A S T N O I T K I V E J E F A S
F L R E R I V A Y U E F A B I H E A D I N G E K I T
R A S M L O I K A Y R P T E S N A M O A T L Y I F I
E Q T H O G O W E R E F E N A D J E C T I V E F S J
S R A F E R T Z L O J I W K I O P L E I R O W E U G
O V Y B R A I N S T O R M I N G A P T O A T D L M X
H I V R A P H Y I D A Y I R E L E K I N T E R N E T
O F O L N H W O M A F E U L R A Q I S T E R T G A S
P E L E G Y E N A S E K Y F H I N L P O L Y S I D A
A T E S A X S E F L I N T E R R O G A T I V E O Q P
Y S I R B O H S E A K H I W O K U M S U T E L R I W
P A R A G R A P H S L W N S F E N S A I F R L J O B
T Y F J E A S H I T Q K S R A R I R P K O B A Z N I
```

Word Hints:

1. A picture of the world
2. A writer's story of his or her own life
3. A daily writing book
4. Made up of two sentences
5. A place to keep your writing
6. Getting meaning from print
7. Main part of a word
8. The words you know
9. Changing your writing
10. Shortened form of a word
11. Thinking freely about a topic
12. A poem about death
13. Several of these make an essay
14. Sender's address in a letter
15. A word that describes a noun
16. Worldwide computer network
17. A sentence that questions
18. A name word
19. A Japanese poem
20. An action word

Answer Key

Scavenger Hunt 1: Find the Fives

1. Five parts of a plot
(page 184) exposition, rising action, climax, falling action, resolution

2. Five steps in the writing process
(page 5) prewriting, writing, revising, editing, publishing

3. Five types of primary sources
(page 263) observation and participation; surveys and forms; interviews; presentations; diaries, journals, and letters

4. Five magazines that publish student writing
(page 41) Creative Kids, Kids Byline: A Magazine for Kids by Kids, Merlyn's Pen, Stone Soup, Writing!

5. Five units of linear measure used in the metric system
(page 467) centimeter, decimeter, meter, dekameter, kilometer

6. Five tips for surfing the Internet
(page 269) stay focused, check your facts, preserve your privacy, protect yourself, use netiquette

7. Five transitions that begin with "a" and show time
(page 106) about, after, at, afterward, as soon as

8. "Five Keys to Good Revision"
(page 69) take a break, keep your purpose in mind, picture your audience, read your work aloud, share your draft

11

Scavenger Hunt 2: What Is It?

1. What is an *oxymoron*? *(page 139) a technique in which two words with opposite meanings are put together for a special effect*

2. What is the "Essentials of Life Checklist"? *(page 49) a list of categories of things that we need to live a full life*

3. What is a *paraphrase*? *(page 216) writing that summarizes a reading selection and includes all the ideas*

4. What is a *phase biography*? *(page 166) writing that focuses on an important time or phase in a person's life*

5. What is a *ballad*? *(page 204) a poem that tells a story*

6. What kind of animal is a *cygnet*? *(page 465) a young swan*

7. What is an *intensive pronoun*? *(page 444) a pronoun that emphasizes a noun or pronoun*

8. What is a *proposal*? *(page 258) a detailed plan for doing a project, solving a problem, or meeting a need*

9. What is the "President's Cabinet"? *(page 508) a group of advisers appointed by the president to help set policies and make decisions*

10. What is a "slice-of-life" commercial? *(page 360) a commercial filmed to look like a home video (real life)*

12

Scavenger Hunt 3: You Need to Know

247 1. Your best friend is spending the summer in Hawaii, and you want to send her a letter. You need to know the correct postal abbreviation for Hawaii.

205 2. Uncle Fred wants everybody to write a limerick to recite at the big family party on New Year's Eve. You need to know what a limerick is.

344 3. Your teacher asks you to write a short story using the "omniscient point of view." You need to know what that means.

172 4. It's your first week on the school newspaper, and the editor asks you to write an editorial about a proposal to require students to wear uniforms. You need to know how to write an editorial.

302 5. To go with your social studies project, you want to make a line graph showing the numbers of tourists who visited your town over a five-year period. You need to know how to make a line graph.

506 6. Your mom says you can call your grandmother in Alaska tomorrow. You
56, 113, and/or 317 know that Alaska is in a different time zone, and you don't want to call too early or too late. You need to know how Alaska's time compares to yours.

390, 399 7. Your teacher asks you to make a cause-and-effect organizer showing what you learned from your science reading. You need to know how to do this.

8. You want to include some dialogue in a story you are writing, but you need to know how to punctuate it correctly.

41 9. Your story is finished, and everybody who has read it says it is the best thing you've ever written. You would like to know how to enter it in a writing contest.

256-257 10. You have been elected secretary of the ecology club. One of your jobs is to take minutes at all the club meetings. You need some guidelines.

13

Write Source Word Find

```
T A S E V I K U Q R A S T K U R E A D I N G I A W D
F U B J A R E Y I A B E I H N O I Q E K N A O X R E
A Q E S T A J O U R N A L Y I O R U A I E I R J I B
S R A C E K U Z E F I R A L O T W O S N I Y G I Z A
P A L R O F E B A K E Y O L G C E I F E R I J O S T
E F I S Y R D N S T A F X V A B V O C A B U L A R Y
A R O L M A P I R I T A U W F E O F U B G E L L E R
L A S H P U H O L R F A L A R Y Y R O B E K I X L I
S H F E S T A V O L E T O S U A R A S R O R E N R O
T O N U C O M P O U N D S E N T E N C E L A D E F L
I P E L A B E E G W A S T N O I T K I V E J E F A S
F L R E R I V A Y U E F A B I H E A D I N G E K I T
R A S M L O I K A Y R P T E S N A M O A T L Y I F I
E Q T H O G O W E R E F E N A D J E C T I V E F S J
S R A F E R T Z L O J I W K I O P L E I R O W E U G
O V Y B R A I N S T O R M I N G A P T O A T D L M X
H I V R A P H Y I D A Y I R E L E K I N T E R N E T
O F O L N H W O M A F F U L R A Q I S T E R T G A S
P E L E G Y E N A S E K Y F H I N L P O L Y S I D A
A T E S A X S E F I N T E R R O G A T I V E O Q P
Y S I R B O H S E A K H I W O K U M S U T E L R I W
P A R A G R A P H S L W N S F E N S A I F R L J O B
T Y F J E A S H I T Q K S R A R I R P K O B A Z N I
```

1. map
2. autobiography
3. journal
4. compound sentence
5. portfolio
6. reading
7. root
8. vocabulary
9. revising
10. abbreviation
11. brainstorming
12. elegy
13. paragraphs
14. heading
15. adjective
16. Internet
17. interrogative
18. noun
19. haiku
20. verb

14

Minilessons for Using *Write Source 2000*

On a regular basis, conduct minilessons that give your students practice using *Write Source 2000*. Minilessons usually take 10-15 minutes of class time. (Sample minilessons follow. Also see pages 225-263 in this guide for additional minilessons.)

Polysyllables .... Improving Vocabulary

- **SURVEY** the section on "Improving Your Vocabulary" (HB 323-340); learn how to use the lists of prefixes (HB 329-330), suffixes (HB 331), and roots (HB 332-339).
  USE the three lists to figure out the definitions of the following words:
  philanthropy
  prestidigitation
  pneumoconiosis
  antidisestablishmentarianism
  CHECK your definitions against an unabridged dictionary.

Quiz Bowl .... Punctuation

- You're in a junior-high "Quiz Bowl." Here are the questions:
  What is the proper punctuation after the salutation in a business letter?
  What punctuation mark do you usually use with an interjection?
  What punctuation mark separates words in a series?

A lot happens in 50 years! .... History

- **REFER** to the "Historical Time Line" (HB 516-525).
  SELECT and study any 50-year period in history.
  LIST the five most important events, from your point of view, that occurred during this period of time.
  Then **WRITE** a paragraph explaining the importance of one of the events.

Seeing Spots .... Clauses

- **STUDY** the explanations of independent and dependent clauses (HB 436.3).
  REFER to the Braille alphabet (HB 460).
  WRITE a complex sentence (a sentence with one independent clause and at least one dependent clause) in Braille.
  Special Challenge: Translate your sentence into cuneiform (HB 460).

Using the Handbook in the Classroom

Where does *Write Source 2000* fit in?

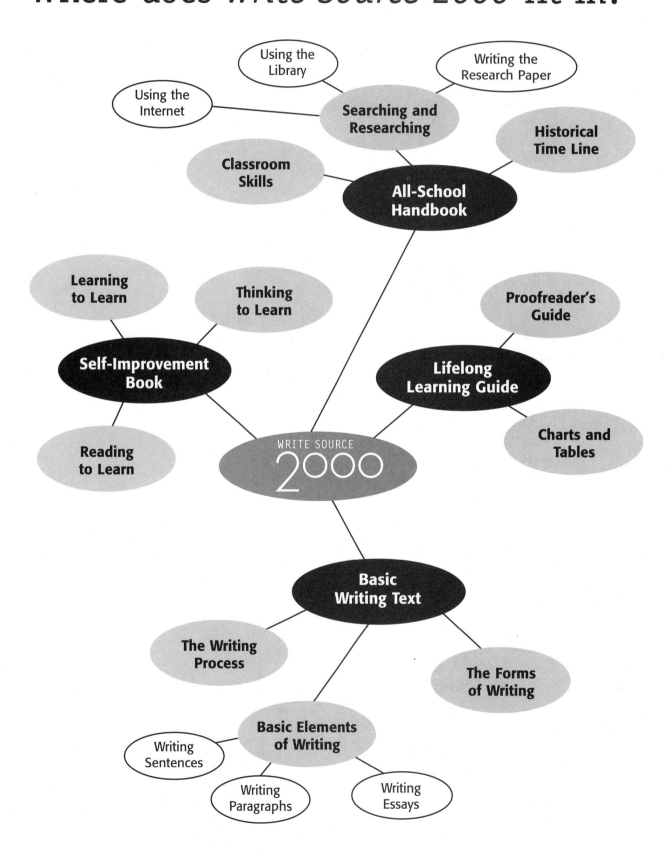

Using the *Write Source 2000* Handbook in the Language Arts Classroom

Q. **Can teachers develop a language program with *Write Source 2000* and the *Teacher's Guide*?**

A. Most definitely. These two resources can serve as the foundation for a language arts program promoting, among other things, student-centered language learning, writing as a process of discovery, and the reading-writing connection. These products can also serve as the foundation for a school-wide writing and learning program.

Q. **How should teachers plan a program with these two resources?**

A. Since *Write Source 2000* functions mainly as a writing handbook, that is where teachers should first focus their attention. Two very basic questions should be answered during initial planning: **How will writing instruction be approached?** Will students engage in writing workshops? Will writing be integrated into thematic units? **What types of writing will be covered?** Will personal forms of writing be emphasized in grade 6? Will paragraphs be of primary importance in grades 6 and 7 and multiparagraph essays in grade 8?

"Effective Writing Instruction," pages 146-148 in this guide, will help teachers answer the first question. Teachers can answer the second question by reviewing the forms of writing covered in the handbook. (Teachers should also refer to the framework of writing activities for grades 6-8 listed on page 20 in this guide.)

Q. **What about the other language arts?**

A. Teachers will find major sections in the handbook related to searching, thinking, and reading skills.

Searching for Information (pages 260-281) • Various primary and secondary sources can be emphasized at different grade levels. In addition, students can explore the Internet and the library in more depth from year to year.

Thinking to Learn (pages 282-299) • This section addresses thinking from a number of different perspectives. The primary focus of attention in one grade might be recalling and understanding information; in another grade, applying and analyzing information; and so on.

Reading to Learn (pages 300-345) • A number of different patterns of nonfiction should be practiced at each grade level. We also suggest that the glossary of prefixes, suffixes, and roots should be the focus of vocabulary study. (See 213-215 in this guide for help.)

Q. **What about learning and study skills?**

A. In the "Learning to Learn" section (handbook pages 346-385), teachers will find a variety of guidelines related to studying and learning. Perhaps writing to learn and note taking could be emphasized in one grade, test taking in the next grade, and individual skills (setting goals, managing time, etc.) in the following grade.

Q. **What else should teachers remember when planning with *Write Source 2000*?**

A. Teachers should always remember to turn to the "Introductory Notes" in the *Teacher's Guide* (pages 31-144) whenever they are planning a unit around a particular chapter in the handbook.

What specific types of writing are covered in *Write Source 2000?*

The chart below lists the types of writing discussed in the *Write Source 2000* handbook. The types of writing are listed in this manner to indicate a possible framework or sequence of activities, moving from personal writing to writing that becomes more inventive and reflective. Teachers can use this framework as a starting point when planning a middle-school writing program (or individual writing activities) with the handbook.

	6	7	8
PERSONAL WRITING			
Recording	Writing to Learn (366) Journal Writing (145)	Creating a SourceBank (47) Journal Writing (145)	Learning Log (366) Journal Writing (145)
Recalling and Remembering	Narrative Paragraphs (101) Writing About an Event (126)	Writing Personal Narratives (154)	Writing Phase Autobiographies (158)
Connecting	Writing Friendly Letters (149)	Writing Friendly Letters (149)	Writing Friendly Letters (149)
SUBJECT WRITING			
Introducing	Writing About a Person (123)	Biographical Stories (161)	Phase Biographies (166)
Describing	Descriptive Paragraphs (100) Describing a Place (124)	Descriptive Paragraphs (100) Describing an Object (125)	Writing Observation Reports (209)
Reporting	Writing News Stories (167)	Writing a Feature (174) Writing Minutes (256)	Writing News Stories (167) Writing Minutes (256)
Corresponding	Letters of Request (248) Memos and E-Mail (252)	Letters of Request (248) Memos and E-Mail (252)	Letters of Application (250) Memos and E-Mail (252)
Informing	Expository Paragraphs (102) Writing an Explanation (127)	Expository Essays (107) Writing an Explanation (127)	Expository Essays (107) Writing Proposals (258)
Searching and Researching	Writing Summaries (213) Personal Research Reports (217)	Writing Summaries (213) Personal Research Reports (217)	Writing Paraphrases (216) Writing Research Papers (223)
CREATIVE WRITING			
Translating and Imagining	Free-Verse Poetry (193) Invented Poetry (206)	Free-Verse Poetry (193) Invented Poetry (206)	Free-Verse Poetry (193) Traditional Poetry (204)
Inventing	Writing Stories (183) Writing Mysteries (192)	Writing Stories (183) Writing Myths (192)	Writing Stories (183) Writing Science-Fiction Stories (192)
REFLECTIVE WRITING			
Analyzing and Classifying	Writing Comparison Essays (112)	Writing Problem and Solution Essays (112)	Writing Cause and Effect Essays (112)
Persuading	Persuasive Paragraphs (103)	Writing Persuasive Essays (115)	Writing Editorials (172)
Reviewing	Responding in a Journal (180) Writing Book Reviews (175)	Responding with a Poem (180) Writing Book Reviews (175)	Responding with a Letter (181) Writing Book Reviews (175)

How are the modes of writing covered in the handbook?

Many language arts curriculums approach writing according to the different modes of writing: *narrative, descriptive, expository,* and *persuasive.* The chart below shows how the modes of writing are covered in the *Write Source 2000* handbook. Teachers may find this chart helpful when planning writing assignments.

NARRATIVE
Narrative Paragraphs **101**
Writing About Events (Guidelines) **126**
Writing Friendly Letters **149-152**
Writing Personal Narratives **153-157**
Writing Phase Autobiographies **158-159**
Writing Stories **183-192**
Writing Personal Research Reports **217-222**

DESCRIPTIVE
Descriptive Paragraphs **100**
Writing About People (Guidelines) **123**
Writing About Places (Guidelines) **124**
Writing About Objects (Guidelines) **125**
Writing Biographical Stories **161-165**
Writing Phase Biographies **166**
Writing Observation Reports **209-212**

EXPOSITORY
Expository Paragraphs **102**
Writing Expository Essays **107-114**
Writing Explanations (Guidelines) **127**
Writing News Stories **167-171**
Writing Summaries **213-216**
Writing Research Papers **223-235**
Writing Business Letters **241-250**

PERSUASIVE
Persuasive Paragraphs **103**
Writing Comparison and Contrast Essays **112-113**
Writing Persuasive Essays **115-122**
Writing Editorials **172-173**
Writing Book Reviews **175-181**
Using Logic to Persuade **291-296**

Using the Handbook as an All-School Writing and Learning Guide

Because there is such a wide range of information covered in the *Write Source 2000* handbook, it can be used in many different ways. For example, in many schools the handbook serves as an **all-school resource**—one that students refer to in every class for help with their writing, study-reading, note taking, test taking, and so on. Once teachers in all subject areas become familiar with the contents of the handbook, they will understand its potential as a writing and learning tool. The following list demonstrates the handbook's cross-curricular value.

Special Note: See pages 159-174 in this guide for more information about writing across the curriculum.

Writing Skills

- Why Write? (1)
- Understanding Writing (3-8)
- Writing with a Computer (25-30)
- Using Graphic Organizers (56)
- Building Paragraphs (97-105)
- Transitions or Linking Words (106)
- Writing Expository Essays (107-114)
- Writing Persuasive Essays (115-122)
- Writing Business Letters (241-250)
- Special Forms of Workplace Writing (251-259)
- Thinking and Writing (283-290)
- Thinking Logically (291-296)
- Writing to Learn (366-367)

Researching Skills

- Using Collection Sheets (57)
- Writing Observation Reports (209-212)
- Writing Summaries (213-216)
- Writing Personal Research Reports (217-222)
- Writing Research Papers (223-235)
- Types of Information (261-264)
- Using the Internet (265-272)
- Using the Library (273-281)

Reading and Speaking Skills

- Reading Charts (301-306)
- Patterns of Nonfiction (308-319)
- Study-Reading Strategies (320-322)
- Improving Your Vocabulary (323-340)
- Preparing a Speech (347-354)

Study Skills

- Viewing Skills (355-360)
- Taking Notes (361-365)
- Group Skills (369-372)
- Taking Tests (373-380)
- Planning Your Time (383)
- Completing Assignments (384)

Helpful Charts and Lists

- Periodic Table of the Elements (466)
- The Metric System (467)
- Math Terms (475-479)
- Maps (493-502)
- Government (507-514)
- Historical Time Line (516-525)

Using the Handbook for Standards-Based Instruction

Today, teachers are expected to use standards to inform instruction. Standards are the tools used to justify and document what is being taught and what students are achieving. As you will see on the next five pages, *Write Source 2000* can serve as an important resource for planning instruction that meets the essential *writing standards* as developed at the national, state, and/or local level. (The performance standards that follow reflect the writing skills and forms that students should understand and employ by grade 8.)

The Process of Writing

Understanding How Writing Works

The student is expected to . . .   *Handbook Pages*

- **use** prewriting strategies, such as freewriting and clustering, to generate and collect ideas for writing.   45-57

- **use** appropriate reference materials and resources as needed during the writing process.   55, 261-264, 265-272, 273-281

- **pay** careful attention to purpose and audience when developing writing.   58, 69, 72

- **establish** a central idea (*topic sentence, focus or thesis statement*), collect details, and organize supporting information for writing.   58-60

- **apply** different methods of support, including paraphrases, quotations, anecdotes, descriptions, sensory details, etc.   64-66, 105, 138-140

- **revise** selected drafts by adding, deleting, and rearranging copy—striving for effective content, logical organization, and appropriate voice.   24, 67-74

- **edit** drafts to ensure smooth-reading sentences, effective word choice, and clear and accurate copy.   79-83

- **use** available technology to support aspects of prewriting, drafting, revising, editing, and publishing texts.   25-30, 37-43

Evaluating Written Work

The student is expected to . . .   *Handbook Pages*

- **assess** writing according to the traits of effective writing.   19-24, 67-74

- **respond** in constructive ways to others' writing.   75-78

- **use** published examples as models for writing.   4, 131-133

- **review** a collection of his or her own writing to determine its strengths and weaknesses, and to set goals as a writer.   31-36

The Forms of Writing

Writing to Share

The student is expected to develop . . .   *Handbook Pages*

- **personal narratives** that . . .   101, 153-159
  - focus on specific experiences.
  - develop three key elements: characterization, setting, and action.
  - begin in the middle of the action, focus on the essential details, and end right after the most important narrative moment.
  - reveal the significance of, or the writer's attitude about, the subject.

- **expository compositions** that . . .   100, 102,
  - engage the interest of the reader and state a clear focus.   107-114,
  - elaborate on the focus with supportive details.   209-212,
  - follow an organizational pattern appropriate to the form.   237-240,
  - conclude with a summary linked to the purpose of the   251-259,
    composition.   377-380

- **news stories** that . . .   167-171, 174
  - focus on timely and important issues.
  - begin with a strong lead and continue with related details and information.
  - follow the newswriting form—important information up front.
  - present clear, accurate, and verifiable finished copy.

- **persuasive compositions** that . . .   103, 115-122
  - state a clear position or focus.
  - include relevant and organized support.
  - differentiate between fact and opinion.
  - anticipate and address readers' concerns and counterarguments.

- **research reports** that . . .   217-222,
  - originate with an important, relevant subject.   223-235
  - focus on a specific part or main idea about the subject.
  - present a clear and organized discussion or argument.
  - use a variety of primary and secondary sources.
  - support the focus or thesis with facts, specific details, and examples from multiple sources.
  - provide clear and accurate documentation.

- **fictional narratives** that . . .   183-192
  - develop an effective story line that builds in suspense.
  - use sensory details and effective word choice to develop the key elements (characterization, plot, setting, and theme).
  - include a meaningful problem that influences the main character and moves the story along.
  - employ a range of narrative strategies (*dialogue, foreshadowing, suspense-building actions,* etc.).

Writing to Share (continued)

The student is expected to develop . . .   *Handbook Pages*

- **poems** that . . .   193-207
  - describe, express, and/or reflect upon the importance of
    a subject.
  - display an understanding of poetic techniques and a
    creative use of language.

- **summaries** that . . .   213-216, 359
  - highlight the main idea and significant details in a reading
    selection.
  - reflect a clear understanding of the selection.

- **responses to literature** that . . .   175-181
  - develop interpretations that exhibit a careful reading and
    understanding of the literary work.
  - take a point of view and support it with textual references.
  - display a personal connection with the literary work.

- **workplace forms** that . . .   237-240,
  - are purposeful and address a specific audience.   241-250, 251-259
  - follow the conventions and style for the respective form.

Writing to Learn

The student is expected to . . .   *Handbook Pages*

- **write to learn** in all subjects in the following ways: 145-148, 180,
  - keeping dialogue journals   213-216, 288,
  - using learning logs   359, 361-368
  - writing response journals
  - making lists
  - summarizing or paraphrasing what is heard or read
  - connecting knowledge within and across the disciplines
  - synthesizing information

The Mechanics of Writing

Research

The student is expected to . . .   *Handbook Pages*

- **organize** prior knowledge about a topic using a graphic organizer or some other prewriting strategy.   52, 54-56

- **generate** questions to direct research.   221, 225

- **use** various reference materials such as the dictionary, encyclopedia, almanac, thesaurus, atlas, and on-line information as an aid to writing.   278-279, 325-327

- **use** print and electronic sources to locate books and articles.   265-272, 273-277, 280

- **understand** and use tables of contents, chapter and section headings, glossaries, indexes, and appendices to locate information in reference books.   281

- **take** notes from sources such as guest speakers, periodicals, books, on-line sites, and so on.   361-365

- **summarize** and organize ideas gained from multiple sources.   57, 213-216, 225-226

- **evaluate** the research and frame new questions for further investigation.   225, 227

- **follow** accepted formats for writing research papers, including documenting sources.   227-235

- **give** credit for quotations and information in a bibliography (*works-cited page*).   229-232, 235

Grammar and Usage

The student is expected to . . .   *Handbook Pages*

- **employ** standard English—including correct subject-verb agreement, pronoun-antecedent agreement, verb forms, and so on—to communicate clearly and effectively in writing.   88-91, 340, 448-449

- **understand** the different parts of speech.   439-457

- **write** in complete sentences (and eliminate sentence errors in writing).   85-87, 434-437

- **vary** the types of sentences in writing (*simple, compound, complex*).   81, 93-96, 437-438

- **use** conjunctions to connect ideas meaningfully.   93-96, 106

Grammar and Usage (continued)

The student is expected to . . .	*Handbook Pages*
• **make** writing precise and vivid using action verbs, specific nouns, and colorful modifiers.	135-136
• **learn** vocabulary-building strategies.	323-340
• **correctly use** commonly misused words.	419-433

Punctuation, Capitalization, and Spelling

The student is expected to . . .	*Handbook Pages*
• **use** correct punctuation and capitalization in writing.	387-403, 404-407
• **spell** accurately in final drafts, including frequently misspelled words, contractions, plurals, and homophones.	402, 408-409, 411-418, 419-433
• **spell** derivatives correctly.	329-339, 411
• **use** syllable constructions and syllable boundary patterns to spell correctly.	412-418
• **understand** the influence of other languages and cultures on the spelling of English words.	461-463

Using *Write Source 2000* to Meet the Needs of Every Student

Teachers can't possibly accommodate all of their students' different learning styles following a standard text, one chapter after another. What works best is a language resource like *Write Source 2000*, providing useful information and guidelines that each student can turn to on his or her own terms.

Students refer to *Write Source 2000* when they have a need for information—in any class, at any time. We like to call *Write Source 2000* a contextbook because students use it in context when they are developing a piece of writing, studying for a test, preparing for an interview, and so on. *Write Source 2000* helps make learning much more student directed than a textbook does. It accommodates all students with their different learning needs.

Reform and Restructuring

We strongly believe that the primary role of instruction should be to help students improve their emerging learning abilities and explore their own interests. Instead of the assembly-line approach to teaching with the products being the students (having survived the system), students should be met on their own terms, with their individual needs at the core of the curriculum. For educators to do this, they must change their approach: How much content to cover should not be their main concern. Rather, they should constantly ask themselves if they are doing enough to help each learner progress.

Student-Centered Learning

Certainly this method of instruction makes the most sense in language arts instruction since no two students progress as writers and readers at the exact same speed or in the exact same way. To make instruction more student centered, many language arts teachers run their classrooms as writing and reading workshops. In workshops, students write at their own pace, read books that interest them, interact, take risks, decide what projects to work on next, and so on.

We've used the workshop approach in our own classrooms, so we know how effective it can be. Former students tell us all the time how they really learned to write and read in our language arts classes. It's also because of the workshop approach that we developed our first handbook. We did it to give our students a basic resource they could refer to when writing and learning.

Meeting Everyone's Needs

Once your students have their own copies of *Write Source 2000*, we can't urge you enough to turn your classroom into a workshop. It is the best way to meet your students' individual needs. Everyone reads, writes, and learns together. When workshops are used effectively, large-scale grouping or tracking isn't necessary.

Making It Work

Workshop teachers must become effective managers of their classrooms, providing an atmosphere conducive to writing and learning. And they must guide students and help them master basic skills during personal conferences and editing sessions, and in occasional whole-class periods of instruction.

Read *In the Middle* by Nancie Atwell and *Seeking Diversity* by Linda Rief for two thorough discussions about the operation and successful management of writing and reading workshops. Both books are available from Heinemann-Boynton/Cook Publishers. In addition, see pages 154-155 in this guide for more information on workshops.

Using the Handbook in the Complete *Write Source 2000 Program*

The *Write Source 2000* handbook works as an extremely effective writing and learning guide all on its own and can be used for a number of different purposes—many of which are discussed on the previous pages in this section of your *Teacher's Guide*.

The handbook also serves as the core resource in the ***Write Source 2000 Language Program***. There is a separate program of activities for each grade level—6, 7, and 8. (See below for more information.)

Working in the Program

Students refer to the *Write Source 2000* handbook to help them complete their work in the program.

Teachers refer to the *Teacher's Guide* (this guide) for basic planning ideas, start-up activities, and minilessons.

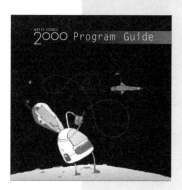

Teachers who purchase the complete program receive a *Program Guide* ring binder for their grade level, providing teaching units for each chapter in the handbook (with daily lesson plans and blackline masters), editing and proofreading practice activities, and much more. All program guide activities are reproducible.

Special Note: The editing and proofreading practice activities are also available in a bound *SkillsBook* for each grade level.

The Process
of Writing **Introductory Notes**

This section introduces "The Process of Writing" chapters in the handbook and provides getting-started ideas to help you with your initial planning.

Understanding Writing

(See handbook pages 3-8.)

This chapter introduces the concept that skilled student writing involves a number of steps. The text gives an overview of the writing process and a concise, detailed explanation of each step in the process.

Of Special Interest

- "Building Good Writing Habits" lists several practices students can utilize to become better writers. (page 4)
- "Reviewing the Writing Process" identifies the separate steps of the process: prewriting, writing, revising, editing, and publishing. (page 5)

Rationale

- Students can improve their writing by emulating attitudes and habits common to experienced writers.
- Writing goes through a series of steps as it is developed from a rough composition into a finished piece.
- The writing process is recursive in nature, going back and forth between steps a number of times before a final piece of writing is produced.

Major Concepts

- There are a number of positive habits students can cultivate that will help them develop as writers. (page 4)
- Writing is a process, not a single event. (page 5)
- Producing a good finished piece requires planning, drafting, and reworking. (pages 5-7)
- Students can gain valuable insights into the writing process from one another. (page 8)

Performance Standards

Students are expected to . . .
- approach writing as a process to help them meet all of their writing challenges.

Getting Started with "Understanding Writing"

Start-Up Activity: Before you read and discuss any part of "Understanding Writing," have your students describe their personal process of writing—that is, the way in which they have generally completed writing assignments in the past. Ask them to compare this process to the one described in the chapter. Later in the quarter, have students describe how their personal process of writing has changed.

Enrichment Activity: Have students list at least four or five important things they do when they write. Here are some of the things we feel are important:

- Writers should approach writing as a process of discovery.
- Writers should write about something that interests them.
- Writers should write for an intended audience, even if that means their fellow writers.
- Writers should write with an honest and sincere voice.

Post a list of "Keys to Good Writing" in your classroom where all of your students can see it. (Your list should include important reminders your students suggest plus additional reminders, including some or all of the suggestions listed above.)

Teaching Resources

Write Source 2000 Teacher's Guide

- Minilessons:
  "Here's help." (page 226)
  "Quote me on that." (page 226)
- "The Process Approach" (pages 149-150)

Write Source 2000 Handbook

- "One Writer's Process," pages 9-18, shows how one student uses the writing process to develop a piece of writing.
- "Using the Writing Process," pages 44-83, addresses each step in the writing process in a separate chapter.

Write Source 2000 Program Guide

- A teaching unit (lesson plans and blackline masters) can be found in the Program Guide ring binder for each grade level.

One Writer's Process

(See handbook pages 9-18.)

This chapter shows how one student used the writing process for a particular assignment. Each step in the process is modeled, from prewriting to publishing. Along the way, some of the "messiness" of the process is demonstrated, with words and ideas being cut or moved and new material added as the writer refines his work.

Of Special Interest
- "Prewriting—Choosing a Subject" demonstrates the use of brainstorming and clustering to choose a subject and generate ideas. (page 10)
- "Revising" shares the comments of a student writer after he rereads his first draft; it also shows the changes he penciled into the text. (pages 14-15)

Rationale
- Taking students through one writer's process helps them to understand how the writing process could work for them.

Major Concepts
- Good writing typically requires multiple drafts. (page 9)
- Planning before writing is essential. (pages 10-11)
- The first draft should be written freely, getting all the ideas on paper without worrying about the best way to say them. (pages 12-13)
- Revising and editing are two different steps. The first focuses on organization and completeness, the second on style and mechanics. (pages 14-17)

Performance Standards
Students are expected to . . .
- do the necessary prewriting, drafting, revising, and editing to produce an effective piece of writing.

Getting Started with "One Writer's Process"

Start-Up Activity: Discuss the following quotations with your students before and after reviewing the chapter:

"You can't wait for inspiration.
You have to go after it with a club."
                    —Jack London

"Unfortunately, you learn from your mistakes. Unless you're a genius,
I don't see how you could do it right the first time."
                    —Lloyd Alexander

"What is written without effort is in general read without pleasure."
                    —Dr. Samuel Johnson

Enrichment Activity: Ask students to save all of their work, from prewriting through editing and proofreading, for at least one of their major writing projects. Then have small groups of students discuss the development of their writing—what they did first, second, and so on. Afterward, ask for volunteers to share their writing process with the entire class.

Teaching Resources

Write Source 2000 Teacher's Guide

- Minilessons:
  "Long Ago and Far Away" (page 226)
  "Take it to heart." (page 226)
- "The Process Approach" (pages 149-150)

Write Source 2000 Handbook

- "Special Forms of Workplace Writing," page 259, shows the proposal that lead to the writing in "One Writer's Process."

Write Source 2000 Program Guide

- A teaching unit (lesson plans and blackline masters) can be found in the Program Guide ring binder for each grade level.

Traits of Effective Writing

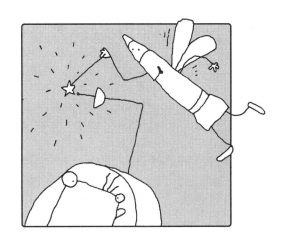

(See handbook pages 19-24.)

Even the best writers can improve their writing by knowing and implementing specific traits, or features, that make writing work. This chapter introduces students to six key traits of good writing: stimulating ideas, logical organization, engaging voice, original word choice, smooth-reading sentences, and correct, accurate copy. Each trait is clearly defined and modeled through examples that show exactly how that trait can make writing come alive for the reader.

Of Special Interest
- The "Quick Guide" defines each trait clearly and concisely, showing why it is important to good writing. (page 20)
- The "Checklist for Good Writing" gives students a quick way to assess the overall effectiveness of any piece of writing. (page 24)

Rationale
- Defining the traits, pointing them out in examples of good literature, and asking students to consider these traits in their assessments will acquaint young writers with the elements of good writing.
- Though some writers may be more talented than others, working with the traits can help all writers expand their writing skills.

Major Concepts
- Effective writing is characterized by six specific features, or traits, that can be identified and described. (page 20)
- Good literature models key traits of effective writing. (pages 21-23)
- Students who know the six traits can use them to identify strengths—or weaknesses—in their own and others' writing. (page 24)

Performance Standards

Students are expected to . . .
- assess writing according to specific standards.
- analyze published examples as models for writing.
- review collections of their own written works to determine strengths and weaknesses and to set goals as writers.

Getting Started with "Traits of Effective Writing"

Start-Up Activity: Share with the class an effective piece of student writing. Ask students to identify elements or features that add to its overall effectiveness. Their comments may be primarily general in nature ("It's funny."). Then, after reviewing the chapter, analyze the writing using the checklist on page 24 in the handbook as a guide.

Enrichment Activity: Students should use the checklist on page 24 as a guide to assess their own writing throughout the school year as well as the writing of others in group-advising sessions. (The traits in the checklist are used as an assessment guide in many state writing tests.)

Teaching Resources

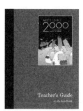

Write Source 2000 Teacher's Guide
- Minilessons:
  "What a voice!" (page 227)
  "The Right Stuff" (page 227)
- "The Trait-Based Approach" (pages 156-157)
- "Assessment Strategies and Rubrics" (pages 175-192)

Write Source 2000 Handbook
- "Revising Your Writing," pages 67-74, links the traits of good writing to the revising process.

Write Source 2000 Program Guide
- A teaching unit (lesson plans and blackline masters) can be found in the Program Guide ring binder for each grade level.

Writing with a Computer

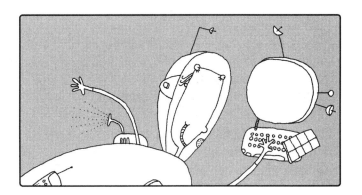

(See handbook pages 25-30.)

This chapter provides an introduction to applying computer technology to the writing process. It instructs students in basic strategies for using computers efficiently and also points out a few of the potential problems involved. Some important issues of page design are also covered, including the wide range of font and style choices students will face. Having read this chapter, students will be better prepared to compose with a computer. (See also handbook pages 483-490.)

Of Special Interest	• "Understanding the Basics" provides students with helpful advice about using the computer effectively and comfortably. (page 26) • "Designing Your Writing" presents a concrete list of strategies for page layout and typography choices when using computers. (page 27)
Rationale	• Students need some "basic training" in order to fully utilize computers and word processors in their writing process.
Major Concepts	• Computers and word processors are great tools for writing, but a writer must use them intelligently. (page 26) • A good page design helps make text clear and easy to follow. (pages 27-29)
Performance Standards	Students are expected to . . . • use available technology to create, revise, edit, and publish texts.

Getting Started with "Writing with a Computer"

Start-Up Activity: If you have access to a computer lab, ask students to prepare a brief piece of writing on a computer from start to finish. Then have them identify the pluses and minuses of composing with a computer. Make their suggestions the focus of a discussion about computers and writing. As part of this discussion, read and discuss "Understanding the Basics," page 26 in the handbook.

Enrichment Activity: Encourage students to practice keyboarding as often as they can. Provide some incentive for practicing—perhaps a certain number of bonus points for 15-30 minutes of practice time.

Teaching Resources

Write Source 2000 Teacher's Guide

- Minilessons:
  "All Dressed Up" (page 227)
  "Keyboard Fluent" (page 227)

Write Source 2000 Handbook

- "Computer Keyboard," pages 484-485, works as a "practice pad" for students who want to practice their keyboarding.

Write Source 2000 Program Guide

- A teaching unit (lesson plans and blackline masters) can be found in the Program Guide ring binder for each grade level.

Developing a Portfolio

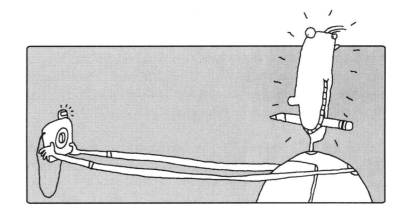

(See handbook pages 31-36.)

Just as a photo album tells more than a single snapshot tells, a writing portfolio reveals more about a student writer than any single piece of writing reveals. This chapter helps students understand the advantages of keeping a portfolio, offers step-by-step guidelines for creating either growth or showcase portfolios, and emphasizes the importance of self-reflection during the process of becoming a writer.

Of Special Interest	• "Creating a Portfolio" lists the key components of a well-constructed portfolio and offers tips for assembling a portfolio that positively reflects a writer's work. (page 34)
	• "Planning Ideas" breaks portfolio design into four steps: collecting, selecting, reflecting, and projecting. (page 35)
	• "Example Portfolio Reflections" offers sample reflections from both students and professional writers. (page 36)
Rationale	• Portfolios provide a more complete and accurate picture of what a writer can do than any single piece of writing provides.
	• Portfolios provide a means by which a writer can show (1) a wide range of skills or (2) growth over time in a specific skill.
	• Keeping a portfolio encourages a writer to be thoughtful and reflective about his or her work and to set goals for improvement.
Major Concepts	• Through a carefully chosen collection of writings, a student portfolio provides a detailed picture of who a writer is. (page 32)
	• Well-constructed portfolios contain a table of contents, dates to show when each piece was written, and a reflective letter or essay to explain why each piece was chosen. (page 34)
	• Four key steps help students design effective portfolios. (page 35)
Performance Standards	Students are expected to . . . • review a collection of their own written works to determine strengths and weaknesses and to set goals as writers.

Getting Started with "Developing a Portfolio"

Start-Up Activity: List the following professions on the board: *graphic designer, advertiser, freelance writer, fashion designer,* and *architect.* Explain to the class that for people in these professions a portfolio is an essential tool. Describe how it is used to showcase their work to prospective clients or employers. If at all possible, invite someone from one of these noted professions to share his or her portfolio with the class.

Enrichment Activity: If your students compile a portfolio, make sure that they share their finished products with their classmates. Also make sure that you meet individually with each student for a discussion about his or her work. (A portfolio takes a great deal of time and effort to compile, and, in the end, it should be treated with comparable admiration and respect.)

Teaching Resources

Write Source 2000 Teacher's Guide

- Minilessons:
  "Only the Best" (page 228)
  "My, how I've grown." (page 228)
- "Using Writing Portfolios" (page 189)

Write Source 2000 Handbook

- "Getting Your Writing Ready," page 38, provides a checklist that will help students prepare their writing for portfolios.

Write Source 2000 Program Guide

- A teaching unit (lesson plans and blackline masters) can be found in the Program Guide ring binder for each grade level.

Publishing Your Writing

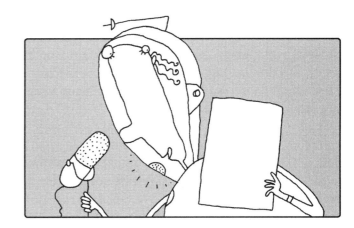

(See handbook pages 37-43.)

This chapter teaches students how to share their writing with an audience. It deals with several different publishing opportunities: participating in a contest, submitting material to a magazine, performing a work in play form, self-publishing on the World Wide Web, and so on. It also points out the importance of polishing a work before publishing.

Of Special Interest
- "Publishing Ideas" shares many different ways for student writers to place their texts before an audience. (page 39)
- "Places to Publish" lists specific contests and magazines that solicit student writing. (page 41)
- "Making Your Own Web Site" gives students an overview of the steps involved in creating their own Web pages to showcase their work. (page 43)

Rationale
- When writing is published, it seems more "real" to young people.
- If students publish their own work, the importance of careful writing becomes more apparent.

Major Concepts
- Good writers are their own most demanding audience. They don't publish a work until it is truly ready. (pages 37-38)
- There are many different ways to publish writing. Student writers, too, can find ways to get their work before an audience. (page 39)

Performance Standards

Students are expected to . . .
- edit drafts to ensure clarity, neatness, and accuracy in content and format.
- use available technology to publish texts.

Getting Started with "Publishing Your Writing"

Start-Up Activity: Inform your students that they are all published writers in one form or another. (Publishing, as presented in this chapter, refers to different ways to share writing.) Then have them read through "Publishing Ideas" (page 39 in the handbook) to identify ways that their work has been published.

Enrichment Activity: The Internet has opened up new publishing opportunities for students. If your class has access to the Net, show different sites where students can post their work. Use our Web site **(thewritesource.com)** as a starting point for this demonstration. Your class, as well as individual students, can also make their own Web sites for publishing. (See page 43 in the handbook.)

Teaching Resources

Write Source 2000 Teacher's Guide

- Minilessons:
  "Learning the Ropes" (page 228)
  "Take it on-line." (page 228)

Write Source 2000 Handbook

- "Publishing," page 201, describes some creative ways to publish poetry.

Write Source 2000 Program Guide

- A teaching unit (lesson plans and blackline masters) can be found in the Program Guide ring binder for each grade level.

Prewriting:
Choosing a Subject

(See handbook pages 45-52.)

This chapter presents writing as a natural human activity, one closely related to thinking. It explains that writing is a process, and the first step is prewriting—choosing a subject and gathering details about it. The bulk of the chapter is devoted to strategies for choosing a subject, which will help students identify topics for both assignments and their own writing enjoyment.

Of Special Interest	• The "Quick Guide" in the handbook provides an overview of prewriting and its relation to the overall writing process. It serves as a handy reminder of the most significant points in the chapter. (page 46) • "Creating a Writing 'SourceBank'" presents ideas for collecting interesting writing topics. (page 47)
Rationale	• Writing is an activity for all people, not for a select few. • Students need strategies for identifying and choosing appropriate writing subjects. • Accomplished writers often collect ideas in a notebook and keep a journal of their thoughts.
Major Concepts	• Prewriting means "getting prepared to write." (page 46) • Writers are always watching for ideas and recording them in a notebook or journal. (page 47) • Strategies such as journal writing, clustering, listing, and freewriting can help to identify a specific writing subject. (pages 48-49)
Performance Standards	Students are expected to . . . • use prewriting strategies such as journal writing, clustering, listing, and freewriting to generate ideas.

Getting Started with "Choosing a Subject"

Start-Up Activity: Early in the year, have your students begin to list possible writing ideas in a small pocket notebook (handbook page 47), or have them create a life map highlighting the highs and lows in their lives up to this point (page 52). Provide students with large sheets of paper for their life maps.

Enrichment Activity: Show your students how to use the "Essentials of Life Checklist" (handbook page 49). To get them started, ask students to imagine the following assignment: *Write about some aspect of a memorable field trip.* Suggest ways in which to use the checklist categories to find specific writing subjects, and then have students (individually or in pairs) generate possible writing ideas. Afterward, ask for volunteers to share some of their ideas with the class.

Teaching Resources

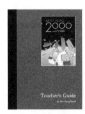

Write Source 2000 Teacher's Guide

- Minilessons:
  "The end becomes the beginning." (page 229)
  "At the Starting Line" (page 229)

Write Source 2000 Handbook

- "Gathering Details," pages 53-60, contains additional prewriting strategies and continues the discussion of prewriting.

Write Source 2000 Program Guide

- A teaching unit (lesson plans and blackline masters) can be found in the Program Guide ring binder for each grade level.

Gathering Details

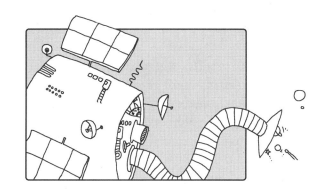

(See handbook pages 53-60.)

This chapter explains that the second part of prewriting is gathering details for writing. It recommends various strategies for gathering, including using graphic organizers. The chapter also emphasizes that students need to recognize when further research is necessary and which ideas should be included in their writing. Finally, this chapter discusses how to arrange details for the best effect.

Of Special Interest

- "Using Gathering Strategies" presents different strategies for researching and collecting facts and details. (pages 54-55)
- "Using Graphic Organizers" provides an overview of seven organizers plus page references for more information on each. (page 56)
- "Planning Your Writing" explains how to find a writing focus and offers five ways to arrange the details in a piece of writing. (pages 59-60)

Rationale

- After choosing a subject, students need to gather information and plan how to use that information in their writing.

Major Concepts

- During prewriting, writers need to identify what they already know about their subject and then do research to find any missing information. (pages 54-55)
- Graphic organizers and collection sheets are effective ways to gather details for writing. (pages 56-57)
- Writing should be planned: It needs a clear focus, specific details, and effective organization. (pages 59-60)

Performance Standards

Students are expected to . . .

- use graphic organizers and other prewriting strategies to gather ideas.
- use an inventory, the 5 W's of writing, graphic organizers, and other prewriting strategies to organize ideas.

Getting Started with "Gathering Details"

Start-Up Activity: List the following categories on the board: *personal writing, subject writing,* and *report writing.* Make sure that students know which forms of writing relate to each category. (See the table of contents, handbook page vi.) Then, after reviewing pages 53-57, ask students to suggest the best gathering strategies to use for each category of writing. (For example, free 46
writing, clustering, and the 5 W's chart work well for most types of personal writing.)

Enrichment Activity: After reviewing "Finding a Focus" (page 59), have students volunteer general subject areas that interest them (*winter sports, Italian food, old movies,* etc.). Then, as a class, identify different specific subjects and focus statements for each subject area. Here's an example:

> General subject area: *Winter sports*
> Specific subject: *Snowboarding*
> Focus statement: *Snowboarding belongs to the young at heart.*

Teaching Resources

Write Source 2000 Teacher's Guide

- Minilessons:
  "Make a list." (page 229)
  "Same and Different" (page 229)

Write Source 2000 Handbook

- "Prewriting: Choosing a Subject," pages 45-52, leads up to "Gathering Details."
- "Study-Reading Skills," pages 307-322, shows how to use a number of important graphic organizers.

Write Source 2000 Program Guide

- A teaching unit (lesson plans and blackline masters) can be found in the Program Guide ring binder for each grade level.

Writing the First Draft

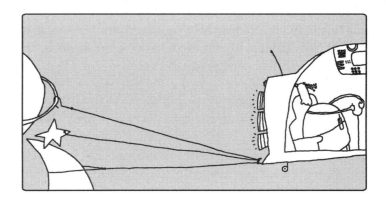

(See handbook pages 61-66.)

This chapter explains how to approach the second step in the writing process—developing the first draft. It also provides guidelines and examples that will help students organize the beginning, middle, and ending of their drafts, plus a special section on the types of support that can be used to develop a piece of writing.

Of Special Interest
- The "Quick Guide" tells how to start a first draft and how to focus on writing freely, with an eye toward ideas, organization, and voice. (page 62)
- "Writing an Opening Paragraph," "Developing the Middle Part," and "Bringing Your Writing to a Close" provide help when dealing with each section of a first draft. (pages 63-66)

Rationale
- Inexperienced writers often try to produce a finished piece in one sitting.
- During the first draft, writers should work with ideas rather than with the fine points of spelling, grammar, and usage.

Major Concepts
- The first draft is a "discovery draft." Its purpose is to get a writer's thoughts down in a connected fashion on paper. (page 61)
- A first draft should be freely written, without much worry about neatness or correctness. (page 62)
- The draft's beginning should introduce the subject and interest readers; its middle should explain and/or support that subject; and its ending should bring the writing to a satisfying close. (pages 63-66)

Performance Standards

Students are expected to . . .
- compose a draft that establishes a central idea (topic sentence) and a clear and well-supported conclusion.

Getting Started with "Writing the First Draft"

Start-Up Activity: After reviewing handbook pages 61-62, share with your students the following quotations, which have to do with drafting as a process of discovery and/or as a process of setting the "real writing" in motion.

> "By the time I finish my first draft, I've written between the lines and around the edges and on the back of the paper. It's a mess."
> —Beverly Cleary

> "A writer keeps surprising himself."
> —Thomas Williams

> "I love first drafts. I just write and write. But I've learned that no matter how good I think my first draft is, it can always be better."
> —Emma Tobin, student writer

Enrichment Activity: Share with students effective opening and closing paragraphs in essays, news stories, and feature articles. Identify the different elements that help make them effective. (Use handbook pages 63 and 66 as guides.) Then ask students to find their own examples to analyze.

Teaching Resources

Write Source 2000 Teacher's Guide

- Minilessons:
  "In Support" (page 230)
  "From Beginning to End" (page 230)

Write Source 2000 Handbook

- "Planning Your Writing," pages 59-60, helps students establish a focus for their first drafts and organize their supporting details.

Write Source 2000 Program Guide

- A teaching unit (lesson plans and blackline masters) can be found in the Program Guide ring binder for each grade level.

Revising Your Writing

(See handbook pages 67-74.)

This chapter presents revision as an important step in the process of writing—for students and professionals alike. It includes specific guidelines for making students' revision work more effective and, through examples and suggestions, links revision to three key traits of good writing: ideas, organization, and voice.

Of Special Interest
- The "Quick Guide" provides a thorough review of revision. (page 68)
- "Five Keys to Good Revision" offers specific, easy-to-follow suggestions for making any piece of writing stronger. (page 69)
- The "Revising Checklist" gives students a quick, "big picture" review of their writing before they go on to the next step: editing. (page 74)

Rationale
- Revision is an important step for all writers.
- While editing focuses on surface changes like correcting spelling and punctuation, revision goes deeper—moving paragraphs around, taking sections out, or putting new information in.
- Students can learn revision strategies to improve their writing.

Major Concepts
- Revision can involve major changes that affect the whole form and tone of students' writing. (page 68)
- Specific strategies, such as waiting a day or two to revise, reading the work aloud, and sharing writing with others, make students' revisions much stronger. (page 69)
- Students who understand the significance of ideas, organization, and voice in writing are far more likely to know what to change in order to improve a piece of writing. (pages 70-72)

Performance Standards

Students are expected to . . .
- revise selected drafts by adding, deleting, combining, and rearranging text while striving for clarity and coherence.

Getting Started with "Revising Your Writing"

Start-Up Activity: After reviewing handbook pages 67-68 with your students, turn to pages 14-15 so they can see actual revising in action. Note that the writer makes many different changes in the text—including some cutting, adding, and rewriting.

Special Note: Review "Revising in Action" on page 73 only after you look over pages 69-72 with your students.

Enrichment Activity: Instruct your students to use the checklist on page 74 as a basic guide whenever they revise a first draft. Also have them save all of their work for important writing assignments, so you can see how much revising they have done and make recommendations for future writing projects.

Teaching Resources

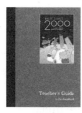

Write Source 2000 Teacher's Guide

- Minilessons:
  "Hit the target." (page 230)
  "Making Big Changes" (page 230)

Write Source 2000 Handbook

- The "Traits of Effective Writing," pages 19-24, shows samples of effective writing that may help students with their revising. This chapter also contains a helpful revising checklist on page 24.

Write Source 2000 Program Guide

- A teaching unit (lesson plans and blackline masters) can be found in the Program Guide ring binder for each grade level.

Group Advising

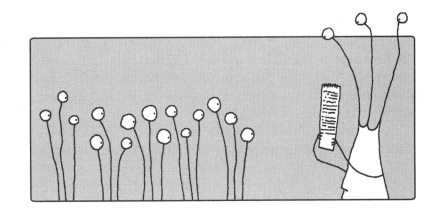

(See handbook pages 75-78.)

This chapter presents group advising as a critical component of the revision process. It includes specific guidelines for students in their alternate roles as writer-reader and listener-responder. In addition, it offers sample comments that will help students respond to their peers' writing.

Of Special Interest
- "Making Helpful Responses" illustrates specific, tactful comments and questions for responding to writing. (page 77)
- The "Checklist for Good Writing" and the "Student Response Sheet" offer two different ways for students to respond to writing. (pages 24 and 78)

Rationale
- Participating in group advising is one good way to discover whether a student's writing has the desired effect on an audience.
- Both writer-reader and listener-responder have specific responsibilities to make the group advising process work well.

Major Concepts
- Sharing writing in a group, though sometimes scary, gives students the chance to receive feedback from a real audience. (page 75)
- Understanding the roles of both writer-reader and listener-responder will help students in group advising sessions. (page 76)
- Specific comments and questions that call for more than simple yes/no answers give student writers useful feedback for revising. (page 77)

Performance Standards

Students are expected to . . .
- respond in constructive ways to one another's writing.
- collaborate with peers to generate ideas and revise drafts.
- confer with other writers about composition, organization, and revision of each other's writing.

Getting Started with "Group Advising"

Start-Up Activity: Have students write freely for 10 minutes about anything they wish. (Refer them to handbook pages 50-51 for ideas.) Then have them share their writing with a classmate, using the "Group Advising Guidelines" on page 76. Instruct listeners to make at least one positive comment and ask at least two questions that would help the writer-reader develop his or her writing.

Afterward, have students work their initial freewritings into finished pieces, or have them move on to another type of writing for additional group practice.

Enrichment Activity: Give each student three pieces of writing. Erase all names and number the papers. Tell students: "One of these samples is a very good piece of writing. A second is average. A third one really needs work. Predict which paper is very effective, which paper is average, and which paper is least effective. Look at content first. Then look at mechanics."

As you discuss their predictions, ask them to talk about the strengths and weaknesses they found in each piece of writing. Then tell the students how you would rate these papers and your reasons for doing so.

Teaching Resources

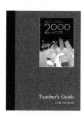

Write Source 2000 Teacher's Guide

- Minilessons:
  "Any comments?" (page 230)
  "In Response" (page 231)

Write Source 2000 Handbook

- The "Checklist for Good Writing," page 24, may prove helpful for students during group-advising sessions.
- "Group Skills," pages 369-372, provides additional information about the dynamics of group work.

Write Source 2000 Program Guide

- A teaching unit (lesson plans and blackline masters) can be found in the Program Guide ring binder for each grade level.

Editing and Proofreading

(See handbook pages 79-83.)

 This chapter instructs students on the fourth step in the writing process: editing and proofreading. It helps them focus on smooth sentence structure, the best word choice, and accuracy in their work. Many specific problems are identified, and specific tactics are suggested for solving them. The chapter ends with a checklist students can use as a guide when editing and proofreading their own writing.

Of Special Interest
- "Checking for Sentence Smoothness" identifies the most common sentence problems and offers a clear listing of what writers can do to avert them. (page 81)
- "Checking for Word Choice" also identifies writing problems related to word choice and tells students what to do to ensure the best selection of words. (page 82)

Rationale
- A writer's message is best conveyed in a form that is carefully edited and proofread.

Major Concepts
- Editing and proofreading involve three important traits of effective writing: sentence smoothness, word choice, and correct, accurate copy. (page 80)

Performance Standards
Students are expected to . . .
- edit drafts to ensure standard usage, grammar, and mechanics, including varied sentence structure, appropriate word choice, and correct spelling, capitalization, punctuation, and format.

Getting Started with "Editing and Proofreading"

Start-Up Activity: After your students read handbook page 79 silently, lead a class discussion about editing and proofreading. Emphasize that editing involves checking revised writing for style and accuracy, while proofreading deals with checking a final copy for errors. Then have students turn to pages 16-17 for an example of editing in action.

Enrichment Activity: Have students check the effectiveness of the sentences in a piece of their writing using the "Testing Your Sentences" strategy in the handbook as a guide (page 81). Discuss the results of their analysis; then remind students that when they edit, they should check their sentences for variety, length, and verb choice.

Teaching Resources

Write Source 2000 Teacher's Guide

- Minilessons:
  "The Right Choice" (page 231)
  "Check it out!" (page 231)
- "What About Grammar?" (pages 190-192)

Write Source 2000 Handbook

- "Composing Sentences" and "Combining Sentences," pages 85-92 and 93-96, provide examples and explanations to help students edit their writing for sentence style and correctness.
- The "Proofreader's Guide," pages 386-457, helps students edit and proofread for punctuation, capitalization, usage, and grammar.

Write Source 2000 Program Guide

- A teaching unit (lesson plans and blackline masters) can be found in the Program Guide ring binder for each grade level.

Composing Sentences

(See handbook pages 85-92.)

   This chapter helps students master the basic sentence. Explanations and examples show students how to avoid common errors in sentence construction, including sentence fragments, run-on sentences, misplaced modifiers, and so on.

Of Special Interest
- "Write Complete Sentences" explains how to avoid fragments, comma splices, run-on sentences, and rambling sentences. (pages 86-87)
- "Write Agreeable Sentences" covers subject-verb agreement involving compound subjects, unusual word order, and so on. (pages 88-89)
- "Write Clear, Concise Sentences" deals with pronoun problems, misplaced modifiers, and nonstandard language. (pages 90-91)

Rationale
- Student writers need to know basic sentence structure.
- As students mature, they need to know how to express themselves with more complicated sentence structures.

Major Concepts
- Sentences are the basic building blocks of writing. (page 85)
- A complete sentence contains a subject and a predicate and expresses a complete thought. (pages 86-87)
- Subjects and predicates must agree in number. (pages 88-89)
- Good sentences avoid the confusion caused by pronoun problems, misplaced modifiers, and nonstandard language. (pages 90-91)

Performance Standards

Students are expected to . . .
- eliminate sentence fragments, run-on sentences, rambling sentences, and comma splices in their writing.
- employ standard English usage when they communicate, including subject-verb and pronoun-antecedent agreement.

Getting Started with "Composing Sentences"

Start-Up Activity: Write the sentences below on the board, but don't introduce them as sentences to the class. Instead, ask students what these groups of words have in common. When someone says that they are all sentences, ask the class members how they know this for sure. Continue the discussion by talking about the working parts of a sentence, sentence length, and so on. Then review handbook page 85 with the students.

Anna keyboards.
Michael plays the trumpet.
Mr. Robertson, our band teacher, belongs to a jazz band.
Many members of the seventh-grade band don't practice on weekends.

Enrichment Activity: On small strips of paper, write a series of possible subjects for sentences. Make sure to include some compound subjects, indefinite pronouns, and collective nouns. Also, on strips of paper, write a series of verbs, including action verbs and linking verbs. Put the subjects in one hat and the verbs in another hat. Then have small groups of students select 5-10 strips from each hat and compose nonsense sentences by combining the different subjects and verbs. (If they select 5 strips from each hat, they should be ready to write 5 sentences and so on.) Ask for volunteers to write some of their sentences on the board.

Teaching Resources

Write Source 2000 Teacher's Guide

- Minilessons:
  "Sentence Doctor" (page 231)
  "It's not definite." (page 231)

Write Source 2000 Handbook

- "Combining Sentences," pages 93-96, continues the discussion of sentences.
- "Writing with Style," pages 129-136, discusses the "art" of writing stylish sentences.
- "Understanding Sentences," pages 434-438, defines and illustrates the basic parts of sentences.

Write Source 2000 Program Guide

- A teaching unit (lesson plans and blackline masters) can be found in the Program Guide ring binder for each grade level.

Combining Sentences

(See handbook pages 93-96.)

This chapter shows students three basic ways to combine short sentences into smoother, more mature sentences: combining with key words, combining with phrases, and combining with longer sentences. Practicing sentence combining is one of the most effective ways for students to improve their writing style.

Of Special Interest
- "Combining with Phrases" shows how to use phrases, compound subjects, and compound verbs to combine sentences. (page 95)
- "Combining with Longer Sentences" explains how to construct compound and complex sentences. (page 96)

Rationale
- Sentence-combining skills help students become more fluent writers.
- Sentence-combining skills help students to better understand the English language.

Major Concepts
- Sentence combining is the act of making one longer sentence out of two or more short sentences. (page 93)
- Short sentences can be combined by moving one or more key words into a new, longer sentence. (page 94)
- Prepositional, appositive, infinitive, and participial phrases can be used to combine sentences. (page 95)
- Simple sentences can be combined to make compound and complex sentences. (page 96)

Performance Standards

Students are expected to . . .
- write in complete sentences, using a variety of types (simple, compound, complex, and so on).
- use conjunctions to connect ideas meaningfully.
- use prepositional phrases to elaborate written ideas.

Getting Started with "Combining Sentences"

Start-Up Activity: Write the sentences below on the board. Point out that they lack style because they are so short and choppy. Then ask for a volunteer to combine these ideas into one longer, smoother sentence. (See the sample below.)

> *Crazy Chris draws.*
> *He draws funny pictures.*
> *He draws them for the local newspaper.*
> *He spends a lot of time doing it.*

> Sample Combined Sentence:
> *Crazy Chris spends a lot of time drawing funny pictures for the local newspaper.*

Instruct students to check each piece of their writing for series of short, choppy sentences, and to combine these ideas into longer, smoother-reading sentences.

Enrichment Activity: Assign students to write sets of short sentences like the ones above. They should also write a sample combined sentence for each set. Collect their work, and then use the sentences as a daily or weekly warm-up for sentence combining.

Teaching Resources

Write Source 2000 Teacher's Guide

- Minilessons:
  "Make it longer." (page 232)
  "Put them together." (page 232)

Write Source 2000 Handbook

- "Checking for Sentence Smoothness," page 81, reminds students to check the style of their sentences during editing.
- "Composing Sentences," pages 85-92, covers basic sentence errors and sentence clarity.
- "Types of Sentences," pages 437.4 - 438.2, explains and illustrates different types of longer sentences: compound, complex, and compound-complex.

Write Source 2000 Program Guide

- A teaching unit (lesson plans and blackline masters) can be found in the Program Guide ring binder for each grade level.

Building Paragraphs

(See handbook pages 97-106.)

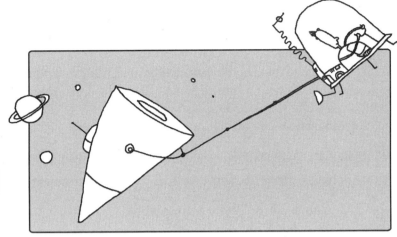

   A student who has mastered the basics of building paragraphs can tackle any academic topic and write to any purpose, whether it be to describe, to explain, to entertain, or to persuade. This chapter covers all the basics to help students write focused, organized paragraphs.

Of Special Interest

- The topic sentence, the body, and the closing sentence are explained and labeled in a sample paragraph. (pages 98-99)
- Sample descriptive, narrative, expository, and persuasive paragraphs are provided. (pages 100-103)

Rationale

- The paragraph forms the structural and conceptual basis of all writing.
- Learning to write good paragraphs helps students focus and organize their thoughts and equips them to write longer, more complex pieces.
- Understanding the different types of paragraphs helps students match their writing to their purpose.

Major Concepts

- A paragraph focuses on a specific topic that is developed and supported with details to give readers a clear understanding of the topic. (page 97)
- There are three parts to a paragraph: the topic sentence, the body, and the closing sentence. (pages 98-99)
- There are four basic types of paragraphs: descriptive, narrative, expository, and persuasive. (pages 100-103)
- Details—the facts and examples that support the topic—are an important part of every paragraph. (page 105)
- Certain words and phrases are useful for making transitions within paragraphs. (page 106)

Performance Standards

Students are expected to . . .
- establish a central idea (topic sentence), collect details, and organize supporting information into a coherent paragraph.

Getting Started with "Building Paragraphs"

Start-Up Activity: Have your students think metaphorically about paragraphs by writing "A paragraph is like . . ." statements. Here is a sample statement: *A paragraph is like a sub sandwich—the more layers you add, the better it tastes.* These statements should be shared and discussed in class.

Enrichment Activity: Give your students the following special challenge: Write a paragraph that includes the following levels of detail. (See handbook page 64.)

(1) Controlling (Topic) sentence
  (2) Clarifying sentence
    (3) Completing sentence
    (3) Completing sentence
  (2) Clarifying sentence
    (3) Completing sentence
    (3) Completing sentence
(1) Closing sentence

Special Note: This is only a suggested pattern. Change it as necessary to meet the needs of your students.

Teaching Resources

Write Source 2000 Teacher's Guide

- Minilessons:
  "Building Blocks" (page 232)
  "Match the topic to the type." (page 232)
- Assessment Rubrics (pages 179, 180-186)

Write Source 2000 Handbook

- "Thinking and Writing," pages 283-290, contains additional sample paragraphs based on different levels of thinking.

Write Source 2000 Program Guide

- A teaching unit (lesson plans and blackline masters) can be found in the Program Guide ring binder for each grade level.

Writing Expository Essays

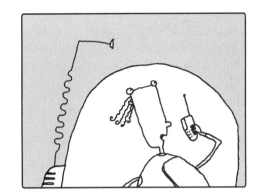

(See handbook pages 107-114.)

This chapter explains what an expository essay is and how to write one. As students write expository essays, they are organizing and presenting factual information in a way that demonstrates what they have learned or understand about a subject.

Of Special Interest
- "Developing Two-Part Essays" explains what a two-part essay is and how to develop one. (pages 112-113)
- "Personalizing Your Essays" outlines nine ways to infuse essays with energy and the writer's distinctive voice. (page 114)

Rationale
- Writing expository essays helps students learn to think clearly.
- Expository-writing skills enable students to share what they know.
- Students will do expository writing throughout their school years—and beyond.

Major Concepts
- An expository essay explains or informs. (page 107)
- Writing an expository essay requires gathering specific details and organizing them into a beginning, middle, and ending that clearly share information with the reader. (pages 108-109)
- A good essay subject is specific, interests the writer, and is carefully developed. (pages 110-111)
- Two-part essays, which require two different types of thinking, are the most challenging essay form. (pages 112-113)
- Writers can personalize their essays. (page 114)

Performance Standards

Students are expected to . . .
- create expository compositions that state a clear purpose and engage the interest of the reader.
- elaborate on the purpose of their composition with supportive details.
- use organizational patterns appropriate to the type of composition.
- conclude with a summary linked to the composition's purpose.

Getting Started with "Writing Expository Essays"

Start-Up Activity: After discussing the chapter opening with your students (page 107), list the following general subject areas on the board:

- *current health care and medicine*
- *careers and professions*
- *recreation and hobbies*
- *community life*

As a class, establish specific writing subjects for expository essays. For example, laser eye surgery is a potential writing idea related to the first general subject area. Remind students that it is important to identify limited, manageable subjects for expository essays.

Enrichment Activity: Review with students "Personalizing Your Essays" on handbook page 114 when they are developing an expository essay. Ask them to try one or more of the ideas listed on this page to add more spark and energy to their writing.

Teaching Resources

Write Source 2000 Teacher's Guide

- Minilessons:
  "For Starters" (page 233)
  "Charting Your Course" (page 233)
- Assessment Rubric (page 182)

Write Source 2000 Handbook

- "Planning Your Writing," page 59, helps students develop focus or thesis statements for their essays.
- "Writing the First Draft," pages 61-66, provides tips, guidelines, and examples that will help students with their essay writing.
- "Gathering Ideas for Essays," pages 123-127, offers guidelines for collecting details for different types of essay subjects.

Write Source 2000 Program Guide

- A teaching unit (lesson plans and blackline masters) can be found in the Program Guide ring binder for each grade level.

Writing Persuasive Essays

(See handbook pages 115-127.)

In this chapter, students are introduced to the challenging task of writing essays designed to persuade readers. Persuasive essays call for the same organizational skills as expository essays do, but also require students to form and express reasonable opinions, to support their opinions with evidence, and to anticipate conflicting opinions and evidence.

Of Special Interest
- "Gathering Ideas for Essays" offers tips for writing essays that focus on a person, a place, an object, a definition, an event, and an explanation. (pages 123-127)

Rationale
- Writing persuasive essays helps students learn how to form sound opinions based on facts and evidence.
- Students need practice stating and supporting opinions.
- Students must learn to anticipate and address counterarguments.

Major Concepts
- A persuasive essay states and supports an opinion. (pages 116-117)
- The subject of a persuasive essay should be specific, timely, debatable, and something the writer feels strongly about. (page 118)
- The beginning of a persuasive essay should introduce the subject, share background information, and give the writer's opinion in an attention-grabbing way. (page 120)
- Opinions are statements of fact, value, or policy. (page 121)
- Opinions must be supported with evidence. (page 122)

Performance Standards

Students are expected to . . .
- create persuasive compositions that state a clear position in support of a proposition or proposal.
- support a position with organized and relevant evidence.
- anticipate and address reader concerns and counterarguments.

Getting Started with "Writing Persuasive Essays"

Start-Up Activity: After discussing handbook pages 115-118, have students practice writing opinion statements—the type that could serve as the focus of persuasive essays. To get started, list the following general categories on the board:

- *school life*
- *sports*
- *U.S. history*
- *technology*

Have students list two or three subjects related to each category. For example, *study halls, lunch hour,* and *homework* are three possible subjects related to school life. Then ask them to write an opinion statement for at least one specific subject under each category. Discuss some of these statements.

Enrichment Activity: Analyze sample essays with your students using "Thinking Through an Argument" (pages 121-122) as a general guide. Encourage students to use the information on these two pages to help them write their own persuasive essays.

Teaching Resources

Write Source 2000 Teacher's Guide

- Minilessons:
  "I object!" (page 233)
  "Keep on schooling?" (page 233)
- Assessment Rubric (page 184)

Write Source 2000 Handbook

- "Newswriting Sampler," page 172, provides a sample editorial, an important type of persuasive writing.
- "Thinking Logically," pages 291-296, helps students understand the difference between fact and opinion and avoid fuzzy or sloppy thinking.

Write Source 2000 Program Guide

- A teaching unit (lesson plans and blackline masters) can be found in the Program Guide ring binder for each grade level.

Writing with Style

(See handbook pages 129-136.)

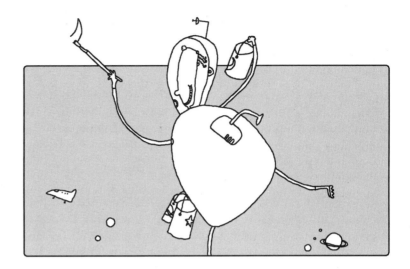

This chapter focuses on how to develop style in one's writing. It explains that style is personal, is somewhat different for every writer, and evolves naturally as an author gains experience. It also contends, however, that writers can improve their style by studying and imitating the polished writing of favorite authors.

Of Special Interest

- "Studying Sentences with Style" identifies four types of sentences and offers examples written by professional writers that students can emulate. (page 131)
- "Modeling the Masters" goes a step further, asking students to mimic sentences and passages they admire in their favorite authors' work. (pages 132-133)
- "Using Strong, Colorful Words" explains how to make writing more active and powerful with careful word choice. (pages 135-136)

Rationale

- Style is personal; it develops naturally as writers practice and gain experience.
- Writers can help their style develop by reading avidly, by writing regularly, and by modeling interesting sentences and passages.

Major Concepts

- Good writers write naturally and freely, letting their own voice come through. Then they revise problematic sentences and polish the whole piece for better style. (page 131)
- Specific nouns, vivid verbs, effective modifiers, and words with feeling add style to a piece of writing. (pages 135-136)

Performance Standards

Students are expected to . . .
- select vocabulary and voice in their writing with an awareness of audience and purpose.

Getting Started with "Writing with Style"

Start-Up Activity: Have students select a writing prompt from handbook page 50 to write about for 5-10 minutes. Afterward, pairs of students may exchange papers and underline two or three phrases or sentences that sound especially stylish or effective. Discuss some of the examples as a class. Then, as you review different parts of the chapter, see if your students' notion of stylish writing changes at all.

Enrichment Activity: Have students submit samples of well-made sentences from books, magazines, and newspapers. Then, at regular intervals, write one of these sentences on the board for modeling practice. (See pages 132-133 for an explanation.)

Teaching Resources

Write Source 2000 Teacher's Guide

* Minilessons:
  "Modeling a Master" (page 234)
  "The Real You" (page 234)

Write Source 2000 Handbook

* "Traits of Effective Writing," pages 19-24, provides samples of engaging writing in action.
* "Editing and Proofreading," pages 79-83, helps students check their writing for sentence smoothness and effective word choice.
* "Combining Sentences," pages 93-96, shows students how to write longer, more stylish sentences.

Write Source 2000 Program Guide

* A teaching unit (lesson plans and blackline masters) can be found in the Program Guide ring binder for each grade level.

Writing Techniques and Terms

(See handbook pages 137-143.)

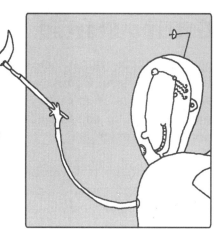

This chapter contains a glossary for students to use when discussing or thinking about writing. It lists common techniques that students will see demonstrated in literature and that they can incorporate into their own writing. It also defines various terms that commonly arise when writing is discussed. Students will find this combined glossary invaluable for looking up unfamiliar words they come across in and out of class.

Of Special Interest
- "Writing Techniques" defines techniques and methods often used in writing to enhance style and improve interest. (pages 138-140)
- "Writing Terms" defines words that writers and readers use to talk about writing. (pages 141-143)

Rationale
- In order to discuss the craft of writing, students need to be familiar with common terms and techniques of writing.

Major Concepts
- Writing techniques are methods used to achieve a particular effect in writing. (pages 138-140)
- Writing terms are words used to discuss the writing process, from prewriting through publishing. (pages 141-143)

Performance Standards
Students are expected to . . .
- select and use reference materials and resources as needed for writing, revising, and editing final drafts.

Getting Started with "Writing Techniques and Terms"

Start-Up Activity: In one column, list on the board writing techniques that students may know about from a previous year. Consider *metaphor, personification, simile, hyperbole,* and *sensory details*. In another column, list in a different order an example of each. (Examples are provided in the chapter.) Then have your students try to match each technique with the appropriate example.

Enrichment Activity: Make pairs of students responsible for presenting minilessons on various terms and techniques. For example, you might have one group provide an explanation and examples of *parallelism* and another group present information on *cliches*.

Teaching Resources

Write Source 2000 Teacher's Guide

- Minilessons:
  "Great Technique" (page 234)
  "Seeing is believing." (page 234)

Write Source 2000 Handbook

- "Traditional Techniques of Poetry" and "Traditional Forms of Poetry," pages 202-203 and 204-205, contain terms and techniques for writing poetry.
- "Understanding Literature," pages 342-344, lists different types and elements of literature.

Write Source 2000 Program Guide

- A teaching unit (lesson plans and blackline masters) can be found in the Program Guide ring binder for each grade level.

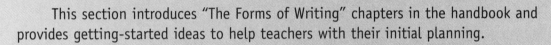

The Forms of Writing

Introductory Notes

This section introduces "The Forms of Writing" chapters in the handbook and provides getting-started ideas to help teachers with their initial planning.

Journal Writing

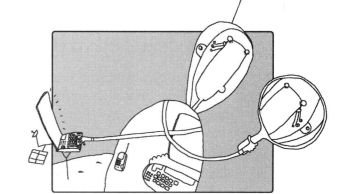

(See handbook pages 145-148.)

Journal writing is a good way to encourage students to write regularly about topics they are interested in. In this chapter, your students will learn about six different types of journal writing as well as how to get started with their own journaling. The chapter also contains a sample journal entry.

Of Special Interest
- Five steps to getting started in journal writing are outlined. (page 146)
- The differences between types of journals are explained. (page 148)

Rationale
- Journal writing is generally an easy, nonthreatening way for even reluctant writers to write on a regular basis.
- Journal writing helps students understand daily experiences, learn about subjects they are studying, try out new ideas, and become more fluent writers.

Major Concepts
- Getting started in journal writing involves collecting the proper tools, choosing a regular time to write, writing about things important to the writer, and keeping track of the writing. (page 146)
- Asking questions and wondering about details help students reflect upon their experiences and feelings. (page 147)
- Students can use many different types of journals: diaries, dialogue journals, learning logs, reader-response journals, specialized journals, and travel logs. (page 148)

Performance Standards

Students are expected to . . .
- write to express, discover, record, develop, and reflect on ideas.
- write to learn in all subjects using tools such as dialogue journals, learning logs, and response journals.

Getting Started with "Journal Writing"

Start-Up Activity: Read and react to pages 145-147 in the handbook. Then help your students lift off into their first journal writing using the countdown that follows: (Before you start, make sure that everyone has his or her notebook open and pen or pencil in hand.)

10 . . . 9 . . . *(Remember, write for the entire time.)*

8 . . . 7 . . . *(Go where your pen and your thinking take you. You don't have to stick to one topic.)*

6 . . . 5 . . . *(If you get stuck, write "I'm stuck " until something comes to mind.)*

4 . . . 3 . . . *(Your hand might get a little stiff near the end, but you can tough it out.)*

2 . . . 1 . . . *(Write!)*

Enrichment Activity: Once your students have written in a classroom journal for a few weeks, have them review their work to date. (Refer them to "Keep track of your writing" at the bottom of page 146.) Also have them exchange an entry with a classmate. Ask the students to comment on at least one interesting or well-stated part in each other's writing.

Teaching Resources

Write Source 2000 Teacher's Guide

- "The Personal Experience Approach" (pages 153-154)
- Minilessons:
  "The Time Machine" (page 235)
  "Dear Diary" (page 235)

Write Source 2000 Handbook

- "Starting Points for Writing," pages 50-51, provides prompts and topics for journal writing.

Write Source 2000 Program Guide

- A teaching unit (lesson plans and blackline masters) can be found in the Program Guide ring binder for each grade level.

Writing Friendly Letters

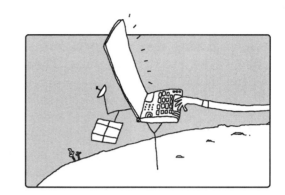

(See handbook pages 149-152.)

Writing a friendly letter is still one of the best ways to keep in touch with friends and family members and, in the process, to improve writing skills. This chapter contains a sample friendly letter and writing guidelines.

Of Special Interest
- "Parts of a Friendly Letter" explains the six common parts of the letter. (page 150)

Rationale
- Despite the rise in popularity of e-mail and the lowering of long-distance phone rates, letter writing is an important and unique form of communication.
- Everyone should learn how to write friendly letters and experience the joy of both writing and receiving letters.

Major Concepts
- Letter writing has several advantages over other forms of communication. (page 149)
- A standard friendly letter includes a heading, a salutation, a body, a closing, a signature, and, sometimes, a postscript. (pages 150-151)
- A friendly letter should be composed in a free and natural manner but checked for smoothness, completeness, and errors. (page 152)

Performance Standards

Students are expected to . . .
- engage the interest of the reader.
- follow an appropriate organizational pattern.
- reflect their personal thoughts, feelings, and experiences.

Getting Started with "Writing Friendly Letters"

Start-Up Activity: Discuss page 149 in the handbook with your students. Then conduct a brainstorming session in which the students offer situations when a friendly letter is an effective way to communicate. (These situations may give them ideas for friendly letters to write.)

You might also have them talk to friends, immediate family members, and relatives about the importance of friendly letters in their lives. Have students share their findings in class.

Enrichment Activity: Discuss with students related forms of friendly communication: phone conversations, personal visits, e-mail messages, fax sheets, etc. Have the class determine the upside and the downside for each form of communication. (Include the friendly letter in your discussion.)

Teaching Resources

Write Source 2000 Teacher's Guide

- Minilessons:
  "Did you hear the one about . . . ?" (page 235)
  "You've got real mail!" (page 235)

Write Source 2000 Handbook

- "Writing Guidelines: E-Mail" pages 254-255, shows students how to write e-mail messages, a common form of friendly correspondence.

Write Source 2000 Program Guide

- A teaching unit (lesson plans and blackline masters) can be found in the Program Guide ring binder for each grade level.

Autobiographical Writing

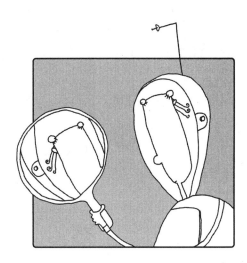

(See handbook pages 153-159.)

Autobiographical writing gives students the opportunity to reflect upon their own personal experiences. This chapter includes models of a personal narrative and a phase autobiography. It also includes writing guidelines and tips on how to choose a subject, gather details, and write, revise, and edit autobiographical writing.

Of Special Interest
- "Making Your Narrative Work" offers tips about including only the best details and about beginning and ending a piece effectively. (page 157)

Rationale
- All students have had experiences that are important to them and worth sharing with others.
- Students can learn to shape their experiences into stories that have a beginning, a middle, and an ending.

Major Concepts
- Students should write about personal experiences that are meaningful to them. (pages 153-155)
- A personal narrative should be written in the writer's natural voice and, through the details of the story, reveal something important about him or her. (page 156)
- Knowing where to begin, knowing what to include, and knowing when to quit are the keys to writing a good narrative. (page 157)

Performance Standards
Students are expected to . . .
- use prewriting strategies to generate and organize ideas.
- create an engaging story line by employing dialogue, sensory descriptions, specific action, and personal feelings.
- revise and edit their writing, striving for completeness, personal voice, specific word choice, and smooth-reading sentences.

Getting Started with "Autobiographical Writing"

Start-Up Activity: Prior to assigning a personal narrative, have students write a series of journal entries that focus on their experiences. (See page 50 in the handbook for writing prompts.) These entries will serve as a valuable resource of writing ideas.

To generate ideas for phase autobiographies, have students create a table of contents for their complete autobiography. Each chapter should focus on an important period, or phase, in their lives.

Enrichment Activity: Have your students praise or ridicule a personal keepsake (*a valued hat, a first baseball glove, an unflattering photograph*, etc.) in a brief speech. With the item as a prop, they should share the experience that makes this keepsake so important.

Teaching Resources

Write Source 2000 Teacher's Guide

- Minilessons:
  "I'll never forget . . . 1" (page 236)
  "I'll never forget . . . 2" (page 236)
- Assessment Rubric (page 181)

Write Source 2000 Handbook

- "Traits of Effective Writing," pages 19-24, serves as a guide to students as they develop their narratives.
- "Gathering Ideas for Essays," pages 123-126, helps students collect details for their writing.
- "Writing Personal Research Reports," pages 217-222, offers students a more challenging type of personal writing in which they investigate a topic of interest and share their results in a detailed narrative report.

Write Source 2000 Program Guide

- A teaching unit (lesson plans and blackline masters) can be found in the Program Guide ring binder for each grade level.

Biographical Writing

(See handbook pages 161-166.)

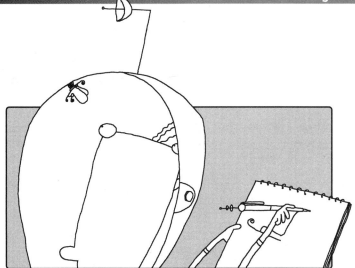

Biographical writing follows naturally from autobiographical writing. This chapter offers writing guidelines plus a sample story and phase biography.

Of Special Interest	• "Special Planning and Writing Tips" offers students ideas for writing effective biographical pieces. (page 165)
Rationale	• Biographical writing helps students appreciate, understand, and learn from other people and the world around them. • Writing biographies is a logical next step after completing one or more autobiographical pieces.
Major Concepts	• Writers may choose people they know, people who have influenced them, or people they have heard or read about as subjects for biographies. (page 163) • Details for a biography may come from the writer's memory, interviews, library research, radio, TV, or the Internet. (page 163) • A biography should clearly state the focus of the writing and answer the 5 W's about the subject in an interesting and entertaining way. (page 164)

Performance Standards

Students are expected to . . .
- use prewriting strategies to generate and organize ideas.
- support a central idea (focus) in a variety of ways: with background information, sensory details, memory details, and the subject's personal thoughts and feelings.
- revise and edit the writing, striving for complete and clear information, appropriate voice, specific word choice, and smooth-reading sentences.

Getting Started with "Biographical Writing"

Start-Up Activity: To generate ideas for biographical writing, have your students write freely about interesting relatives, ancestors, or acquaintances. Also, have them read and react to the two sample biographies in the chapter (pages 162 and 166).

Enrichment Activity: Once your students write a biographical story or a phase biography, have them change the point of view of their writing so it becomes a form of autobiographical writing—that is, so the subject tells his or her own story. This doesn't mean that students should completely rewrite their papers. Instead, they should focus on one significant part.

Teaching Resources

Write Source 2000 Teacher's Guide

- Minilessons:
  "Subject Gathering" (page 236)
  "Who's who in my life?" (page 236)
- Assessment Rubric (page 181)

Write Source 2000 Handbook

- "Traits of Effective Writing," pages 19-24, serves as a helpful guide to students as they develop their biographical stories.

Write Source 2000 Program Guide

- A teaching unit (lesson plans and blackline masters) can be found in the Program Guide ring binder for each grade level.

Writing News Stories

(See handbook pages 167-174.)

After students have written autobiographical and biographical stories, they should be ready to write stories about the world around them. In "Writing News Stories," students will learn how to write and revise timely stories that answer the 5 W's accurately and responsibly.

Of Special Interest
- The sample news story, editorial, editorial cartoons, and feature article show students the main types of newswriting. (pages 168 and 172-174)
- The 5 W's chart provides a simple graphic that students can use to gather details for their news stories. (page 170)

Rationale
- News stories help people learn about and understand what is going on in the world.
- Newswriting is an important way to get information to real audiences.
- Newswriting teaches students the importance of accuracy, point of view, and conciseness.

Major Concepts
- Subjects for newswriting should be chosen on the basis of timeliness, importance, local angle, and human interest. (page 169)
- Successful interviews require careful planning, attentive listening, note taking, reviewing, and following up. (page 170)
- Extra time and attention should be devoted to the lead in a news story. (page 171)
- Editorials, editorial cartoons, and feature articles are three other types of newswriting. (pages 172-174)

Performance Standards

Students are expected to . . .
- include significant information in the body of the news story.
- begin their feature news article with a strong lead that grabs the reader's attention.

Getting Started with "Writing News Stories"

Start-Up Activity: Review with your students the model news story and writing guidelines in the handbook (pages 167-171). Then give your students newswriting practice by having them write a brief news story about a memorable event in their lives.

Enrichment Activity: For an extended period of time, ask students to contribute effective news stories, editorials, editorial cartoons, and feature articles for a classroom scrapbook of good newswriting. On each example, students should label at least one effective element: strong lead, clear explanation, timely subject, interesting angle, etc. Periodically share these examples with the class.

Teaching Resources

Write Source 2000 Teacher's Guide

- Minilessons:
  "Give me the facts." (page 236)
  "Just give the news." (page 237)

Write Source 2000 Handbook

- "Writing Persuasive Essays," pages 115-122, includes writing guidelines that will help students write editorials.

- "Gathering Ideas for Essays," pages 123-127, provides tips for collecting information for different types of subjects—people, places, objects, events, and explanations.

- "Types of Information," pages 261-264, helps students understand their source options when they are ready to investigate a subject for a news or feature story.

Write Source 2000 Program Guide

- A teaching unit (lesson plans and blackline masters) can be found in the Program Guide ring binder for each grade level.

Writing About Literature

(See handbook pages 175-181.)

Writing about literature is an active experience that demands critical and evaluative skills. This chapter shows students how to evaluate literature and write book reviews. A model review is included as well as three other ways of responding to literature.

Of Special Interest
- A list of ideas for reviews is organized under the elements of plot, characterization, setting, and theme. (page 176)

Rationale
- Writing can help students think about and evaluate literature.
- Writing about literature can turn students into critical readers.
- Writing about literature can increase students' enjoyment of literature.

Major Concepts
- Plot, characterization, setting, and theme are the four most important elements to consider when evaluating literature. (page 176)
- A book review is a type of persuasive writing that gives the writer's opinion, supported by details from the literature itself. (pages 177-178)
- Some other ways of responding to literature are writing in a journal, writing a poem, or writing a letter to the author or a specific character. (pages 180-181)

Performance Standards

Students are expected to . . .
- develop interpretations that exhibit careful reading and understanding of plot, character, theme, and setting.
- take a point of view and support it with references from the literature.

Getting Started with "Writing About Literature"

Start-Up Activity: Using handbook page 176 as a guide, have the class brainstorm for review ideas for a novel or a short story that they have all read. They should come up with ideas for all four main elements of literature: *plot, characterization, setting,* and *theme*.

Enrichment Activity: Encourage your students to develop some creative book reviews, especially after they have written one in traditional essay form. You might have your students . . .

- write a poem expressing a strong feeling about a piece of literature. (See page 180.)
- write a thoughtful letter to the author. (See page 181.)
- create bookmarks or posters for a particular book, as if they were marketing agents trying to sell it.
- present an oral reading.
- write the "next chapter" (*stanza, scene,* etc.), maintaining the original style, tone, and story line.

Teaching Resources

Write Source 2000 Teacher's Guide
- Minilessons:
  "Great Plot, Mr. Dickens" (page 237)
  "Just Like in Real Life" (page 237)

Write Source 2000 Handbook
- "Writing Techniques and Terms," pages 137-143, defines a wide range of concepts related to literary style.

Write Source 2000 Program Guide
- A teaching unit (lesson plans and blackline masters) can be found in the Program Guide ring binder for each grade level.

Writing Stories

(See handbook pages 183-192.)

"Writing Stories" encourages young writers to use their imaginations and recapture the ability they had as young children to invent stories. This chapter contains a clear explanation of how stories develop, together with a model story, writing guidelines, a sample story map, tips on how to improve a story, plus a short-story sampler.

Of Special Interest
- The five basic parts of a plot are diagrammed in a plot line explained and illustrated with sample copy. (pages 184-185)
- A sample story further illustrates the basic short-story plot. (pages 186-187)
- "A Short-Story Sampler" offers brief descriptions of five popular types of fiction. (page 192)

Rationale
- Writing stories encourages and strengthens creative thinking in young learners.
- Inventing and sharing stories is an enjoyable and worthwhile activity for all students.

Major Concepts
- The plot of a story consists of the exposition, rising action, a climax, falling action, and a resolution. (pages 184-185)
- Students should identify the characters, the plot line, and the setting when they are planning a story. (page 188)
- Stories should start in the middle of the action, build to a climax, and come to an effective, believable resolution. (pages 190-191)

Performance Standards
Students are expected to . . .
- establish and develop plot, characterization, and setting.
- include sensory details and specific concrete language.

Getting Started with "Writing Stories"

Start-Up Activity: Have students in pairs share surprising, amusing, and/or important personal experiences. Afterward, ask for one or two volunteers to share their stories with the class. Map out the key elements for each on the board, using the story map in the handbook as a guide (page 189). Show students how they can fictionalize their stories by altering some of the key elements.

After reviewing the guidelines for story writing in the handbook, have students develop their personal stories into pieces of fiction.

Enrichment Activity: Have students individually or in pairs use a story map to plan a story for one of the story types listed on page 192 in the handbook. Encourage students to develop their plans into completed stories. Compile the results in a classroom publication.

Teaching Resources

Write Source 2000 Teacher's Guide

- Minilessons:
  "Create a Frankenstein." (page 237)
  "It's a fight!" (page 238)
- Assessment Rubric (page 185)

Write Source 2000 Handbook

- "Publishing Your Writing," pages 37-43, provides guidelines and tips for students interested in sharing their stories beyond the classroom.

Write Source 2000 Program Guide

- A teaching unit (lesson plans and blackline masters) can be found in the Program Guide ring binder for each grade level.

Writing Poetry

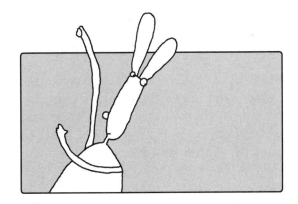

(See handbook pages 193-207.)

Poetry comes in many shapes, sizes, and forms. This chapter offers students a thoughtful explanation of just what poetry is, showing them how to read and appreciate it, too. Writing guidelines, sample poems, four pages on traditional techniques and forms, and two on modern forms of poetry complete this chapter.

Of Special Interest
- Several excerpts of poems, with explanation, illustrate the difference between prose and poetry. (pages 194-195)

Rationale
- Poetry gives student writers the opportunity to express their thoughts and feelings with exact, succinct language.
- Poetry awakens the senses.

Major Concepts
- Poetry differs from prose in its emphasis on the senses, feelings, sound, and form. (pages 194-195)
- Good poets revise their poems many times before declaring them finished. (pages 198-199)
- Free-verse poetry does not follow usual capitalization and punctuation rules. (page 200)
- Poetry can be shared in many creative ways. (page 201)
- Learning some of the traditional techniques and forms of poetry helps students read, understand, and write traditional poetry. (pages 202-205)
- Students think creatively when they write invented forms of poetry. (pages 206-207)

Performance Standards

Students are expected to . . .
- describe and express the importance of a subject.
- display an understanding of poetic techniques and a creative use of language.

Getting Started with "Writing Poetry"

Start-Up Activity: Here's an easy and almost foolproof way for students to produce a brief free-verse poem. Have them take a close look at your school and record three or four brief scenes that draw their attention. Ask your students to write one sentence for each observation.

Next, have your students "pull the rug" from under one or more of their sentences so that the words spill into a *tumble-down poem* as in the example that follows:

Sentence: These dusty stairs lead to the attic where old, forgotten band uniforms lay.

Tumble-Down Poem: These dusty stairs
                 lead to the attic
                 where
                 old, forgotten
                 band uniforms
                 lay.

Enrichment Activity: Each month, celebrate one traditional form of poetry. (See pages 204-205 in the handbook.) Have students look for and share samples of each form. Also encourage them to write samples of their own.

Teaching Resources

Write Source 2000 Teacher's Guide

- Minilessons:
  "Toot your horn." (page 238)
  "A Snake-Shaped Poem" (page 238)

Write Source 2000 Handbook

- "Publishing Your Writing," pages 37-43, provides tips for students interested in sharing their poems beyond the classroom.
- "Writing Techniques and Terms," pages 137-143, defines and illustrates many of the writing devices that poets use.

Write Source 2000 Program Guide

- A teaching unit (lesson plans and blackline masters) can be found in the Program Guide ring binder for each grade level.

Writing Observation Reports

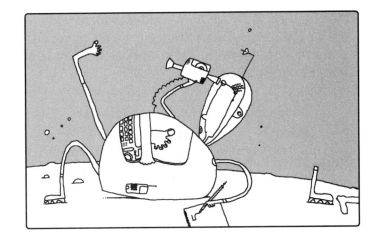

(See handbook pages 209-212.)

Professionals such as detectives, doctors, and artists have always known the value of careful observation, but it is just as important a skill for writers. This chapter contains two model observation reports and guidelines for gathering details, writing a first draft, and revising and editing an observation report.

Of Special Interest	• The "Five Senses Organizer" gives students an orderly form for collecting sensory details. (page 211)
Rationale	• Observation is an important method of gathering information about the world.
	• Observation is a skill that can be learned and refined.
	• Observation is an essential aspect of scientific writing.
Major Concepts	• All of the senses should be used in observation reports. (pages 210-211)
	• Any location with interesting sights, sounds, and action can serve well as the subject of an observation report. (pages 211-212)
	• A science report usually states the problem, offers a hypothesis, describes the procedure, shares observation, and puts forth a conclusion. (page 212)
Performance Standards	Students are expected to . . .
	• engage the interest of the reader.
	• elaborate with supporting details.
	• follow an organizational pattern appropriate to the type of composition.

Getting Started with "Writing Observation Reports"

Start-Up Activity: To help students focus on sensory details, have them study the details used in the model observation report on page 210 in their handbooks. Next, ask students to show proper respect for their own senses by listing their most enjoyable sensations. (The examples below should help.)

* Smells
  Examples: just-baked bread, pine trees
* Textures
  Examples: freshly poured cement, smooth stones
* Tastes
  Examples: a tart apple, chocolate
* Sights
  Examples: your weekly allowance, a sparkling lake
* Sounds
  Examples: the 3:00 dismissal bell, a cat's purr

Enrichment Activity: Ask students to observe some place over a series of days and report their findings in a series of separate entries or in a compiled report.

Teaching Resources

Write Source 2000 Teacher's Guide

* Minilessons:
  "What's the sense of it?" (page 238)
  "Look at that!" (page 239)

Write Source 2000 Handbook

* "Writing News Stories," pages 167-174, serves as an effective "next chapter" after students have written observation reports.

Write Source 2000 Program Guide

* A teaching unit (lesson plans and blackline masters) can be found in the Program Guide ring binder for each grade level.

Writing Summaries

(See handbook pages 213-216.)

Writing good summaries contributes to academic success because such an ability shows that the student understands what he or she has read or heard. This short chapter contains writing guidelines as well as models of a summary and a paraphrase, plus an explanation that compares the two forms.

Of Special Interest

- An original reading selection and its summary show students how one is derived from the other. (page 215)
- The same reading selection is paraphrased so that students compare summarizing with paraphrasing. (page 216)

Rationale

- Writing summaries helps students to understand what they read and hear.
- Writing summaries is a way for students to demonstrate their understanding of a complex subject.
- Summarizing is a complex thinking skill and should be practiced.

Major Concepts

- Writing a summary helps students identify the main idea in a reading selection. (page 214)
- Summaries contain only the most important details from a selection. (pages 214-215)
- Paraphrases restate a reading selection in simpler words and may be as long as the original selection. (page 216)

Performance Standards

Students are expected to . . .
- write summaries that contain the material's main ideas and most significant details.
- write summaries in their own words.
- reflect the underlying meaning of the source, not just the superficial details.

Getting Started with "Writing Summaries"

Start-Up Activity: After you've discussed the guidelines for summary writing with your students, read aloud the sample expository essay in the handbook (pages 108-109). Instruct students to follow along carefully and, perhaps, list a few main ideas. Then have them review the reading on their own and write a brief summary of the essay. Ask volunteers to share their summaries in class.

Enrichment Activity: Have students cut out news stories, editorials, and feature articles for extended summary-writing practice. The articles should be comparable in length to the samples in the handbook (pages 168, 172, and 174). Then, periodically, have students pick an article out of a hat to summarize.

Teaching Resources

Write Source 2000 Teacher's Guide

* Minilessons:
  "It's about buffalo." (page 239)
  "In Your Own Words" (page 239)

Write Source 2000 Handbook

* "Viewing Skills," pages 355-360, contains a sample summary of a television documentary.

Write Source 2000 Program Guide

* A teaching unit (lesson plans and blackline masters) can be found in the Program Guide ring binder for each grade level.

Writing Personal Research Reports

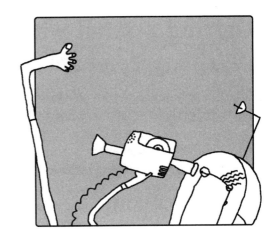

(See handbook pages 217-222.)

Everyone has questions about things they are especially interested in. Writing a personal research report is one way to find the answers. The chapter begins with a model report and follows up with writing guidelines, including a list of suggestions for gathering information, a handy grid for organizing the material, and a checklist of questions students should ask themselves after they finish their reports.

Of Special Interest
- A model shows how to construct a personal research report. (pages 218-219)

Rationale
- Personal research reports help channel students' natural curiosity into research and writing projects.
- A writing form that requires students to choose their own subjects encourages a committed effort.

Major Concepts
- A research plan can include some or all of the following: talking to friends and family, library research, interviews, advice from experts, and research on the Internet. (page 220)
- A grid with sectors for "What I Knew," "What I Wanted to Know," "What I Found Out," and "What I Learned" can help students organize their reports. (page 221)
- A personal research paper should contain a beginning that arouses the reader's curiosity, a middle that shares the writer's discoveries, and an ending that explains how the research affected the writer. (page 222)

Performance Standards

Students are expected to . . .
- include a beginning, a middle, and an ending in their writing.
- support the main ideas with facts, details, explanations, and examples from more than one authoritative source.

Getting Started with
"Writing Personal Research Reports"

Start-Up Activity: Set aside plenty of time for students to generate possible subjects for their reports. They should use the prewriting guidelines on page 220 in the handbook to help in their search. Also share with students a number of engaging personal research reports that you find in newspapers and magazines. Many feature articles in periodicals tell the story of the writer's quest for information.

Enrichment Activity: After students have written one personal research report, challenge them later in the year to develop another report, with one of the following general topics as their starting point: *apples, cats, dogs, bees, stars, cars, houses, clothes,* or *trees.*

Teaching Resources

Write Source 2000 Teacher's Guide

- Minilessons:
  "Ten Wonders of Your World" (page 239)
  "Go to your corner." (page 239)
- Assessment Rubric (page 186)

Write Source 2000 Handbook

- "Interviewing Tips," page 170, helps students plan for and carry out interviews, the main source of information for most personal research reports.

- "Types of Information," pages 261-264, discusses the difference between primary and secondary sources. (When collecting material for their reports, students should first focus on primary resources.)

Write Source 2000 Program Guide

- A teaching unit (lesson plans and blackline masters) can be found in the Program Guide ring binder for each grade level.

Writing Research Papers

(See handbook pages 223-235.)

"Writing Research Papers" is packed with all the information your students need to write successful research papers. Included are guidelines on writing, tips on organizing information, and instruction on documenting a report. The chapter concludes with a model research paper.

Of Special Interest	• The "Documenting" section shows students how to credit sources in the text of their papers and avoid plagiarism. (page 229) • Instructions for the works-cited page and a list of the most common entries (including Internet entries) are provided. (pages 230-232) • An annotated sample paper completes the chapter. (pages 233-235)
Rationale	• Research and report writing are important academic skills required in school and the workplace. • Writing a research report involves students in higher-level thinking skills (analyzing, synthesizing, and evaluating).
Major Concepts	• Writing webs can help students zero in on an aspect of a topic that interests them. (page 224) • Asking questions, selecting a main point, and creating an outline help students gather and organize their information. (pages 225-226) • Students need to learn the difference between common knowledge and new information to avoid plagiarism. (page 229) • Accurate, precise documentation adds credibility and authenticity to research reports. (pages 229-232 and 235)
Performance Standards	Students are expected to . . . • select relevant topics narrow enough to be thoroughly covered. • include a good beginning, middle, and ending in their reports. • support the main ideas with facts, details, explanations, and examples from multiple authoritative sources. • include a works-cited page with their reports.

Getting Started with "Writing Research Papers"

Start-Up Activity: Have students search for possible subjects in the following way: Ask them to investigate three general subject areas that interest them. For each one, have them locate at least three or four possible sources of information (primary and secondary, print and electronic). Also have them list two or three interesting things they discovered during their initial search. (This activity should point students toward a specific subject for their research paper.)

Enrichment Activity: Have your students put their research and report-writing experience to good use by making your classroom the research and resource center for your school and the community. Teachers, students, and community members may submit questions they want answered, information they want compiled, and references they want checked. Then your students can search for answers and information and develop their findings into mini-reports.

Teaching Resources

Write Source 2000 Teacher's Guide

- Minilessons:
  "Why is this here?" (page 240)
  "To Put It Another Way" (page 240)
- Assessment Rubric (page 186)

Write Source 2000 Handbook

- "Writing with a Computer," pages 27-29, offers students designing tips for finished products.
- "Searching for Information," pages 260-281, helps students to better understand the many available resources and how to access them.

Write Source 2000 Program Guide

- A teaching unit (lesson plans and blackline masters) can be found in the Program Guide ring binder for each grade level.

Writing in the Workplace

(See handbook pages 237-240.)

At least 90 percent of your students will become professional writers. How? They will earn their living, in part, by writing: letters, memos, e-mail messages, proposals, reports, and so on. This chapter shows the types of workplace writing students will do now and in the future. The traits of good workplace writing are cross-referenced to models found elsewhere in the handbook.

Of Special Interest

- A chart at the end of the chapter correlates six traits of good school-based writing to good workplace writing. Student-written models illustrating each trait are cross-referenced. (page 240)

Rationale

- Students' success in school depends on their ability to write.
- Workplace writing forms help students communicate with teachers, classmates, and people throughout their communities.
- The same composition skills required for workplace writing help students with school writing now and in years to come.

Major Concepts

- Workplace writing skills are practical. (pages 237-239)
- Effective workplace and school-based writing share key traits: stimulating ideas, a logical organization, an engaging voice, original word choice, sentence fluency, and correct, accurate copy. (pages 19-24, 240)

Performance Standards

Students are expected to . . .

- recognize a variety of workplace writing forms.
- see how workplace writing can help them succeed in school.
- choose appropriate forms for their writing: letters, memos, reports, and so on.
- use writing as a tool for learning in all subjects.
- learn traits of good workplace writing, which they can use as a benchmark for their own writing and that of their peers.

Getting Started with "Writing in the Workplace"

Start-Up Activity: Show students examples of workplace writing from a variety of different businesses and organizations, including your school. Discuss the basic qualities of this type of writing: objective, concise, purposeful, clear, etc.

Enrichment Activity: As an extra-credit project, have students collect and analyze samples of workplace writing. Their analysis should be based on the basic qualities of business writing as discussed in the start-up activity above as well as the traits listed in the handbook (page 240).

Teaching Resources

Write Source 2000 Teacher's Guide

- Minilessons:
  "Don't forget to say thanks." (page 240)
  "Mission Accomplished" (page 240)
- "Schoolwide Writing" (pages 159-174)

Write Source 2000 Handbook

- "Writing Business Letters" and "Special Forms of Workplace Writing," pages 241-250 and 251-259, continue the discussion of workplace writing.

Write Source 2000 Program Guide

- A teaching unit (lesson plans and blackline masters) can be found in the Program Guide ring binder for each grade level.

Writing Business Letters

(See handbook pages 241-250.)

Letter writing gives students an opportunity to connect with people outside the classroom—to do research for a report, to promote a school activity, to apply for a job, or to thank someone. This chapter gives students all the information they'll need to write a letter, from prewriting to addressing the envelope. Student-written samples are also included.

Of Special Interest
- "Parts of a Business Letter" and "Sample Basic Business Letter" show students how to format a letter. (pages 242-243)
- "Using Clear, Fair Language" gives students examples of fair, gender-free language. (page 245)

Rationale
- Writing good business letters can help students succeed now in school and later in the workplace.
- Students need experience with a variety of letter types—from simple requests to explaining a problem.

Major Concepts
- A business letter is practical writing that—if done well—gets results. (page 241-243, 246-247)
- Business letters should be organized, concise, professional, polite, and free of errors. (pages 244-245)

Performance Standards

Students are expected to . . .
- use the writing process to produce and send a letter.
- select style and voice that fit the audience and purpose.
- edit for standard usage, grammar, and mechanics (sentence structure, word choice, format, capitalization, punctuation, and spelling).

Getting Started with "Writing Business Letters"

Start-Up Activity: Before students review the chapter, ask them to suggest different reasons to write business letters (*making a request, solving a problem, giving information, applying for a job, asking for help*, etc.). Write their suggestions on the board. Also ask them to share any memorable business letters they have received or sent.

Enrichment Activity: Have students write letters to a business or institution of their choice, introducing themselves and asking for information about the organization. Class time should be provided so students can share any information they receive.

Teaching Resources

Write Source 2000 Teacher's Guide

- Minilessons:
  "Dear Sir" (page 241)
  "Satisfaction Guaranteed" (page 241)

Write Source 2000 Handbook

- "Writing in the Workplace" and "Special Forms of Workplace Writing," pages 237-240 and 251-259, continue the discussion of workplace writing.

Write Source 2000 Program Guide

- A teaching unit (lesson plans and blackline masters) can be found in the Program Guide ring binder for each grade level.

Special Forms of Workplace Writing

(See handbook pages 251-259.)

First, this chapter gives guidelines and models for the two most common forms of communication between workers: memos and e-mail messages. Second, the chapter gives guidelines and models for two specific workplace forms: proposals and meeting minutes.

Of Special Interest
- Writing guidelines for memos, messages, minutes, and proposals help students walk through the writing process. (pages 252, 254, 256, 258)
- The sample memo and e-mail message do double duty as progress reports. (pages 253 and 255)

Rationale
- Workplace writing can help students do their course work more efficiently.
- Workplace writing, tied to student projects, helps students take ownership of their learning.

Major Concepts
- Workplace writing can help students and teachers communicate as they do their work. (page 251)
- Following the workplace writing process can help students develop effective writing skills. (pages 252, 254, 256, 258)
- Students benefit from experiencing the traits of workplace writing in action: accurate content, clear explanations, and effective organization. (pages 253, 255, 257, 259)

Performance Standards

Students are expected to . . .
- correspond with peers and others.
- choose appropriate forms for their writing (memos, e-mail, etc.).
- select a style and voice to fit the audience and purpose.
- use technology to produce and publish writing.

Getting Started with "Special Forms of Workplace Writing"

Start-Up Activity: To introduce this chapter, list the following special forms on the board: *memos, e-mail messages, minutes,* and *proposals.* Ask students what they know about these forms and how they might use them in school. Then turn to each of the samples in the chapter.

Enrichment Activity: Encourage students to write memos or e-mail messages to you whenever they feel a need to share their thoughts and concerns about the class, ask questions about challenging concepts, update you on their work, and so on. Make sure to respond to their correspondence as promptly as possible.

Teaching Resources

Write Source 2000 Teacher's Guide

- Minilessons:
  "You need to know." (page 241)
  "In a Minute" (page 241)
- "Schoolwide Writing" (pages 159-174)

Write Source 2000 Handbook

- "One Writer's Process," pages 9-18, shows the development of a piece of writing based on the student proposal on page 259.
- "Writing in the Workplace" and "Writing Business Letters," pages 237-240 and 241-250, continue the discussion of workplace writing.

Write Source 2000 Program Guide

- A teaching unit (lesson plans and blackline masters) can be found in the Program Guide ring binder for each grade level.

The Tools of Learning

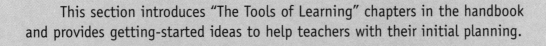

Introductory Notes

This section introduces "The Tools of Learning" chapters in the handbook and provides getting-started ideas to help teachers with their initial planning.

Types of Information

(See handbook pages 261-264.)

This chapter introduces students to the difference between primary and secondary information sources. Students are encouraged to consider using primary sources to add first-hand information to their research projects. The chapter concludes with guidelines for evaluating information.

Of Special Interest
- "Types of Primary Sources" lists five common kinds of primary sources. (page 263)
- "Evaluating Sources of Information" lists six questions students need to ask to judge the reliability of their sources. (page 264)

Rationale
- Students need to be aware of the difference between primary and secondary sources and the strengths and weaknesses of each.
- Students need to (1) understand that not all published information is reliable and (2) know how to evaluate it for reliability.

Major Concepts
- For any topic students look into, they will find a wide variety of sources and kinds of information. (page 261)
- All sources are either primary (original, firsthand) or secondary (gathered from primary sources). (page 262)
- There are five common types of primary sources. (page 263)
- Students need to be thoughtful "consumers" of information, because not all information is equally reliable. (page 264)

Performance Standards
Students are expected to . . .
- use information accurately.
- evaluate information critically.

Getting Started with "Types of Information"

Start-Up Activity: Before you review the chapter, write two interesting occupations on the board (*pilot, architect, television producer*, etc.). Then ask students to identify a few sources of information about each occupation. After reviewing this short chapter, ask students if there are any sources of information they could add to the list.

Enrichment Activity: For any major research project, have students prepare a list of sources they will consult. (Whenever possible, they should have one or two primary sources in the list.) Then ask them to evaluate the trustworthiness of each source using page 264 in the handbook as a general guide.

Teaching Resources

Write Source 2000 Teacher's Guide

- Minilessons:
  "From the Horse's Mouth" (page 242)
  "List of Books" (page 242)

Write Source 2000 Handbook

- "Using the Internet" and "Using the Library," pages 265-272 and 273-281, continue the discussion of information resources.

Write Source 2000 Program Guide

- A teaching unit (lesson plans and blackline masters) can be found in the Program Guide ring binder for each grade level.

Using the Internet

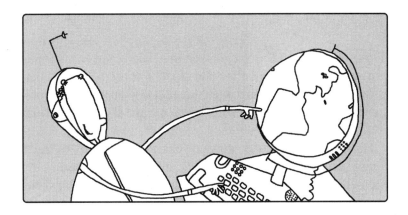

(See handbook pages 265-272.)

This chapter is a basic guide to using the Internet as a research tool, discussion forum, and publishing outlet. The chapter includes tips for evaluating, saving, and crediting information found on the Net.

Of Special Interest

- "A Guide to the Internet" explains the basic components of the Internet. (pages 266-267)
- "Searching for Information" gives detailed information about how to search the Net. (pages 270-271)

Rationale

- The Internet is an important, effective research tool that students need to understand.
- Students also need to know about the problems associated with Internet use (loss of privacy, unreliability of information, and so on).

Major Concepts

- The Internet is comprised of several different systems that work together to provide on-line communication. (pages 266-267)
- Students can use the Internet to conduct research, discuss ideas, and publish their writing. (page 268)
- Because there are millions of Web pages, students must search, either through their ISP (Internet Service Provider) or a search engine, for the information they need. (pages 270-271)
- Once students find useful information, they need to save it, evaluate it, and credit it. (page 272)

Performance Standards

Students are expected to . . .
- access electronic information efficiently.

Getting Started with "Using the Internet"

Start-Up Activity: Write these categories on the board: *science, social studies,* and *math.* Then call on students to name specific topics or subjects related to each category. For example, one student may offer the science topic "earthquakes." Next, demonstrate how to carry out a word search for this topic on the classroom computer. Continue with other topics as time permits. (This activity will demonstrate that the Internet contains a wealth of information.)

Enrichment Activity: Weekly, assign a student to be the Internet guide to current events (or some other subject under study in your classroom). It will be this student's responsibility to surf the Net for information that may add to everyone's understanding of the event (or subject). The Internet guide should report on his or her findings to the rest of the class.

Teaching Resources

Write Source 2000 Teacher's Guide

- Minilessons:
  "On the Web" (page 242)
  "See Hunt" (page 242)

Write Source 2000 Handbook

- "Publishing On-Line" and "Making Your Own Web Site," pages 42-43, suggest different ways for students to share their best writing via the Internet.

- "Sample Internet Entries," page 232, serves as a documentation guide for on-line resources.

- "Writing Guidelines: E-Mail" and "Sample E-Mail Message," pages 254-255, demonstrate how students can correspond on-line.

Write Source 2000 Program Guide

- A teaching unit (lesson plans and blackline masters) can be found in the Program Guide ring binder for each grade level.

Using the Library

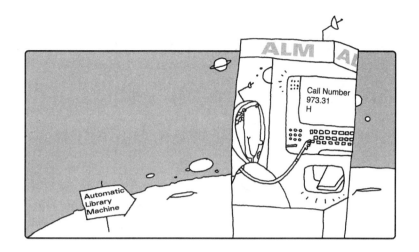

(See handbook pages 273-281.)

Many students can find their way on the Internet but don't know how to track down materials in a library. This chapter covers basic library skills, including how to use a card or computer catalog, read call numbers, explore the reference section, and more.

Of Special Interest
- "Using the *Readers' Guide*" explains how to use this index. (page 280)
- "Understanding the Parts of Books" lists the parts of nonfiction books and tells how each part can be useful. (page 281)

Rationale
- Libraries are an essential research resource that students need to know how to use.

Major Concepts
- The library is an important source of information. (page 273)
- In the library, the search for information begins with the catalog, either on cards or on computer. (page 274)
- Both the card and computer catalogs contain three kinds of entries: title, author, and subject. (pages 275-276)
- Nonfiction books are shelved by call number. (page 277)
- Reference books are in a separate section. (pages 278-279)
- The *Readers' Guide* is an index of magazine articles arranged by subject and author. (page 280)
- Understanding the parts of books can help students use them more efficiently. (page 281)

Performance Standards
Students are expected to . . .
- access information efficiently.

Getting Started with "Using the Library"

Start-Up Activity: Have each student submit a reasonable question that they want answered. Something on the order of "How long do mosquitoes live?" not "What is the last word in the third paragraph in chapter fourteen in *The Adventures of Huckleberry Finn*?" Students should then pick a question out of a hat to answer, using the resources in the school library to find the answer. They should present to the class not only an answer (or non-answer) but also the story of their search.

Enrichment Activity: If at all possible, have your school, community, or university librarian discuss with your students the influence of technology on library services. There are a lot of fascinating things happening in today's libraries because of technology.

Teaching Resources

Write Source 2000 Teacher's Guide

- Minilessons:
  "It has to be here somewhere." (page 243)
  "Hide and Seek" (page 243)

Write Source 2000 Handbook

- "Types of Information" and "Using the Internet," pages 261-264 and 265-272, also discuss information resources.

Write Source 2000 Program Guide

- A teaching unit (lesson plans and blackline masters) can be found in the Program Guide ring binder for each grade level.

Thinking and Writing

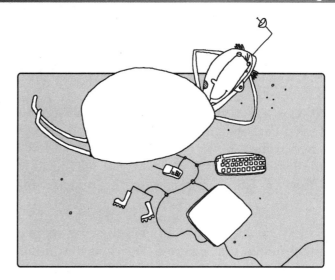

(See handbook pages 283-290.)

This chapter explains the different kinds of thinking that students need to do when they write. The six levels of thinking that were identified by Benjamin S. Bloom, known as Bloom's taxonomy, are discussed. Students learn what each kind of thinking involves and how to use it in their writing assignments.

Of Special Interest

- Each level of thinking is presented on a separate page with an explanation, information about how students can use that type of thinking, and a sample writing assignment.
- "Guidelines for Thinking and Writing" is a table that summarizes the six levels of thinking. (page 290)

Rationale

- Students need to know that thinking skills are as essential to good writing as grammar, mechanics, and other skills are.
- Students must learn to apply different kinds of thinking to different kinds of assignments.
- Thinking skills help students do well on assignments and face challenges both in and outside of the classroom.

Major Concepts

- Recalling is the most basic type of thinking. (page 284)
- Understanding means being able to explain something in one's own words. (page 285)
- Applying means being able to use what one has learned. (page 286)
- Analyzing means breaking information down into smaller parts. (page 287)
- Synthesizing means combining information with new ideas to create something. (page 288)
- Evaluating means forming and expressing an opinion of something. (page 289)

Getting Started with "Thinking and Writing"

Start-Up Activity: Have students briefly describe one of their most challenging thinking tasks. Perhaps one student memorized a lengthy list of difficult terms. Another student may have argued for a new lunch-hour policy, and still another student may have organized a club fundraiser. Use this activity as a lead-in for a discussion of the different levels of thinking. (Refer to "Guidelines for Thinking and Writing," handbook page 290, during your discussion.)

Enrichment Activity: If your students write in journals, periodically provide them with writing prompts that promote the levels of thinking you want to emphasize throughout the school year. For example, a prompt such as "A classmate I will never forget" emphasizes basic recall and understanding. A prompt such as "What if I never forgot?" emphasizes speculating or synthesizing, a more complex level of thinking.

Teaching Resources

Write Source 2000 Teacher's Guide

- Minilessons:
  "A Matter of Chance" (page 243)
  "What next?" (page 243)
- "Teaching Thinking" (pages 211-212)

Write Source 2000 Handbook

- "Thinking Logically" and "Thinking Better," pages 291-296 and 297-299, continue the discussion of effective thinking.

Write Source 2000 Program Guide

- A teaching unit (lesson plans and blackline masters) can be found in the Program Guide ring binder for each grade level.

Thinking Logically

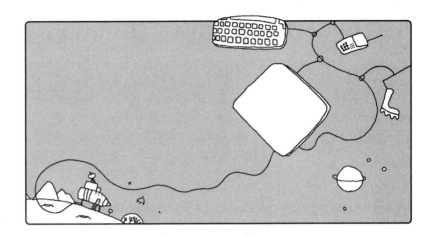

(See handbook pages 291-296.)

This chapter introduces the basics of logical thinking. Students learn how to use sound logic to strengthen their persuasive writing. They are also shown how to avoid the "fuzzy thinking" that leads to weak writing. The chapter concludes with general guidelines for logical thinking and a chart that offers questions to consider when dealing with various types of subjects.

Of Special Interest

- "Using Logic to Persuade" gives step-by-step guidelines, with examples, for using logical thinking in persuasive writing. (pages 292-293)
- "Avoiding Fuzzy Thinking" explains seven common types of misleading statements, with examples of each. (pages 294-295)
- "Asking Questions" contains a chart that will help students gather information for their persuasive-writing tasks. (page 296)

Rationale

- It is important for students to understand the difference between facts and opinions.
- Students need to know how to form, express, and support opinions.
- Students need to avoid making weak, misleading statements in their writing and to recognize such statements in the materials they read.

Major Concepts

- Logical thinking is reasonable, reliable, and believable. (page 291)
- Good persuasive writing begins with good logic. (page 292)
- To be persuasive, an opinion must be worded effectively and supported with facts. (page 293)
- Good persuasive writing avoids fuzzy thinking and the resulting illogical, misleading statements. (pages 294-295)
- Asking questions is an effective way to gather information for persuasive writing. (page 296)

Getting Started with "Thinking Logically"

Start-Up Activity: Have some "good thinkers"—maybe a panel of good thinkers—speak to your class. Perhaps you could have an attorney explore how he or she prepares a convincing case. A physician could describe how he or she makes a diagnosis, prepares and carries out an operation, and/or proposes a plan for recovery. A car mechanic could describe what it means to "troubleshoot" and share some challenging car problems he or she has dealt with. A coach could describe how he or she plans a strategy for an upcoming opponent, and so on.

Enrichment Activity: Have pairs or small groups of students stage debates that focus on topical and controversial issues. The rest of the class should evaluate the performances. Have them pay special attention to the strength of each debater's argument.

Teaching Resources

Write Source 2000 Teacher's Guide

- Minilessons:
  "In My Opinion" (page 244)
  "Let's get fuzzy." (page 244)
- "Teaching Thinking" (pages 211-212)

Write Source 2000 Handbook

- "Thinking Through an Argument," pages 121-122, provides additional information about persuasive thinking.
- "Thinking and Writing" and "Thinking Better," pages 283-290 and 297-299, also discuss effective thinking.

Write Source 2000 Program Guide

- A teaching unit (lesson plans and blackline masters) can be found in the Program Guide ring binder for each grade level.

Thinking Better

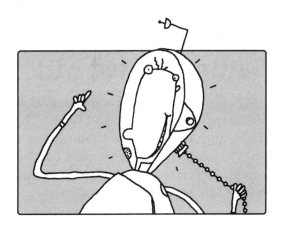

(See handbook pages 297-299.)

This short chapter gives students three pages packed with information that will help them think better and write better. There are suggestions for thinking more broadly and deeply as well as more creatively.

Of Special Interest
- "Basic Writing and Thinking Moves" is a process chart showing the different levels of thinking that students need to bring to their writing. The chart includes examples of how to apply each level of thinking. (page 299)

Rationale
- Learning different ways to think about ideas, issues, and problems will help students do better on all their assignments and in the challenges they face in life.
- Students can be more creative and thorough when they apply many different levels of thinking.

Major Concepts
- Thinking better means being more creative, logical, and thoughtful. (page 297)
- Becoming a better thinker is a matter of practicing different ways of thinking. (page 298)
- Students use many levels of thinking in their writing. (page 299)

Getting Started with "Thinking Better"

Start-Up Activity: Have pairs of students create and briefly describe a group of bad thinkers—perhaps a classroom of bad thinkers, a game show for bad thinkers, a ship of fools, and so on. Have them list at least four or five characteristics of their bad thinkers.

One group might create a baseball team of bad thinkers: The best hitter bats last in the lineup, the strongest hitter always tries to bunt, the manager changes pitchers when they have their best control, and so on.

Enrichment Activity: Ask students to write a specific opinion statement concerning school life, fashions, sports, movies, or television. (Example: *We need an afternoon break between fifth and sixth hours.*) Then have students ask and answer four or five *why* questions about their statements. Afterward, discuss the value of asking *why* questions.

Teaching Resources

Write Source 2000 Teacher's Guide

- Minilessons:
  "Be creative." (page 244)
  "Good move!" (page 244)

Write Source 2000 Handbook

- "Thinking and Writing" and "Thinking Logically," pages 283-290 and 291-296, also explore effective thinking.

Write Source 2000 Program Guide

- A teaching unit (lesson plans and blackline masters) can be found in the Program Guide ring binder for each grade level.

Reading Charts

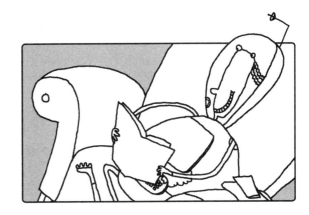

(See handbook pages 301-306.)

This chapter is a minicourse on common kinds of charts. Software that makes it easy to create charts has made these graphics much more common in reading material. However, to use charts correctly, students need to understand the principles that govern the creation and interpretation of graphs, tables, and diagrams.

Of Special Interest

- "Understanding Graphs" gives examples of four graphs and explains what kind of data each one presents. (pages 302-303)
- "Understanding Tables" explains and illustrates three kinds of tables and also suggests that students use tables to record and organize the data they gather for assignments. (pages 304-305)
- "Understanding Diagrams" explains and illustrates picture diagrams and line diagrams. (page 306)

Rationale

- Charts are increasingly common in materials in and out of school.
- Skills needed to read and create charts differ from skills used to read and create verbal texts.
- Students need to know how to read charts correctly and how to create accurate charts to organize and present information.

Major Concepts

- Charts can make complex information easy to understand. (page 301)
- Graphs are pictures of information, and different kinds of graphs show different kinds of information. (pages 302-303)
- Tables organize different kinds of information so readers can easily see how one set of data relates to another. (pages 304-305)
- Diagrams are drawings that show how things are put together or how things work. (page 306)

Getting Started with "Reading Charts"

Start-Up Activity: Have students submit sample charts from newspapers and magazines. Then ask students to pick two of these charts out of a hat to analyze. The following questions will help them carry out their analysis. (Students should share their findings afterward.)

What type of chart is it?

What is the general subject of the chart?

What specific information does it provide?

Enrichment Activity: Challenge students to develop a graph based on any part of page 471 in the handbook (or on some other common set of facts). The finished products should be neat, clear, colorful, and fill a standard piece of paper. Post the finished products in the room.

Teaching Resources

Write Source 2000 Teacher's Guide

- Minilessons:
  "That's 'chartable.'" (page 245)
  "Line up." (page 245)

Write Source 2000 Handbook

- The "Student Almanac," pages 458-525, contains many different types of charts for students to analyze.

Write Source 2000 Program Guide

- A teaching unit (lesson plans and blackline masters) can be found in the Program Guide ring binder for each grade level.

Study-Reading Skills

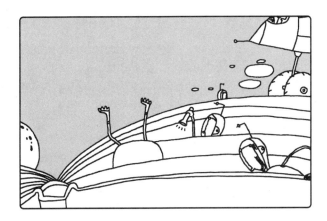

(See handbook pages 307-322.)

With each passing year, middle-school students will encounter increasing variety and complexity in the materials they read. To maintain a high level of reading comprehension and enjoyment, students must become more sophisticated readers. This chapter offers a broad range of strategies that will help students understand and learn from many different kinds of texts.

Of Special Interest
- "Patterns of Nonfiction" explains six patterns of organization that students will often encounter in their nonfiction reading. For each pattern there is a brief explanation, a sample text, and an example of a graphic organizer that students can use when taking notes. (pages 308-319)
- "Study-Reading Strategies" outlines two strategies for learning from reading assignments: "Think and Read" and "KWL." (pages 320-321)
- "Adjusting Your Reading Rate" explains how students can vary their reading speed to fit their reading purpose. (page 322)

Rationale
- All students, even those who read well, need strategies to help them learn from what they read.
- Knowing how to approach different kinds of texts and how to take notes efficiently gives students a sense of mastery and makes study-reading more enjoyable and productive.

Major Concepts
- Recognizing the pattern by which material is organized makes it easier to understand the material and to take good notes. (pages 308-319)
- Using reading strategies such as "Think and Read" and "KWL" saves time and improves comprehension. (pages 320-321)
- Reading speed should be adjusted to fit the purpose for reading. (page 322)

Getting Started with "Study-Reading Skills"

Start-Up Activity: Review handbook pages 307 and 310-311 with your students. Then, as a class, study the second paragraph of the sample research paper on page 233. Have students take notes on this paragraph using a table organizer. (See page 311 for an example.) Afterward, discuss their finished work.

Enrichment Activity: On a regular basis, provide students with brief sample articles that exemplify different patterns of nonfiction: *description, main idea/supporting details,* etc. As a class, analyze each article; then have students use the appropriate organizer to take notes on their reading. Discuss the results of their work.

Teaching Resources

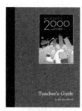

Write Source 2000 Teacher's Guide

- Minilessons:
"Setting a Table" (page 245)
"It's very hot there." (page 245)

Write Source 2000 Handbook

- "Taking Reading Notes" and "Reviewing Your Notes," pages 364-365, offer additional study-reading tips.

Write Source 2000 Program Guide

- A teaching unit (lesson plans and blackline masters) can be found in the Program Guide ring binder for each grade level.

Improving Your Vocabulary

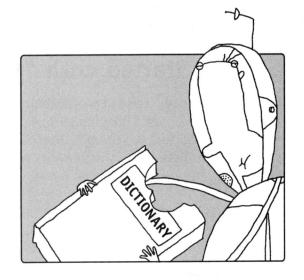

(See handbook pages 323-340.)

This chapter gives students strategies for building their working vocabularies and for learning more about the words they already know. Seven common types of context clues are listed. A sample thesaurus entry and dictionary page demonstrate how to use these references. Students are given several models for keeping personal dictionaries. The chapter concludes with a discussion of levels of diction.

Of Special Interest
- "Using Prefixes, Suffixes, and Roots" includes a glossary of word parts, plus lists of numerical prefixes and word roots that name parts of the human body. (pages 329-339)

Rationale
- Students need to expand their vocabularies as they progress to higher-level reading material.
- Knowing how to improve their word knowledge makes students more confident and independent readers.

Major Concepts
- Surrounding words that give information about the meaning of an unknown word are called "context clues." (page 324)
- A thesaurus is a reference book of synonyms and antonyms. (page 325)
- A dictionary, besides giving the meanings of words, is loaded with useful information about language. (pages 326-327)
- A personal dictionary is a good vocabulary-building tool. (page 328)
- Prefixes, suffixes, and roots are word parts that can help students figure out the meanings of words. (pages 329-339)
- English has different levels of diction that are appropriate for different kinds of writing. (page 340)

Getting Started with "Improving Your Vocabulary"

Start-Up Activity: Select two vocabulary words to analyze. Write each word and a sentence using it on the board. Have students volunteer a definition for each word, explaining how the word's context helped them to define it. Then, as a class, explore the words using a thesaurus; a dictionary; the glossary of prefixes, suffixes, and roots (handbook pages 329-339); and so on. On a regular basis, post additional words on the board for students to analyze.

Enrichment Activity: Challenge students to combine word parts they have studied into as many words as possible (perhaps within 5 minutes). Special cards can be used for this purpose. (See below.) Also invite students to share "new words" with their classmates, who then will attempt to define or explain each one.

de	flex	ion
re	flect	or
in		ible

Teaching Resources

Write Source 2000 Teacher's Guide

- Minilessons:
  "Keep griddle cakes off gridirons." (page 245)
  "Root got you stumped?" (page 246)
- "Building Vocabulary" (pages 213-215)

Write Source 2000 Handbook

- "Using Strong, Colorful Words," pages 135-136, helps students use the best words in their writing.

Write Source 2000 Program Guide

- A teaching unit (lesson plans and blackline masters) can be found in the Program Guide ring binder for each grade level.

Understanding Literature

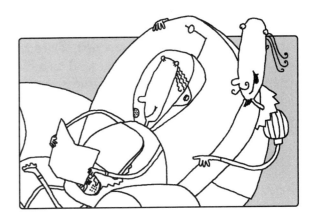

(See handbook pages 341-345.)

This chapter introduces students to the vocabulary of literature, giving them tools to better understand, enjoy, and respond to the literature they read. The chapter concludes with guidelines for discussing literature in a book group.

Of Special Interest
- "Types of Literature" is a glossary of common literary forms. (page 342)
- "Elements of Fiction" is a glossary of basic terms for literary analysis. (pages 343-344)

Rationale
- Students need to know the language of literature in order to understand and respond to it.

Major Concepts
- Literature is writing that has universal themes, wide appeal, and a powerful impact. (page 341)
- There are many different forms of literature. (page 342)
- Literature has its own vocabulary, which students can use to understand, discuss, and write about what they read. (pages 343-344)
- Participating in a book group is a good way to understand and enjoy literature. (page 345)

Getting Started with "Understanding Literature"

Start-Up Activity: On the board, write the titles of one or two pieces of fiction (short stories or novels) your students have read as a class. Then, without referring to their handbooks, ask them to answer the following questions for each title:

- What *type* of literature is it?
- Who is the *antagonist*? The *protagonist*?
- What is the main *conflict*?
- When does the *climax* occur?
- What is the *setting* for this story?

Discuss your students' ability to answer the questions, and then have them turn to handbook pages 342-344 to check their responses.

Enrichment Activity: Develop fiction-analysis sheets, including questions like the ones above or including other questions or terms from pages 343-344 in the handbook. Then encourage students to complete such a sheet for each book they read.

Teaching Resources

Write Source 2000 Teacher's Guide

- Minilessons:
  "Ups and Downs of Fiction" (page 246)
  "Book Talk" (page 246)

Write Source 2000 Handbook

- "Writing Techniques and Terms," pages 137-143, defines additional words and phrases that may be used in the analysis of literature.
- "Writing About Literature," pages 175-181, helps students use key elements of fiction as the starting point for book reviews.

Write Source 2000 Program

- A teaching unit (lesson plans and blackline masters) can be found in the Program Guide ring binder for each grade level.

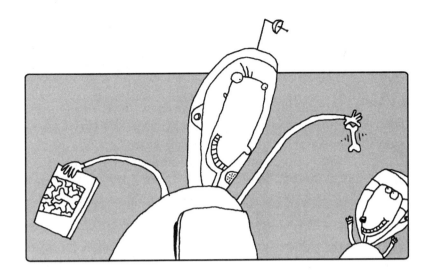

Preparing a Speech

(See handbook pages 347-354.)

Speaking to classes and other groups is something students will be called on to do throughout their school years and adult lives. The ability to speak clearly, confidently, and persuasively is a skill that will serve students well. This chapter is a step-by-step guide to preparing and giving a speech, from knowing the purpose of your speech to delivering it well.

Of Special Interest
- "Planning Your Speech" tells students what to do before they start writing: know your purpose, choose and narrow your subject, gather details. (pages 348-349)
- "Writing Your Speech" explains how to write a strong beginning, middle, and ending, and culminates with a student model. (pages 350-353)
- "Practicing and Giving Your Speech" is a checklist of what students need to do from the time they finish writing their speeches until they finish presenting them. (page 354)

Rationale
- Public speaking is a skill students will use throughout their lives.
- Speaking before a group is less intimidating when students know how to prepare.

Major Concepts
- To plan a speech, a student should know the purpose; choose a specific, appropriate subject; and collect interesting details from many sources. (pages 348-349)
- To write a good speech, a student should let his or her personality come through in an attention-getting beginning, a well-organized body, and an interesting ending. (pages 350-353)
- To ensure a strong presentation, students should make a readable final copy of their speeches and practice, practice, practice. (page 354)

Getting Started with "Preparing a Speech"

Start-Up Activity: Have students interview someone in class whom they don't know very well. Encourage students to be creative in the types of questions they ask: *What three things have you never done? What will be your address in 20 years?*

Each student should develop and present a brief introductory speech for the person he or she interviewed. Point out that the manner in which they introduce their subject is up to them. They may want to develop a campaign speech, make a toast, file a complaint, etc.

Enrichment Activity: Have your students observe and evaluate experienced speakers in action. (Use videotapes if in-person observations are impossible.) Review "Skills for Listening" with your students (page 370 in the handbook) before having them observe a speaker.

Teaching Resources

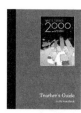

Write Source 2000 Teacher's Guide

- Minilessons:
  "Talk to me!" (page 246)
  "Performance Tips" (page 247)

Write Source 2000 Handbook

- "Skills for Listening," page 370, offers tips that will help students stay "on task" when one of their classmates is giving a speech.

Write Source 2000 Program Guide

- A teaching unit (lesson plans and blackline masters) can be found in the Program Guide ring binder for each grade level.

Viewing Skills

(See handbook pages 355-360.)

Television has a big impact on what students know and think about the world. The average American child spends much more time with TV than with parents. This chapter gives students the insight and skills they need to be more thoughtful viewers.

Of Special Interest
- "Watching the News" includes an excerpt from an actual network news program and explains how to watch for completeness, correctness, and point of view in TV news stories. (pages 356-357)
- "Watching Documentaries" tells how to get the most out of educational programs and includes a sample summary written after viewing a documentary. (pages 358-359)
- "Watching Commercials" explains four selling methods often used in TV commercials. (page 360)

Rationale
- Students need to be aware that different kinds of TV programs have different purposes.
- Students can be better informed when they know the benchmarks of good reporting and how to watch for them.
- Students will learn more from documentaries if they are active viewers.
- Students need to understand the purpose of commercials and the selling methods used.

Major Concepts
- Television influences what people know and how they think, so it is important to be a critical viewer. (page 355)
- When watching the news, it's important to watch for completeness, correctness, and point of view. (pages 356-357)
- Students learn more from documentaries when they are active viewers. (pages 358-359)
- Commercials use a variety of selling methods to achieve their purpose of persuading viewers to buy products. (page 360)

Getting Started with "Viewing Skills"

Start-Up Activity: For a week, have your students keep track of the time they spend watching TV. You may want to provide them with a viewing log to complete this task. (See the partial sample below.) Discuss the results of their viewing habits for the week.

TV-Viewing Log					
	Started watching at:	Stopped watching at:	Started watching at:	Stopped watching at:	Total Hours Watched
Sunday					
Monday					

Enrichment Activity: Have students compare how an important news story is covered on television and in a newspaper. Suggest that they compile their data using a graphic organizer. (See pages 113 and 313 in the handbook for examples.) As a class, discuss the merits and drawbacks of each medium.

Teaching Resources

Write Source 2000 Teacher's Guide

- Minilessons:
  "I witness the news." (page 247)
  "TV Time" (page 247)

Write Source 2000 Handbook

- "Thinking Logically," pages 291-296, offers students background information that will help them evaluate news stories, documentaries, and commercials.

Write Source 2000 Program Guide

- A teaching unit (lesson plans and blackline masters) can be found in the Program Guide ring binder for each grade level.

Classroom Skills

(See handbook pages 361-368.)

As students progress through school, they will spend more and more of their class time taking notes. This chapter gives tips and guidelines to help students develop good note-taking skills, as well as skills for reviewing and revising their notes.

Of Special Interest

- "Setting Up Your Notes" illustrates a well-designed page of notes. (page 362)
- Tips for taking both lecture and reading notes are listed. (pages 363-364)
- Learning logs are explained and illustrated with sample science and math entries. (pages 366-368)

Rationale

- Students will spend more and more of their class and study time taking notes as they move to higher grade levels.
- Taking good notes helps students learn more and do better on tests.
- Learning logs can enhance understanding in all content areas.

Major Concepts

- Taking notes is an important skill that helps students pay attention, learn, and remember. (page 361)
- Setting up notes in an efficient way is important. (page 362)
- Taking good lecture notes involves listening carefully. (page 363)
- Taking reading notes is easier than taking lecture notes, because students can stop and reread, look up new words, etc. (page 364)
- Students should review their notes each day to look up new words, note questions they have, and so on. (page 365)
- A learning log is a place for reflective notes about the student's thoughts, feelings, and questions. (pages 366-368)

Getting Started with "Classroom Skills"

Start-Up Activity: Have students set up a page for notes, following the example in the handbook on page 362. Then ask them to take lecture notes in class, following the guidelines on page 363, and afterward, to review their work following the tips on page 365. Discuss the value of this note-taking process with your students.

Enrichment Activity: Make admit slip/exit slip forms for your students. At the beginning of class, students respond on an admit slip to a prompt related to the day's lesson. At the end of class, they use an exit slip to reflect upon something related to the lesson.

Teaching Resources

Write Source 2000 Teacher's Guide

- Minilessons:
  "Make a note of it." (page 247)
  "Logging On" (page 248)
- "Writing-to-Learn Activities" (pages 164-165)

Write Source 2000 Handbook

- "Study-Reading Skills," pages 307-322, includes graphic organizers for taking notes about reading material.

Write Source 2000 Program Guide

- A teaching unit (lesson plans and blackline masters) can be found in the Program Guide ring binder for each grade level.

Group Skills

(See handbook pages 369-372.)

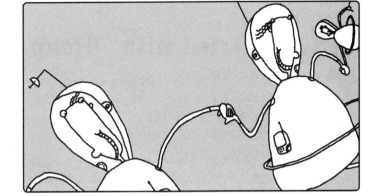

This chapter explains five "people skills": listening, observing, cooperating, clarifying, and responding. These skills will help students work more smoothly and productively in groups.

Of Special Interest
- "Skills for Listening" not only features active and accurate listening, but also covers when and how to interrupt and how to respond to being interrupted. (page 370)
- "Communicating with Respect" gives tips for respecting oneself and others when working in a group. (page 372)

Rationale
- Learning and practicing "people skills" will help students be more productive when they work in groups.
- Knowing how to work with others is an important life skill.

Major Concepts
- The five essential "people skills" are listening, observing, cooperating, clarifying, and responding. (page 369)
- Good listening requires skill and practice. (page 370)
- Observing (watching body language), cooperating (working toward a shared goal), and clarifying are important group skills. (page 371)
- Responding thoughtfully and courteously can help group members disagree without resorting to arguing. (page 372)
- Group work depends on members showing respect for themselves and other group members. (page 372)

Getting Started with "Group Skills"

Start-Up Activity: Show a videotape of a group discussion from a television show. Afterward, analyze the dynamics of the discussion. Did the group members listen carefully, cooperate with each other, respond tactfully, and so on? In what ways did the discussion really seem effective? In what ways did it seem to break down?

Special Note: You may also want the students to report on one of their own group experiences. Ask them to comment on the strengths and weaknesses of the experience.

Enrichment Activity: Provide plenty of opportunities for group discussions (writing groups, study groups, and so on). Also provide a checklist (based on the main points covered in the chapter) for students to use afterward to evaluate the effectiveness of each group experience.

Teaching Resources

Write Source 2000 Teacher's Guide

- Minilessons:
  "What's the story?" (page 248)
  "Everybody listen!" (page 248)
- "Collaborative Learning" (pages 209-210)

Write Source 2000 Handbook

- "Group Advising," pages 75-78, covers the skills needed in effective writing groups.

Write Source 2000 Program Guide

- A teaching unit (lesson plans and blackline masters) can be found in the Program Guide ring binder for each grade level.

Taking Tests

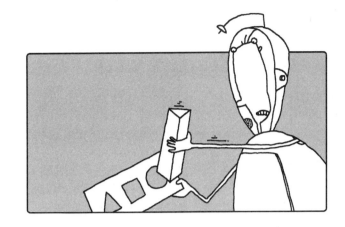

(See handbook pages 373-380.)

As every teacher knows, doing well on a test is partly a matter of knowing the material and partly a matter of knowing how to take a test. This chapter helps students with both. It begins with a few tips for learning and remembering material and then focuses on test-taking skills, from how to read true/false questions to how to write a long essay answer.

Of Special Interest
- "Preparing for a Test" provides a brief list of study tips as well as helpful guidelines for taking tests. (page 374)
- The four common kinds of objective tests are explained and illustrated with example questions. (pages 375-376)
- A glossary of key words used in essay test questions helps students with their first task—understanding the question. (page 377)

Rationale
- Students need test-taking skills, as well as knowledge of the material, to do well on tests.
- Students with good test-taking skills can face tests with confidence, and their performance will be a more accurate measure of their knowledge.

Major Concepts
- Taking tests can cause jitters, but good test-taking skills make it easier to relax and do well. (page 373)
- The first step in doing well is knowing the test material. (page 374)
- Objective tests require factual knowledge, not opinions. (pages 375-376)
- Essay tests require several steps: understanding the question, thinking about what is known, planning the answer, and writing the answer. (pages 377-380)

Getting Started with "Taking Tests"

Start-Up Activity: Ask students to write 5-10 objective questions for a current unit of study, based on the examples in the handbook on pages 375-376. These questions can form the basis for a unit review session. Students may also choose to write an essay-test question or two, using the key words found on page 377.

Enrichment Activity: Give students many opportunities to practice writing impromptu essays. You might, for example, have students answer essay prompts every two weeks or so. Have students practice evaluating their writing, too, using the checklist on page 24 in the handbook as a general guide. (This is good practice for state assessment tests.)

Teaching Resources

Write Source 2000 Teacher's Guide

- Minilessons:
  "Ask me anything." (page 248)
  "Be prepared!" (page 249)

Write Source 2000 Handbook

- "Writing Expository Essays" and "Writing Persuasive Essays," pages 107-114 and 115-122, provide basic writing guidelines that will help students answer essay-test questions.
- "Guidelines for Thinking and Writing," page 290, addresses many of the key words used in essay-test questions.

Write Source 2000 Program Guide

- A teaching unit (lesson plans and blackline masters) can be found in the Program Guide ring binder for each grade level.

Planning Skills

(See handbook pages 381-385.)

As students' assignments—and their lives—become more complex, they need to know how to set goals, plan their time well, and manage stress. This chapter offers strategies and guidelines that will get them started.

Of Special Interest

- Five important guidelines for setting and working toward long-range goals are spelled out. (page 382)
- Steps in the process of time management, including a sample weekly planner form, are outlined for students. (page 383)
- Guidelines for getting assignments done on time are explained. (page 384)
- "Managing Stress" lists some causes and symptoms of stress and ways students can reduce it. (page 385)

Rationale

- Students need special skills to set and reach academic and life goals.
- Time-management skills help students complete important tasks.
- Recognizing the causes and symptoms of stress and knowing how to deal with them can improve students' well-being and school performance.

Major Concepts

- There are a number of guidelines students can use to help them set and reach long-range goals. (page 382)
- Time management is an important lifelong skill that can help students accomplish all tasks and activities. (page 383)
- Completing assignments on time is a matter of planning ahead and developing good study habits. (page 384)
- Students can identify the causes and symptoms of stress in their lives and take steps to deal with them. (page 385)

Getting Started with "Planning Skills"

Start-Up Activity: At the beginning of the year, have your students set some realistic goals for the year. These goals could cover the number and type of books they will read, the journal-writing routine they will try to keep, the types of writing they will complete, and so on. Periodically, have them revisit these goals.

Enrichment Activity: For extra credit, ask students to read and report on articles or books dealing with the skills covered in this chapter: setting goals, planning your time, completing assignments, and managing stress.

Teaching Resources

Write Source 2000 Teacher's Guide

- Minilessons:
  "Time is on my side." (page 249)
  "Make it easy on yourself." (page 249)

Write Source 2000 Handbook

- "Building Good Writing Habits," page 4, emphasizes the importance of planning time for writing.

Write Source 2000 Program Guide

- A teaching unit (lesson plans and blackline masters) can be found in the Program Guide ring binder for each grade level.

Proofreader's Guide

Introductory Notes

This section introduces the "Proofreader's Guide" in the handbook and provides getting-started ideas to help you with your initial planning.

	Teacher's Guide	Student Handbook
Marking Punctuation	139	387–403
Editing for Mechanics		404–410
Improving Spelling		411–418
Using the Right Word		419–433
Understanding Sentences		434–438
Understanding Our Language		439–457

Proofreader's Guide

(See handbook pages 387-457.)

The "Proofreader's Guide" is placed near the end of the handbook to emphasize the fact that writing shouldn't begin with the study of grammar. This placement is not meant to downplay the importance of mechanics and grammar. Students must have a good working knowledge of the standard conventions of our language. However, we do suggest that you put the study of these conventions in proper perspective and not make it the main focus of your writing program. The "Proofreader's Guide" covers the conventions in the following order: punctuation, mechanics, spelling, usage, sentences, language (*parts of speech*).

Of Special Interest
- This section is color coded, so students can quickly flip to it when they have a questions about punctuation, capitalization, mechanics, usage, and so on.

Rationale
- Students need an easy-to-use reference to answer their questions about the standard conventions of the language.
- Knowing how to use a reference tool such as the "Proofreader's Guide" is an important learning skill.

Major Concepts
- "Marking Punctuation" and "Editing for Mechanics" cover everything students need to know about punctuation, capitalization, plurals, abbreviations, and numbers. (pages 387-410)
- "Improving Spelling" and "Using the Right Word" include the words that students commonly misspell and misuse. (pages 411-433)
- "Understanding Sentences" and "Understanding Our Language" help students learn about sentences and the parts of speech. (pages 434-457)

Performance Standards

Students are expected to . . .
- employ standard English to communicate clearly and effectively.
- understand the different parts of speech.
- write in complete sentences.
- correctly punctuate and capitalize their writing.

Getting Started with the "Proofreader's Guide"

Start-Up Activity: Take students on a quick tour of the "Proofreader's Guide" by having them answer a wide range of questions such as the following:

1. What punctuation mark is used between items in a series?
2. Should you capitalize all of the words in a title?
3. When should you use the word "capital"?
4. Does an imperative sentence give a command?

Enrichment Activity: Create scenarios that allow students to learn about grammar for themselves, logically and deductively. For example, the following scenario lets students discover the relationship between a pronoun and its antecedent.

Step 1: Read this sentence: *The day will begin with a breakfast when they will meet the camp counselors who will direct them during the week.*

Step 2: Respond to each of the following questions or statements (orally or in writing).

1. What are the two pronouns in this sentence?
2. What noun could you substitute for these pronouns?
3. _____ (the noun) is an antecedent for the pronouns "they" and "them."
4. Define antecedent.

Teaching Resources

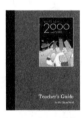

Write Source 2000 Teacher's Guide

- Minilessons:

  Pages 250-260 contain 40 minilessons for the "Proofreader's Guide."

- "What About Grammar?" (pages 190-192)

Write Source 2000 Handbook

- "Composing Sentences," pages 85-92, covers sentence errors, subject-verb agreement, and confusing sentences.

Write Source 2000 Program Guide

- SkillsBook activities for all parts of the "Proofreader's Guide" can be found in the Program Guide ring binder for each grade level.

Student Almanac

Introductory Notes

This section introduces the "Student Almanac" in the handbook and provides getting-started ideas to help you with your initial planning.

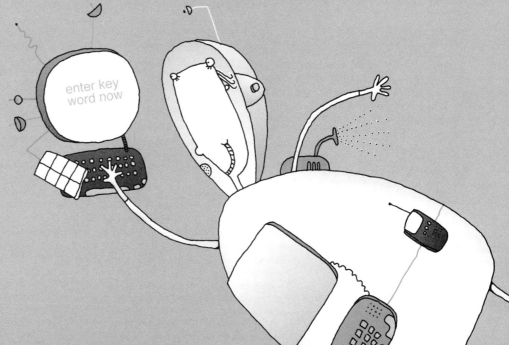

enter key word now

Student Almanac

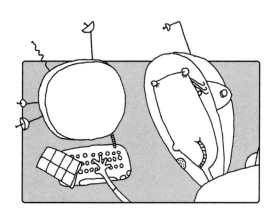

(See handbook pages 459-525.)

The "Student Almanac" is a cross-curricular source of information that students will use for many different purposes. This section is organized under seven subject areas (*language, science, mathematics, computers, geography, government,* and *history*) and contains a wealth of helpful and interesting information. For example, students can learn sign language, study the "American to Metric Table," learn how to solve word problems in math, check out maps from different parts of the world, and have access to many important facts about the U.S. government.

Of Special Interest
- The language map shows all of the world's major language families. (pages 462-463)
- The glossary of math terms covers everything from basic computation to geometry. (pages 475-479)
- The "Historical Time Line" lists interesting inventions and important events from the 1500s to the present. (pages 515-525)

Rationale
- An almanac appeals to students' natural curiosity about many subjects.
- Students should be able to interpret visual information.
- Learning how to use an almanac is an important learning skill.

Major Concepts
- "Language" covers everything from English around the world to symbols of correction. (pages 459-464)
- "Science" includes helpful tables comparing the metric system to basic U.S. measurements. (pages 467-469)
- "Computers" contains a sample keyboard that students can use to practice their keyboarding skills. (pages 484-485)

Performance Standards
Students are expected to . . .
- use various reference materials such as a dictionary, encyclopedia, almanac, thesaurus, atlas, etc.

Getting Started with the "Student Almanac"

Start-Up Activity: Have students list all of their classes across the top or along the side of a piece of notebook paper. Then have them identify parts of the "Student Almanac" that will help them in each of their classes. Also ask them to identify other parts of the handbook that will help them across the curriculum.

Enrichment Activity: Use the "Student Almanac" as a starting point for general-knowledge minilessons. For example, you can form questions such as the following ones for students to answer using the almanac: *Where is Puerto Rico? What is a centimeter? When did the Panama Canal open?* Proceed from there with a discussion of the questions and the students' answers.

Teaching Resources

Write Source 2000 Teacher's Guide

- Minilessons:
  Pages 261-263 contain 14 minilessons
  for the "Student Almanac."

Write Source 2000 Handbook

- "The Tools of Learning," pages 261-385, covers all of the important study skills that students will use across the curriculum.

Write Source 2000 Program Guide

- Blackline masters and minilessons for all parts of the "Student Almanac" can be found in the Program Guide ring binder for each grade level.

Writing Programs

The writing programs described on the following pages offer you an opportunity to use a variety of approaches to meet the individual needs of your students.

Effective Writing Instruction

How is writing taught today?

If you are up on your contemporary writing research, you know writing isn't really taught. That is, writing isn't a set of facts, forms, or formulas that a teacher imparts, and it certainly isn't worksheet busywork. We now know that it is (or should be) a student-centered activity that is learned through a variety of writing experiences.

So where does this put the teacher? Not behind a desk lecturing or correcting yesterday's assignments. It puts her or him right alongside the students; teachers and students write and learn together.

And if writing is not taught, then how is it learned? There are a number of approaches that promote writing as a student-centered learning activity. All of these approaches have a number of things in common in addition to being student centered.

First of all, writing programs don't require a textbook.

Most textbooks by their very nature are prescriptive. That is, they are designed as much to tie students and teachers to the textbook as they are to help students develop as independent thinkers and writers. In an effective writing classroom, the students' own writing serves as the textbook.

Second, writing programs are individualized.

In most contemporary writing classrooms, students work and learn individually and in small groups. Instruction is based on need and given when one or more students need help with a basic skill or rhetorical concept. The form of the instruction is usually a 10- to 15-minute minilesson. (See pages 225-263 in this guide for sample minilessons.)

They are lively and active.

Today's writing programs promote active learning. On any given day, students might spend their time in a group-critiquing session or writing or reading on their own. There's no hiding in the last row of the classroom as the teacher lectures.

They are well planned.

Just because effective writing programs are student centered doesn't mean that students can simply do as they please. Even the most motivated students will take advantage of too much freedom. Deadlines, support materials, methods of instruction, methods for measuring writing progress, and sensible classroom management procedures all have to be established for a program to be successful. Programs must also be flexible enough to meet the needs and interests of the students (obviously within reason) as the course work progresses.

They are adaptable.

A contemporary writing program must be flexible enough to accommodate new methods of instruction or assessment. If an existing method or routine doesn't work with a particular group of students, changes are made. If a different method of assessment seems more appropriate, it is integrated. The best writing teachers pay constant and close attention to the atmosphere and productivity of their classrooms.

They are integrated.

Contemporary writing programs draw from all of the significant research. A particular program won't, for example, be based solely on the writing process approach or on thematic units. Instead, it will most likely be a combination of approaches. What follows is a brief description of six of the most significant approaches to writing.

> "A writer is a person whose best is released in the accomplishment of writing. . . . He writes, and the best of him, in spite even of his thoughts, will appear on the page even to his surprise."
>
> —William Carlos Williams

An Overview of the Approaches

 THE PROCESS APPROACH

While using the process approach, students learn that writing—real writing—is a process of discovery and exploration rather than an end product or a series of basic skills. As students develop their writing, they make use of all steps in the writing process—prewriting, drafting, revising, editing and proofreading, and publishing. And the writing they develop, for the most part, stems from their own thinking.

Students use prewriting activities to discover writing ideas they know and care about. They are encouraged to talk about their ideas and create a community of writers within the classroom. They write first drafts freely and quickly, and they revise carefully. After editing and proofreading, students share or publish their work.

Write Source 2000 includes a complete discussion of the writing process (starting on page 3). Also note that the guidelines for the specific forms of writing are organized according to the steps in the writing process. (See pages 149-150 in this guide for more on the writing process.)

 THE THEMATIC APPROACH

When using this approach, the teacher (with student input) chooses a theme that serves as the focal point for an experience that immerses students in a variety of integrated reading, writing, and speaking activities.

The teacher provides pieces of literature and other prewriting activities as starting points for the thematic study. Writing projects evolve from these activities. The process approach and usually some form of the writing workshop approach are incorporated into thematic programs. (See pages 151-152 in this guide for more on the thematic approach.)

> "Some students don't accept the invitation [to write] as readily. . . . They need to find out who they are as learners. We need to know and trust each other. It takes time."
>
> —Linda Rief

 THE PERSONAL APPROACH

The focus of this approach is simple: Students enjoy writing and find it meaningful if it stems from their personal experiences and observations. Students usually keep a journal in a personal experience (*experiential*) program so they always have a number of potential writing ideas to draw from. As with most contemporary approaches, the writing process and some form of a writing workshop are incorporated into the program.

Freewriting (*rapid writing, spontaneous writing*) plays an integral part in this approach to writing as well. Both journal writing and freewriting help students write honestly about their personal experiences in assigned writing. And it helps students eventually produce writing that readers will find interesting and entertaining.

Review the forms of writing in *Write Source 2000* (page vi), and you will note that we generally address personal forms of writing before we address more detached, content-oriented forms of writing. It follows that the more students write from personal experience, the better able they are to address increasingly more complex experiences in more complex forms of writing. This writing eventually becomes more and more public, the kind of writing students often have to produce before they're ready. (See pages 153-154 in this guide for more information.)

4 THE WRITING WORKSHOP APPROACH

In a writing workshop, students write or work on writing-related issues every day (*reading, researching, critiquing, participating in collaborative writing*, etc.). They are expected to keep all of their work in writing folders, and they are expected to produce a specified number of finished pieces by the end of the term. They are encouraged to take risks, to experiment with new forms and techniques. Support during each writing project comes from both peer and teacher conferences. Students utilize the steps in the writing process to develop their writing and share their work with the group.

The teacher acts as a guide and facilitator. She or he creates a classroom environment that is conducive to the workshop approach. Desks and chairs are arranged to make student interaction easy. The classroom is stocked with an ample supply of relevant reading and writing materials. Instruction and advice are given as they are needed on an individual basis, in small groups, or to the entire class. (See pages 154-155 in this guide for more information.)

> "The discipline of real learning consists of The Self and The Others flowing into each other."
> —Ken Macrorie

5 WRITING-ACROSS-THE-CURRICULUM APPROACH

When a writing-across-the-curriculum program (WAC) is implemented, students begin to experience writing as an important part of the learning process. The writing students do will vary from subject to subject and from situation to situation. In one class, students may be freely recording their observations about a new concept. In another class, students may be summarizing a magazine article. And in still another class, students may be writing a memo or an e-mail message.

The *Write Source 2000* handbook serves as an excellent student resource for cross-curricular writing. It provides guidelines and models for many forms of writing. It discusses the writing process, workplace writing, writing to learn, and journal writing. It offers a complete proofreader's guide to help students take writing to finished form. The handbook makes it possible for all teachers to become writing teachers.

This guide also contains a great deal of additional information related to WAC starting on page 159. Included in this discussion are tips for implementing a WAC program, a list of writing-to-learn activities, guidelines for designing effective writing assignments, and lists of ideas for content-area writing projects.

6 THE TRAIT-BASED APPROACH

Students who learn to write using a trait-based approach become confident, competent managers of their own process of writing. They understand how to approach revision because they know what makes writing work.

Trait-based instruction focuses on six key features—or *traits*—that most writers, editors, and thoughtful readers agree are essential to writing success. These traits are as follows:

- ✔ stimulating ideas
- ✔ logical organization
- ✔ engaging voice
- ✔ original word choice
- ✔ smooth-reading sentences
- ✔ correct, accurate copy

Students are taught each trait individually, but eventually they combine all six in revising and editing their work. They learn to look and listen for examples of each trait in the writing all around them, assessing their own and others' writing for the six key features. The greatest strength of trait-based instruction lies in its power to make writing and revision manageable for students. Like a good athletic coach, a trait-based writing instructor helps students develop their overall proficiency one critical skill at a time. (See pages 156-157 in this guide for more information.)

The Process Approach

What is writing?

- Writing is thinking on paper.
- Writing is "chasing thinking and turning it into thought."
- Writing is "the exposed edge of thought."

What is the "writing process"?

- The "writing process" is the best way we know of to turn thinking into writing.
- The process is usually broken down into manageable steps, allowing students to concentrate on one thing at a time.
- The steps in the process break down into prewriting, writing, revising, editing and proofreading, and publishing.

Why do students write?

Traditional Objectives

- Students write to demonstrate the retention of information.
- They write to improve language skills, especially surface skills (punctuation, handwriting, spelling, . . .).
- They write to please the teacher.

Writing-Process Objectives

- Students write to explore, to understand, to learn, to discover, to clarify thinking, and to pass along information.

How is writing encouraged?

Teacher-Centered Approach

- Assign a topic, length, time limit.
- Assign an outline and/or a thesis statement.
- Assign an introduction; check for compliance.
- Expect students to produce a correct paper.
- Mark, grade, comment.
- Return papers, marked for all errors.
- Request that some students rewrite their assignments until they get them right.

> "The wrong word, the clumsy clause, the misplaced modifiers, may simply be evidence of language still leading to meaning."
>
> —Donald Murray

Student-Centered Approach

- Students use prewriting activities to discover a topic they know and care about. (See pages 45-52 in *Write Source 2000* for examples.)
- Students are encouraged to talk about their topics to help them develop a sense of purpose for writing.
- Students write for real audiences—usually their peers—rather than for their teachers.
- When students write a first draft, they focus on getting ideas down on paper.
- They think as they go, crossing out, switching directions, using abbreviations, writing rapidly.
- Students revise their writing by going back over what they have written—adding, cutting, replacing, and moving information.
- They read aloud what they have written and discuss it with their peers and/or teacher.
- At this stage, the focus is on ideas, order, clarity, and voice. (See pages 67-74 in *Write Source 2000* for more.)
- Students edit and proofread their work only after they have their ideas straight.
- Students work on mechanical problems in small groups, in individual conferences, with the whole class, or by using a handbook of mechanics and usage.
- Students publish their work, which might simply mean that their writing is displayed for peers to read.
- The teacher, with student input, evaluates the finished product.

What are the results of using the writing process?

- Students find writing more meaningful because it becomes a reflection of their own thinking.
- Students develop a feel for real writing.
- Students develop independent thinking skills and take pride in their work.
- Students develop a better attitude toward writing, which results in better writing from students of all abilities.
- Using the writing process means less work for teachers.

What do curriculum guides say about writing and the writing process?

(We happen to be located in Wisconsin. Our Department of Public Instruction produces an excellent guide to curriculum planning from which the following information was taken.)

The Language Arts Task Force makes the following recommendations:

- Curriculum and instruction in writing should reflect the knowledge that we learn language holistically, through whole problems in creating meaning, rather than through practice in isolated skills.
- Texts reinforce the teaching that has already gone on within the writing process.
- Writing should be a schoolwide activity, integrated into content-area learning at all levels.
- Students at all levels do original writing every week, gaining consistent experience in working through the entire writing process.
- Teachers view writing as a developmental process rather than an accumulation of skills.
- Curriculum and instruction recognize the contribution of current research.
- Each district should develop a consistent K-12 philosophy for the teaching of writing.

The Task Force also recognizes the following:

- "Grammar" ought to be taught in the context of actual oral and written communication.
- Sentence diagramming, labeling parts of speech, and having students memorize lists of rules are traditional practices that should be avoided.
- Sentence combining, sentence expansion, and sentence transformation are worthwhile classroom practices.
- Students must be taught how to revise, then given regular opportunities to practice.

Why is it important for all teachers to know about the writing process?

- When implemented properly, it can change the effectiveness of the entire school —in all areas.
- A districtwide implementation of the writing process would provide continuity within the K-12 writing program.
- Using the writing process in all its forms enhances learning in all subjects.
- The writing process works well with all forms of learning, especially thinking and cooperative learning.

Why is it also important for teachers to know about NCTE's English language arts standards?

(The following information comes from *Standards in Practice Grades 6-8,* an NCTE publication, written by Jeffrey D. Wilhelm.)

- Standards help define what students should be able to know and do.
- Standards can be met through a variety of teaching styles and strategies, including the writing process.
- Standards should help teachers decide what to teach and how to teach it.

The Thematic Approach

Thematic teaching isn't just for language arts teachers. Teachers of music, social studies, art, math, or any other subject can also be thematic teachers. By choosing a theme and integrating related writing, reading, speaking, and listening activities into specific content areas, teachers can provide students with complete language experiences, ones that will actively involve them in learning.

Here's how teachers can integrate different strands of language into the curriculum:

Incorporate writing . . .

- Allow students the freedom to choose their specific writing subjects.
- Share with students samples of interesting writing related to the theme.
- Promote writing as a process (rather than a set of skills or an end product).
- Let students write for different audiences: classmates, contest judges, newspaper and magazine editors, friends and relatives.
- Promote writing to learn by implementing journal writing, stop 'n' write, learning logs, exit slips, admit slips, etc. Writing-to-learn activities are ungraded and free from traditional teacher evaluation. (See 164-165 in this guide for more information.)

Incorporate reading . . .

- Provide plenty of reading material relevant to your theme or subject area. (Magazines, journals, and biographies are great resources.)
- Allow students to choose some of their own reading material.
- Give time for SSR (sustained silent reading).
- Provide students time to react to and share their reading.
- Encourage the reading of a wide variety of primary and secondary research materials.

Incorporate speaking . . .

- Provide students with a wide range of speaking opportunities.
- Stimulate discussion by asking questions and providing feedback.
- Give students at all levels frequent opportunities to create classroom dramas.
- Make use of video and audio equipment, overhead projectors, computers, and other technological equipment.

Incorporate listening . . .

- Make listening an important part of the daily activities.
- Practice listening techniques and help students develop skills for effective listening. (See page 370 in the handbook.)
- Build listening skills within the context of the thematic study.
- Encourage students to interview people during each unit of study.
- Arrange for speakers who are willing to share their experiences.
- Help students identify their own purpose for listening to each speaker.

Here's how thematic teachers approach learning in their classrooms:

- You'll find teachers and students working together as active participants in the learning process.
- Writing, reading, speaking, and listening are everyday tools for learning.
- Teachers see reading, writing, speaking, and listening as complementary strands of language learning, and incorporate them throughout the day.
- The students' classroom experiences are open-ended, shaped by their input.
- Teachers provide many opportunities for students to connect with real-life events.
- There is shared decision making. Everyone participates in the decision-making process, including decisions about materials, activities, and evaluation.

> "The secret of education is respecting the pupil."
> —Ralph Waldo Emerson

- Students have opportunities for peer conferencing. (See pages 75-78 and 369-372 in the handbook.)
- There is respect for the ideas and interests of others. It is understood that each learner has something to contribute.
- Instruction is student directed; students influence what is talked about and what is being taught.
- Every child works at his or her ability level and therefore experiences success.
- Activities are considered "invitations" rather than assignments. Students are invited to read, write, and explore thematic topics that are of interest to them.
- Errors are considered a source of information rather than a sign of failure. Students learn by making errors.
- Evaluation for projects and activities is ongoing. Evaluations are made primarily on a personal basis, and each student is seen as unique.
- Teachers observe students and continually evaluate and improve their programs based on those observations.

> "A school should not be a preparation for life. A school should be life."
> —Elbert Hubbard

Here are some important themes that teachers use to provide complete language experiences in their classrooms:

- Aging
- Astronomy
- Careers
- Community Service
- Democracy
- Diversity
- Environment
- The Future
- Holocaust
- Math in Daily Life
- Rainforest
- Space Exploration
- Sports
- Technology
- Wellness

The Personal Experience Approach

> "I can tap into [my students'] human instincts to write if I help them realize that their lives and memories are worth telling stories about, and if I help them zoom in on topics of fundamental importance to them."
>
> —Writing Teacher June Gould

We know from firsthand experience that the personal stories young learners love to share can serve as the basis of an effective and lively writing program. Here's how we did it:

Getting Started

At the beginning of the school year, we introduced in-class journal writing. We knew that the most effective way to get students into writing was simply to let them write often and freely about their own lives, without having to worry about grades or turning their writing in. This helped them develop a feel for writing that originates from their own thoughts and feelings.

That's where journals come in. No other activity that we know of gets students into writing more effectively than journal writing. All your students need are notebooks, pens, time to write, and encouragement to explore their thoughts. (See pages 145-148 in the handbook for more information.)

We provided our students with four or five personal writing prompts each time they wrote. They could use one of these prompts as a starting point for their writing if they wished. The choice was theirs.

Writing Prompts

Here's a typical list of writing prompts: Write about . . .
- a memorable kitchen-related experience,
- coping with younger brothers or sisters,
- being home alone, late at night, or
- what you did over the past weekend.

We would ask our students to write every other day for the first 10 minutes of the class period. Students knew that every Monday, Wednesday, and Friday were writing days.

Keeping It Going

After everyone was seated and roll was taken, the journals were passed out, the prompts were given, and everyone wrote. We expected students to write for the complete 10 minutes nonstop. And we made sure that they did. They knew that they would be given a quarter journal grade for the number of words they produced. This made a contest out of the writing sessions. Each time they wrote, they wanted to see if they could increase their production from past journal entries. (Only legible words were counted.)

Wrapping It Up

On days that we weren't writing, we shared journal entries. First, students would exchange journals with a classmate. They would count the number of words in the entry, read it carefully, and then make comments on things they liked or questioned. Then they shared their comments among themselves, and we would talk about the entries as a class.

The writers themselves would be reluctant to share their entries with the entire class. But the readers had no problem sharing someone else's entry ("You've got to hear Nick's story") and reading it out loud. The students loved these readings and the discussions that followed.

Personal Experience Papers

Periodically, we would interrupt the normal course of journal writing and sharing and make formal writing assignments. That is, we would ask students to review their entries and select one to develop into a more polished, complete personal experience paper. Usually, those entries that readers enjoyed and wanted to know more about would be the ones the young writers would choose to develop.

We wanted to make sure that their writing went through at least two thorough revisions, so we gave our writers plenty of class time to work on their papers. They also were required to turn in all of their preliminary work with their final drafts. (See "Autobiographical Writing," pages 153-159 in the handbook, for guidelines for this type of writing.)

> "In a very real sense, the writer writes in order to teach himself, to understand himself, to satisfy himself."
>
> —Alfred Kazin

The experience papers were shared with the entire class at the end of the project. This was an enjoyable activity, one that students came to appreciate as an important part of the entire composing process. It was their day. They were on stage. They were sharing the end products of all of their work—special moments in their own lives.

The Writing Workshop Approach

See a writing workshop in action by studying the sample schedule on the following page. Here you will see how one teacher organized his writing workshop. This schedule reserves time for minilessons, status checks, individual or group work, and sharing sessions.

Since this schedule is designed for one of the first weeks of a workshop, all students are asked to participate in the minilessons. In time, you can meet the needs of your students by inviting only those attempting certain goals to do mini-lessons. All other students will be actively engaged with a piece of writing or another option you have offered.

Instructor Checklist— A Management Tool

One management technique that teachers of workshops advocate is the use of a checklist similar to the one shown on the right. The teacher designs the checklist after he or she has set up a weekly schedule. Such a checklist serves as a quick reference for you as the week unfolds; it also serves as a history as the year proceeds.

SAMPLE CHECKLIST

✔ **Cover minilessons**

 ____ 3-8 (Introduction to writing process)

 ____ 45-52 (Activities to help discover and select a subject)

 ____ 145-148 (Journal keeping)

 ____ 61-66 (Writing the first draft)

✔ **Teach two reading-to-learn strategies**

 ____ Tell/retell

 ____ Smart

✔ **All students . . .**

 ____ received writing folders.

 ____ experimented with freewriting and clustering.

 ____ made three journal entries

 ____ worked on a first draft.

 ____ wrote exit slips.

Writing Workshop: Weekly Schedule

This schedule can vary depending on your needs. You might, for example, conduct writing workshops for three days a week and reading workshops for the other two days. The sample schedule below focuses exclusively on writing.

Monday	Tuesday	Wednesday	Thursday	Friday
Writing Minilesson 10 MIN.	**Writing Minilesson** 10 MIN.	**Writing Minilesson** 10 MIN.	**Writing Minilesson** 10 MIN.	**Quiz Review of Minilessons** 10 MIN.
Status Check 2 MIN. (Find out what students will work on for the day.)	**Status Check** 2 MIN. (Find out what students will work on for the day.)	**Status Check** 2 MIN. (Find out what students will work on for the day.)	**Status Check** 2 MIN. (Find out what students will work on for the day.)	**Status Check** 2 MIN. (Find out what students will work on for the day.)
Individual Work Writing, Revising, Editing, Conferencing, or Publishing 30 MIN.	**Individual Work** Writing, Revising, Editing, Conferencing, or Publishing 30 MIN.	**Individual Work** Writing, Revising, Editing, Conferencing, or Publishing 30 MIN.	**Individual Work** Writing, Revising, Editing, Conferencing, or Publishing 30 MIN.	**Individual Work** Writing, Revising, Editing, Conferencing, or Publishing 30 MIN.
Whole Class Sharing Session 5 MIN.	**Whole Class Sharing Session** 5 MIN.	**Whole Class Sharing Session** 5 MIN.	**Whole Class Sharing Session** 5 MIN.	**Whole Class Sharing Session** 5 MIN.

The Trait-Based Approach

For many students of past decades, writing was a mystery to be solved: What did the teacher *want* anyway? What *was* good writing? Trait-based writing instruction takes the mystery out of the situation by showing students from day one exactly what makes writing work. It helps them recognize good writing when they see it and also teaches them, step-by-step, the skills they need to succeed as writers.

Enhancing the Process

Trait-based instruction is not meant to take the place of other approaches to writing. It is meant to enhance those approaches by providing students with a way to assess, reflect upon, and improve their work. Specifically, trait-based instruction supports . . .

- **prewriting** by helping students think about, explore, research, discuss, and brainstorm *ideas*.

- **drafting** as students begin to identify a main idea, come up with supporting details, *organize* information in a way that makes sense, and project a *voice* suited to topic and audience.

- **revision** as students think about strengths and weaknesses in their *idea* development, *organization,* and *voice*.

- **editing** as students reflect on the best *word choice* for their topic and audience, review *sentences* for fluency and form, and check *conventions* to ensure their copy is clear and correct.

Getting Started

First, as a teacher, *you* need to understand the traits, inside and out. It is useful to look at rubrics or scoring guides for explanations of the traits as they relate to the different modes of writing. Write Source offers several copies of such rubrics, for both teachers and students. (See pages 181-186 in this guide.)

In *Write Source 2000,* pages 19-24, you will also find excerpts from well-written books that demonstrate the skillful use of each trait. These samples will put you and your students on a path to reading in a new way—noticing moments of voice or excellent word choice, deciding whether information is sufficiently detailed and adequately organized, and so on. Then you can begin collecting other writing samples that your students can assess according to the traits.

Collecting Samples

Samples of excellent *and* perfectly terrible writing abound in the world of print all around you. To teach the traits well, you will need to search out strong *and* weak examples that your students can assess and discuss. *Write Source 2000* contains many samples of excellent student writing that you and your students can assess. Here are some other good sources:

Ideas
- Newspaper articles
- Textbooks

Organization
- Cookbooks
- Manuals

Voice
- Friendly letters
- Reviews

Word Choice
- Greeting cards
- Poems

Sentence Smoothness
- Song lyrics
- Short stories

Correct, Accurate Copy
- Research reports
- Business letters

Sharing Rubrics

The whole idea behind the trait-based approach is that students know from the beginning exactly what teachers expect in good writing. So any basic assessment tool that a teacher plans on using—a rubric or scoring guide—must also be in the hands of the students. Students refer to their rubrics . . .

- as they write and revise,
- as they meet in groups to share their writing, and
- as they assess and discuss collected samples.

The more you use "trait" language—which is nothing more than the vocabulary writers use to talk about their work—the more familiar it becomes to students, and the easier it becomes for them to . . .

- think about and plan writing,
- respond to the writing of others,
- revise and edit effectively, and
- succeed in any writing assessment situation.

Teaching the Traits

Teachers often ask, "In what order should I teach the traits of good writing? And how long should I spend on each one?"

Order: We suggest beginning with *ideas* because it is the foundational trait. After all, don't writers begin with a message to deliver, a point to make, a story to tell? After that, *voice* and *organization* can be taught in either order. Both relate to audience and purpose and shift as those key considerations shift.

Word choice and *sentence smoothness* can be taught next—again, in either order. Both are significant components of editing. *Correctness* is taught by most teachers on an ongoing basis. This means that students will have multiple opportunities to practice editing and proofreading.

Time: Don't rush. Give students time to reflect on each trait, to assess various forms of writing for that trait, to look at the trait in samples of literature, to discuss the trait in a writing group, and to use a rubric in revising their own work for that trait. This variety of activities might mean spending *three weeks or more on one trait*. Don't worry. It takes time to learn the secrets of good writing.

A Traits Classroom in Action

If you would observe a six-trait classroom in action, here are the kinds of things you'd see happening:

1. A room filled with trait posters, trait rubrics, and conversation using trait language.

2. Students writing frequently, creating drafts on various topics and tucking them away in a writing folder (*Some* will be revised and *perhaps* assessed formally; others will never go beyond the draft stage.)

3. The teacher collecting and sharing samples of writing from a wide range of sources

4. Students talking about "strong voice," "good leads," "smooth sentences," and other features of writing

5. Students periodically choosing drafts from their writing folders, assessing them using their own rubrics, and revising accordingly

6. Students choosing to add revised drafts to a portfolio, reflecting upon those revisions, identifying their strengths as writers, and setting goals for themselves

7. The teacher assessing some of the students' revised and edited writing

Why traits make a difference

- Students become responsible for reviewing and assessing their own work.
- Students know what to do to revise, so their second drafts show substantial improvements and are not just empty rewrites.
- Knowing how to assess makes students stronger writers—even of first drafts.

Schoolwide Writing

The strategies and guidelines discussed in this section will help you make writing an important part of your curriculum, no matter if you teach mathematics, science, or language arts.

Introduction to Writing Across the Curriculum

> "In the best of all possible worlds, language study should be part and parcel of the entire school curriculum. The whole school day should be a learning workshop."
>
> —Nancie Atwell

Q. What is writing across the curriculum?

A. Writing across the curriculum (WAC) is the use of writing as a teaching and learning tool in all courses. Based on his or her course content and learning goals, each teacher chooses which writing activities to use, and how often to use them.

Q. What types of WAC activities work best?

A. WAC activities come in many types: graded or nongraded; short or long; school-based forms or workplace forms; and writing that's revised and edited, or writing that isn't. For example, *Write Source 2000* includes more than 40 forms of writing, and any one of them—from journals to research papers—could be an effective writing activity in any course. In addition, pages 164-165 in this guide have 23 informal writing-to-learn activities that are useful across the curriculum.

Q. Why should students write in all courses?

A. Cross-curricular activities help students in three ways:

1. to think through and find meaning in their learning,
2. to retain what they learn, and
3. to develop their writing skills.

In his book *Smart Schools,* David Perkins argues that writing is a smart teaching tool because it presses students to think. In addition, writing helps students construct a network of meaning that connects lessons within a course, courses within a curriculum, and a curriculum to the student's plans for the future. When students find meaning in their learning, they work hard and retain what they learn.

In their book *Writing to Learn/ Learning to Write,* authors Mayher, Lester, and Pradl also argue that writing helps students learn. But WAC, say the authors, has an additional benefit: while students are writing to learn, they are also learning to write. WAC activities give students practice in writing skills such as gathering and organizing information, evaluating arguments, and supporting ideas.

Q. How does writing enhance learning?

A. Whether the assignment is a 10-minute freewriting or a full-blown research paper, writing helps students learn by enabling them to do things like . . .

- develop and record their thoughts,
- connect and analyze their ideas,
- receive a classmate's or teacher's input,
- revise specific points or arguments,
- take ownership for what is said and how it is said.

Q. To grade or not to grade?

A. Teachers choose whether and how to grade an assignment by considering the assignment goals, the type of writing done, and the amount of time that students have to write. For ideas on how to assess all types of writing, see pages 175-189.

Setting Up a Writing-Across-the-Curriculum Program

Writing across the curriculum (WAC) is the whole faculty's assignment—teachers and administrators alike. Every educator in the school can contribute to the effort that builds and implements a strong WAC program. Therefore, while the guidelines below describe how individual teachers can use WAC techniques, they are also addressed to the whole community of educators in your school.

Write Source 2000 and this *Teacher's Guide* are powerful tools for building a program.

The handbook helps students learn writing skills in English class and develop those skills in all other classes. The *Teacher's Guide* is designed to help instructors use writing as a learning tool in all courses. To get the best benefit from both books, make sure that . . .

- each student has a personal copy of the handbook for use in all classes,
- each teacher has a handbook and a *Teacher's Guide,* and
- the faculty learns how to use both tools well.

Know and understand the five reasons for writing.

Teachers can identify reasons that would warrant writing in their classes by looking at these five reasons to write:

1 Writing to share learning

Having students share their writing lets them interact with an audience and builds a healthy learning community. The school-based forms listed on page 166 are often used for this purpose.

2 Writing to show learning

The most common reason content-area teachers have students write is to show learning. For forms of writing commonly used for this purpose, see the following sections in *Write Source 2000:* essay tests (pages 377-380), summaries and paraphrasing (pages 213-216), and reports (pages 208-235).

3 Writing to learn new concepts and ideas

Popular writing-to-learn assignments are unrehearsed and ungraded activities like those listed on pages 164-165 of this guide. The purpose is not to produce a finished piece of writing but rather to record one's thoughts on paper in order to organize, explore, and understand them.

4 Writing to explore personal thoughts and feelings

Exploring personal thoughts and feelings works well in social studies, science, and language arts. Common forms assigned for this purpose are found in the following sections of *Write Source 2000:* journal writing (pages 145-148), learning logs (pages 366-368), personal narratives (pages 154-157), and poetry writing (pages 193-207).

5 Writing to plan and complete classroom tasks

Writing to plan is a beneficial lifelong skill. When assigning writing for this purpose, teachers usually choose forms of workplace writing. Workplace writing helps students (1) organize materials, develop plans, and budget time; (2) correspond with others regarding progress on course work; and (3) learn how to use writing to do work in business.

Study the school-based writing forms in *Write Source 2000*.

For example, the persuasive essay (pages 116-117) is an effective tool for helping students develop an argument related to a topic discussed in class. For additional forms, check out the guidelines and models below, noting that many of them illustrate writing assignments in courses other than English:

School-based writing forms:	*Write Source 2000 Handbook Pages*
* autobiography	155-159
* biography	161-166
* book review	175-179
* editorial	172
* expository essay	107-114
* feature article	174
* journal	145-148
* narrative	153-157
* news story	167-171
* observation report	209-212
* paraphrase	216
* persuasive essay	115-122
* poetry	193-207
* report	28-29
* research paper	223-235
* research report	217-222
* story	183-192
* summary	213-215

Consider how the workplace forms help students think through content.

For example, look at the proposal for a history project (pages 258-259). Then consider how writing the proposal helps the student (1) get an overview of the project, (2) organize his ideas, (3) budget his time, (4) request specific help, and (5) complete the project. Finally, consider how the elements in the proposal help the teacher evaluate the process used, and the product produced.

Workplace writing forms:	*Write Source 2000 Handbook Pages*
* application letter	250
* business letter	241-243
* problem letter	249
* request letter	248
* e-mail	254-255
* memo	252-253
* minutes	256-257
* proposal	258-259

Look through the guidelines and/or models below, noting how each will help students.

Writing about . . .	*Write Source 2000 Handbook Pages*
* a definition	125
* an event	126
* an object	125
* a person	123
* a place	124

Writing according to modes or patterns:	
* cause and effect	316-317
* chronological order	314-315
* classroom notes	362-365
* comparison/contrast	312-313
* documentary	358-359
* essay test	377-380
* explanation	127
* learning log	366-368
* process	318-319

"We do not teach writing effectively if we try to make all students and all writing the same."
—Donald Murray

Know how writing techniques can improve the quality of student's work.

For example, if students are writing a compare/contrast paper, invest 30 minutes to teach how a Venn diagram (see *Write Source 2000,* pages 312-313) will help them organize their information. Your investment will pay double dividends: (1) the papers will be stronger, and (2) you'll save hours evaluating them.

Ask students to write for a variety of audiences.

Students can write letters (to research sources), editorials (to newspapers), workplace forms (to parents and teachers), and stories (to students). When students know that a person other than the teacher will read their writing, they usually work harder at the task. They also experience real-world writing firsthand when they have a real audience.

Read "Writing for Specific Courses" (pages 168-170 in this *Teacher's Guide*), paying special attention to the WAC activities suggested for your discipline.

Identify activities used in your area and discuss the thinking and writing skills required for each. Finally, consider whether students are getting a balanced program of written work in your discipline, and make the necessary changes.

Help students understand how to write and revise their work.

Look carefully at (1) the course goals and (2) the assessment criteria for each writing assignment. Students should always have a clear understanding of the purpose of their writing and how it will be evaluated. For more on this topic, see "Designing a Writing Assignment" on pages 171-173 and "Assessment Strategies and Rubrics" on pages 175-192 in this guide.

> "Writing across the curriculum helps students practice the ground rules for citizenship in a literate society. Encourage both students and teachers to promote literacy in your school."
>
> —Verne Meyer

Add books written by authorities on writing across the curriculum to the faculty's professional library.

Each semester, reserve a faculty meeting to discuss the advice given in one of the books. (See page 172 in this guide for suggested titles.) For example, you could discuss the following tips offered by Donald Graves in his book, *Investigate Nonfiction:*

- Allow students to work on their writing in class. Students need sustained periods of time to immerse themselves in their work.

- Reserve class time for sharing sessions. When students have opportunities to talk about their writing in progress, they put more effort into their work.

- Encourage students who are writing reports to work with a subject through two sequences of data gathering, discussing, and exploratory writing before they establish a definite form and focus for the writing.

- Give students a number of gathering experiences. Firsthand data-gathering experiences (like interviewing and direct observation) should be given priority.

- Help students learn to analyze the data they gather.

Writing to Learn

- appropriate in all courses
- needs no preparation or prewriting
- often used spontaneously to enhance class discussion
- commonly read aloud to the class
- may be collected and placed in a student's file, but is rarely graded
- usually is not revised
- similar to prewriting activities described on pages 48-49 of *Write Source 2000*

Admit Slips: Admit slips are brief pieces of writing (usually fit on half sheets of paper) that can be collected as "admission" to class. The teacher can read several aloud (without naming the writer) to help students focus on the day's lesson. Admit slips can be a summary of last night's reading, questions about class material, requests for teachers to review a particular point, or anything else students may have on their minds.

Bio-poems: Bio-poems enable students to synthesize learning because they must select precise language to fit into this form. (Note: Even though the bio-poem is set up to describe "characters," it can also be used to describe complex terms or concepts such as *photosynthesis, inflation,* etc.) Bio-poems encourage metaphorical and other higher-level thinking. A bio-poem follows this pattern:

Line 1. First name
Line 2. Four traits that describe the character
Line 3. Relative ("brother," "sister," etc.) of _____
Line 4. Lover of _____ (list three things)
Line 5. Who feels _____ (three things)
Line 6. Who needs _____ (three things)
Line 7. Who fears _____ (three things)
Line 8. Who gives _____ (three things)
Line 9. Who would like to see _____ (three things)
Line 10. Resident of _____
Line 11. Last name

Brainstorming: Brainstorming is done for the purpose of collecting as many ideas as possible on a particular topic. Students will come away with ideas that might be used to develop a writing or discussion topic. In brainstorming, everything is written down, even if it seems to be weak or irrelevant.

Class Minutes: One student is selected each day to keep minutes of the class lesson (including questions and comments) to be written up for the following class. That student can either read or distribute copies of the minutes at the start of the next class. Reading and correcting these minutes can serve as an excellent review, as well as a good listening exercise.

Clustering: Clustering begins by placing a key word (nucleus word) in the center of the page and circling the word. Students then record other words related to this word. Each word is circled, and a line is drawn to connect it to the closest related word. (See the cluster example on page 48 of *Write Source 2000*.)

Completions: Students complete an open-ended sentence (provided by other students or the teacher) in as many ways as possible. Writing completions helps students look at a subject in different ways, or focus their thinking on a particular concept.

Correspondence: One of the most valuable benefits of writing to learn is that it provides many opportunities for students to communicate with their teachers, often in a sincere, anonymous way. Teachers should set up a channel (suggestion box, mailbox, special reply notes, etc.) that encourages students to communicate freely and honestly.

Creative Definitions: Students are first asked to write out definitions for new words. Other students are then asked to figure out whether the definition is fact or fiction. When students are given the actual definition, there is a much better chance they will remember it.

Dialogues: Students create an imaginary dialogue between themselves and a character (a public or historical figure, or a character from literature). The dialogue brings to life information being studied about the subject.

Dramatic Scenarios: Students imagine themselves to be historical characters during key moments in these people's lives, and then write dialogues that capture the moment. For example, students might put themselves in President Truman's shoes the day he decided to bomb Hiroshima, or in Amelia Earhart's shoes the day before she flew across the Atlantic.

Exit Slips: At the end of class, students write a short piece in which they summarize, evaluate, or question something about the day's lesson, and then turn in their exit slips before leaving the classroom. Teachers use the exit slips to assess students' learning or the success of a lesson.

First Thoughts: Students write or list their immediate impressions (or what they already know) about a topic they are preparing to study. The writing helps students focus on the topic, and it serves as a reference point for measuring learning.

Focused Writings: Writers concentrate on a single topic (or one particular aspect of a topic) and write nonstop for a time. Like brainstorming, focused writing allows students to see how much they have to say on a particular topic, as well as how they might go about saying it.

How-to Writing: To help them clarify and remember information about a task, students write instructions or directions on how to perform the task. Ideally, they then test their writing on someone who is unfamiliar with the task.

Learning Logs: A learning log is a journal (notebook) in which students keep their notes, thoughts, and personal reactions to the subject. (See pages 366-368 in the handbook for samples.)

Listing: Freely listing ideas is another effective writing-to-learn activity. Students can begin with any idea related to the subject and simply list all the thoughts and details that come to mind. Listing can be very useful as a quick review or progress check.

Predicting: Students are stopped at a key point in a lesson and asked to write what they think will happen next. This works especially well with lessons that have a strong cause-and-effect relationship.

Question of the Day: Writers are asked to respond to a question ("What if?" or "Why?") that is important to a clear understanding of the lesson. To promote class discussion, the writing is usually read in class.

Stop 'n' Write: At any point in a class discussion, students are asked to stop and write. The writing helps them to evaluate their understanding of the topic, to reflect on what has been said, and to question anything that may be bothering them.

Student Teachers: Students construct their own math word problems, science experiments, and discussion questions (which can be used for reviewing or testing). This writing task is a great way to replace routine end-of-the-chapter or workbook questions with questions that students actually wonder about or feel are worth asking.

Summing Up: Students are asked to sum up what was covered in a particular lesson by writing about its importance, a possible result, a next step, or a general impression left with them.

Unsent Letters: Letters can be written to any person on any topic related to the subject being studied. Unsent letters allow students to become personally involved with the subject matter and enable them to write about what they know (or don't know) to someone else, imagined or real.

Warm-ups: Students can be asked to write for the first 5 or 10 minutes of class. The writing can be a question of the day, a freewriting, a focused writing, or any other writing-to-learn activity that is appropriate. Warm-ups not only help students focus on the lesson at hand, but also give them a routine that helps break social contact at the beginning of each class.

> "I think one is constantly startled by the things that appear before you on the page while you write."
> —Shirley Hazzard

School-Based Writing Forms

- traditional forms of writing taught in school
- commonly introduced in English class
- appropriate for learning course material in all classes
- usually revised and polished
- usually collected and graded
- often used as part of a unit or project
- guidelines and models are shown in *Write Source 2000*

While each activity below is illustrated by an assignment for a specific course, the form can be used in any course. (The page numbers indicate the location of guidelines and models in *Write Source 2000*.)

Autobiography (page 158) *Health Class:* Write an autobiography about a phase in your life when you were very conscious about your health, or the health of someone close to you.

Biography (pages 161-166) *History:* Write a story of an individual who has played a role in the history of your community.

Book Review (pages 175-179) *Music:* Write a review of a book written about a musician or type of music that you like.

Definition (pages 125) *Math:* Write a definition of "distributive property."

Documentary (pages 358-359) *Geography:* Watch a documentary on a geographical topic, and then summarize it.

Editorial (pages 172) *Current Events:* Write an editorial in which you explain what a current news event means to people your age.

Essay Test (pages 377-380) *Physical Education:* Explain how a good exercise program can help your heart stay fit. Support your answer with specific details.

Expository Essay (pages 107-114) *History:* Write an essay explaining why the American people need a president whom they respect.

Feature Article (pages 174) *Art:* Develop a feature article on an artist that you like.

Journal (pages 145-148) *Health:* During the next week, record in your journal each item of food that you eat, and its related food group.

Learning Log (pages 366-368) *Math:* Each Friday, write an entry in your learning log identifying a concept you learned that week and reflecting on how that concept could help solve math problems when doing workplace activities like building a bridge, reading a gauge, measuring a pipe, etc.

Narrative (pages 153-157) *Physical Education:* Write a narrative in which you relate how you learned to love (or hate) a specific sport.

News Story (pages 167-171) *Science:* Write a news story on a school or community policy that you believe is either environmentally friendly or unfriendly.

Note Taking (pages 361-365; 306) *Science:* In your class notes, draw each insect that you study, and label the body parts.

Observation Report (pages 209-212) *Social Studies:* Write an observation report about using posters to influence student voters in the school's election. Include your hypothesis and postelection survey.

Persuasive Essay (pages 115-122) *Current Events:* Write an essay arguing for or against state-financed school-voucher programs.

Poetry (pages 193-207) *Art:* Write a poem that describes a work of art and shares your feelings about it.

Research Paper (pages 223-235) *History:* Write a research paper on a Native American you studied, explaining how this person influenced history.

Research Report (pages 217-222) *Health:* Write a research report on one or more ways that TV advertisements influence our health.

Story (pages 183-192) *History:* Imagine that you were in junior high on the day Japan bombed Pearl Harbor. Write a story about how that event affected your life.

Summary (pages 213-216) *Science:* Write a summary or paraphrase of your textbook's explanation of photosynthesis.

Workplace Writing Forms

- forms of writing used to do work in business
- appropriate for completing work in all classes
- appropriate for a workplace-writing unit in English
- appropriate for tasks that are part of extracurricular activities
- usually revised and polished
- usually collected and graded
- often used as part of a larger unit or project
- used with guidelines and models in *Write Source 2000*

While each activity below is illustrated by an assignment for a specific course, the form of writing could be used in any course. (Page numbers indicate the location of guidelines and models in *Write Source 2000.*)

Application Letter (page 250) *Science:* Write an application letter to Western Community College's Engineering Camp. Include with your letter the proposal for your science project, along with your project report.

Business Letter (pages 242-248) *Math:* Write a letter to a businessperson asking to interview him or her regarding how the person uses math in business. Report your findings to the class.

E-mail (pages 254-255) *History:* After you have chosen a topic for your speech, send me an e-mail message describing your thesis and requesting permission to proceed. I shall send you my response via e-mail.

Editorial (page 172) *Health:* We discussed the research showing that the light used in tanning beds causes skin cancer. Write an editorial in which you argue for or against the use of tanning beds in health clubs.

Feature Article (page 174) *Art:* During the next two weeks, interview your assigned classmate about the artwork that he or she has produced this semester, and then write a brief feature article about this person and his or her work. All the articles will be published in a newspaper entitled *Meet the Artists.*

Memo (pages 252-253) *Current Events:* Work with your partner to view the evening news each day this week, listening for examples of the ad hominem attacks discussed in class. Take notes on each example, recording the date, TV network, speaker's name, and summary of the topic. Report your findings in a memo that you read to the class next Monday.

Problem Letter (pages 242, 244, 249) *Geography:* If you have a complaint in this class about a subject or an activity, present it to me in the form of a problem letter, and I shall respond in a memo.

Proposal (pages 258-259) *Science:* Begin work on your science project after you have written a project proposal and I approve it. The proposal must include the following: date, teacher's name, your name, subject, project description, materials needed, deadlines and procedure, and outcome. After your project is finished, use the proposal to write the project report. Place both documents in your project folder.

Request Letter (pages 242-248) *History:* After I inform your group that your project proposal is approved, write a letter to the librarian, requesting a short meeting with her and me to discuss library resources for your project. She will reply by e-mail.

> "[Writers must] first work hard to master the tools. Simplify, prune, and strive for order."
>
> —William Zinsser

Writing for Specific Courses

The activities that follow are designed for one of six specific courses—art, health and phys ed, language arts, social studies, science, or math. They are the kinds of activities that are usually revised and polished by the students and collected and graded by the teacher. Each activity can be tied to guidelines and models in *Write Source 2000* (page numbers are provided).

Arts (Music, Theater, Visual Art)

Arts in Review Write a review of an art exhibit, concert, play, or film. For models, refer to reviews in newspapers and magazines. (For additional help, see "Writing About Literature," pages 175-179.)

Guess who's coming to school? Choose an artist you would like to see perform in a school assembly program. Write a letter to the school's program committee or principal describing the person's work and asking that he or she be invited to perform. (See "Request Letter," page 248.)

How do you get ideas? Write a letter to an artist, musician, or actor, discussing your thoughts and feelings about his or her work. (See "Writing Friendly Letters," pages 149-152.)

Meet the Artist Choose an artist (in music, theater, or visual arts) whose work you admire. Research and write a first-person narrative in which you are that person, and in which you describe your art and the process you use to develop it. (See "Autobiographical Writing," pages 153-157.)

Practice Makes Perfect Interview an artist, musician, actor, dancer, or writer, focusing your questions on how the person refines his or her skills. Present your findings in a feature article. (See "Writing News Stories, pages 167-174).

Technology and the Arts Investigate some aspect of technology and the role it plays in visual art, theater, or music. Write your findings in a research report that you share with the class. (See "Writing Personal Research Reports," pages 217-222.)

Health/Physical Education

False Ads Many foods marketed to young people have a high fat or sugar content. Choose one of these foods, research its contents, and write a letter to the producing company explaining your concern about the quality and/or benefits of this food.

Ms. or Mr. Manners Develop a 1990s-style book of etiquette for students in your school. Focus on classroom conduct, group skills, lunchroom manners, male/female roles and relationships, and so on.

Paraphrasing Lifestyles Find an article in a magazine or on the Internet that covers some phase of leading a healthful lifestyle. Write a paraphrase of the material, and be ready to share your writing with the class. (See pages 214-216.)

Proposing Your Project Write a proposal for your class project to interview people about their exercise routines. (See "Writing Guidelines: Proposals," pages 258-259.)

Real Heroes Professional athletes have the power to influence young people in many ways. Choose an athlete who you think uses his or her power well. Then write a one-page feature showing how and why the athlete is a positive influence. (See "Feature Articles," page 174.)

What's for supper? Compile a cookbook of your class's favorite healthful recipes. Distribute or sell the finished product. A potluck dinner featuring many of the recipes could be organized.

You are what you eat. Maintain a diet log or journal for a week, noting everything that you have consumed. Discuss the results of this "field study" in a summary report. (See "Writing Personal Research Reports, pages 217-222.)

Language Arts

Great American Novel Write the opening pages of your first novel, a novel stemming from your own experiences. (See "Making Your Narrative Work," page 157.)

Great Moments in Sports Re-create a great (or not-so-great) moment in sports. Write the piece as a news story, diary entry, letter, story, or poem. (Check the index of *Write Source 2000* for guidelines and a model for each form.)

Have I got a story for you! Write a tall tale, exaggerating some activity or event that recently took place in your school. (See "Writing Stories," pages 183-192.)

Newsworthy Books Write a news story about a book you like, featuring qualities of the book that would entice your classmates to read it. Rehearse reading the story so that you can read it smoothly in class. (See "Writing News Stories," pages 167-174.)

Slice of Life Interview an elderly family member, neighbor, or acquaintance about growing up and/or working during an earlier time. Present the results of the interview in a character sketch or biographical essay. (See "Interviewing Tips," page 170, and "Biographical Writing," pages 161-166.)

Very Interesting! Observe (and take notes on) the action in a popular spot—cafeteria, store, restaurant, gym, etc. Then write your findings in an observation report that you read to the class. (See "Writing Observation Reports," pages 209-211.)

You were saying? Develop a conversation between yourself and a character from one of your favorite books or movies. Then rehearse the dialogue with a friend, and read it to the class. (See "Writing Dialogue," page 190).

You-Were-There Stories Write a short story based on a brief human-interest story you find in the newspaper. (See "Writing Stories," pages 183-192.)

Social Studies

Community-Leader Digest Develop a portfolio of profiles of all the elected or appointed leaders in the community. (See "Writing About a Person," page 123.)

Fads and Fashions Write a feature article about a former (or present) fad discussed in class, focusing on how it related (or relates) to social or political ideas of the time. (See "Writing News Stories," pages 167-174.)

Good Causes Promote National Education Week, MADD (Mothers Against Drunk Driving), or another cause by writing letters, designing banners, and creating posters. (See "Writing Business Letters," pages 241-250.)

History Around Us Research the history of a building, company, church, store, or restaurant, and present your findings in a news story or feature article. (See "Writing News Stories," pages 167-174.)

Movers and Shakers Read a biography, an autobiography, or articles about an important social thinker, spiritual or religious leader, humanitarian, or citizens' advocate. Report your findings in an essay (or paragraph) about this person. (See "Writing About a Person," page 123.)

My Life Think of some aspect of American culture (family, church, friends, city life, schools) that helps you be what you want to be. Then write about this topic in a personal essay. (See "Autobiographical Writing," pages 153-159.)

Poetic Justice Select a serious issue studied in history (slavery, poverty, war, etc.) and write about it in a poem that you share with the class. (See "Writing Poetry," pages 193-207.)

The Reading/Writing Connection Read a contemporary novel that explores a significant cultural, social, or personal issue. Then write a book report that you share with the class. (See "Writing About Literature," pages 175-179.)

Science

Both Sides Now Study both (or all) sides of a controversial, science-related issue using the Venn diagram as a guide. Compile the results in a paragraph, letter, or essay. (See "Venn Diagram," page 313.)

Dear Benjamin Write an imaginary letter to an important person in science, discussing the individual's accomplishments. Prepare to read the letter to class. (See "Writing Friendly Letters," pages 149-152.)

Great Moments in Science Research Using reference books, magazines, newspapers, and other resources, research a great moment in the science world. Use these facts to write a news story on the topic. (See "Writing News Stories," pages 167-174.)

Mr. or Ms. Wizard Select a scientific concept (gravity, density, or laser light) as a topic for a speech to the class. Research the subject, write the speech, prepare props, and rehearse the presentation. (See "Preparing a Speech," pages 347-354.)

New Equipment Interview a local business about its newest piece of equipment. Learn why the item was purchased, how it works, and how it has affected the business. Report your findings in a brief research paper. (See "Interviewing Tips," page 170, and "Writing Personal Research Reports," pages 217-222.)

Newsworthy Science Read and summarize an important science-related article in either a newspaper or magazine. Read your summary to the class, and be ready to answer questions. (See "Writing Summaries," pages 213-216.)

Tracer Trace the history of an important invention (ink pens, computers, X-ray machines, etc.). Present your findings in a personal research report. (See "Writing Personal Research Reports," pages 217-222.)

Weather in Writing Research an aspect of weather that interests you and write a report on your findings. (See "Writing Personal Research Reports," pages 217-222.)

Mathematics

Backed into a Corner In your math log, ask yourself a question about a significant concept discussed in class, and then answer the question. (See "Sample Math Log," page 368.)

Defining Math Write a definition of a term, concept, or procedure discussed in class. (See "Writing a Definition," bottom of page 125.)

Dramatic Math Write a dialogue between a teacher and a student as they discuss a tough concept or procedure in math. (See "Writing Dialogue," bottom of page 190).

Newsworthy Math Prepare and distribute a biweekly (or monthly) newsletter discussing a variety of math-related issues. (See "Writing Stories," pages 183-192.)

Plain English Translate a challenging math concept into easy-to-understand English so even the most right-brained people can understand the concept. (See "Writing a Definition," bottom of page 125.)

Poetic Math Write a poem (acrostic, limerick, or other form) explaining some main idea or procedure in math. Read the poem to the class, and display it on the bulletin board. (See "Writing Poetry," pages 193-207.)

Poster Math Design a poster illustrating a main idea, definition, or procedure in math. Display the poster.

Sports Records Compile an accurate and comprehensive manual of sports records and statistics for your school.

Story Problems Create story problems about concepts discussed in class. In class, exchange problems with a classmate and solve each other's problems.

Workplace Math Interview an adult in the workplace about how he or she uses math on the job. Take notes during the interview, and present your findings to the class. (See "Interviewing Tips," page 170.)

Designing a Writing Assignment

Students rarely take off on writing assignments—not willingly at least—unless the work seems worth the effort. One way to show the work's value is to design meaningful course goals, connect the assignments to the goals, and evaluate the assignments with goal-related criteria. When students see that doing an assignment helps them achieve something valuable to you and them, the task seems worth the effort.

On the following pages is a list of four middle-school courses: science, social studies, math, and English. Beneath each course you will find (1) one of the course's goals, (2) a writing assignment that helps students achieve the goal, and (3) evaluation criteria that writers can use to refine their writing.

English

Course Goal: To respond to literacy pieces by writing a variety of forms, including book reports, character sketches, and freewritings.

Assignment: For today's class, you were asked to finish reading your biography of a famous person. Imagine that this person just happens to pay you a visit.

For 10 minutes, freewrite a dialogue recording what you say to this person, and what he or she says in reply.

Evaluation: The freewriting shows that the student has . . .

1. read the assignment,
2. imagined herself or himself in the world created by the author, and
3. responded thoughtfully to that world.

Mathematics

Course Goal: To learn basic concepts or techniques of math, and to understand how we use them to solve daily problems.

Assignment: In your science class today, you analyzed the quality of two Wisconsin Fast Plants. In your math journal, describe three ways in which you used numbers to do that

work. (Use the guidelines and model on pages 145-148 in *Write Source 2000*.)

Evaluation: The journal entry clearly and accurately describes three ways in which the student used numbers to do the analysis.

Science

Course Goal: To learn how plants grow and how scientific methods can measure and affect that growth.

Assignment: During the next four weeks, we will study the effects of sunlight on plant life. Working with your partner, do the following:

1. Plant the Wisconsin Fast Plant in the soil tray provided. (The composition of soil is the same in all trays.)
2. Set the timer on your grow light for the number of hours and minutes stated on the yellow tab attached to the soil tray. Each day, the grow light will go on for that length of time. Each lab team has a different number, so each plant will be lit for a different span of time.
3. Each day, analyze the health of the plant by counting leaves, measuring leaf sizes, grading leaf color, and measuring plant height. Using the guidelines and model for note taking (pages 362-365 in *Write Source 2000*), record all procedures and measurements.
4. Using your notes, along with the guidelines and model on pages 211-212 of *Write Source 2000*, write an observation report.

Evaluation: The notes and report (1) are well organized and clear, (2) include accurate information requested in the assignment, (3) show that the writer understands factors involved in plant growth, and (4) show how scientific methods can measure and influence plant growth.

Social Studies

Course Goal: To learn how the check-and-balance structure in our three branches of government has both strengths and weaknesses that affect our lives.

Assignment: In class we learned that our check-and-balance structure of government has (1) strengths—like limiting the abuse of power, and (2) weaknesses—like leading to gridlock and inefficiency.

Choose an incident caused by this structure, one discussed in class. Then research and write a persuasive essay in which you (1) describe the incident, (2) prove that it illustrates a strength or weakness of our government, and (3) show how the incident affects our lives.

Note: Use the guidelines and model on pages 115-122 in *Write Source 2000.*)

Evaluation: The essay (1) describes a relevant incident, (2) proves that the incident reflects a strength or weakness in our governmental structure, and (3) shows how the incident affects our lives.

ADDITIONAL SOURCES:

The books listed below will help your faculty build a writing-across-the-curriculum program.

Gere, Ann Ruggles, ed. *Roots in the Sawdust: Writing to Learn Across the Disciplines.* National Council of Teachers of English, 1985.

Langer, Judith A., and Arthur N. Applebee. *How Writing Shapes Thinking: A Study of Teaching and Learning.* National Council of Teachers of English, 1987.

Mayher, John S., Nancy Lester, and Gordon M. Pradl. *Learning to Write: Writing to Learn.* Portsmouth: Boynton/Cook, 1983.

Perkins, David. *Smart Schools: From Training Memories to Educating Minds.* New York: The Free Press, 1992.

Wiggens, Grant, and Jay McTighe. *Understanding by Design.* Alexandria, VA: Association for Supervision and Curriculum Development, 1998.

Yancey, Kathleen Blake, and Brian Huot, eds. *Assessing Writing Across the Curriculum: Diverse Approaches and Practices.* Greenwich, CT: Ablex, 1997.

Young, Art, and Toby Fulwiler, eds. *Writing Across the Disciplines.* Portsmouth: Boynton/Cook, 1986.

Zinsser, William. *Writing to Learn.* New York: Harper & Row, 1986.

Helping Students Succeed

Students can complete any writing assignment more successfully if they know the following information about the assignment: **subject, audience, purpose, form of writing, necessary prewriting,** and **criteria for evaluation.** Based on your course goals, choose which of these items you should provide, and which the students should come up with themselves. Then present the information in an assignment form like the one on page 173.

For example, if your goals call for writing that is prescriptive in focus and form, you may give students all the information above. However, if your goal is to have students respond freely to an idea, you may give them only a writing prompt and guidelines for evaluation. Students come up with the rest of the information, and all forms of writing are acceptable—from poems to memos.

In either case, students should understand that having the assignment information will help them in two ways: (1) it gives them a clearer view of the assignment and (2) it saves them time while writing.

Designing Your Own Assignments

Subject:

Audience:

Purpose:

Form of Writing:

Prewriting Activities: (Prewriting activities are important, especially if the assignment does not grow out of information or concepts already covered in class.)

  1.

  2.

Evaluation Guidelines: (Include appropriate checklists and guidelines in *Write Source 2000*.)

  1.

  2.

  3.

  4.

Assessment Strategies and Rubrics

The information in this section covers a number of areas related to assessing student writing, including using assessment as a teaching tool, using peer assessment, and using writing portfolios.

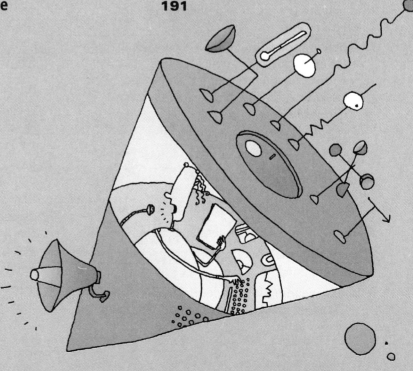

An Overview—
Assessment and Instruction

> "We must constantly remind ourselves that the ultimate purpose of evaluation is to enable students to evaluate themselves."
>
> —Arthur Costa

In past decades, writing assessment was generally held to be the province of the teacher. Students turned in work—then waited to see what grades they would receive. Now it is widely recognized that learning to be a good assessor is one of the best ways to become a strong writer. In order to assess well, students must learn to recognize good writing. They must know and be able to describe the difference between writing that works and writing that does not work. Students learn to assess, generally, by going through three key steps:

1. Learning about the traits of writing by which their work—and that of others—will be assessed

2. Applying the traits to a wide variety of written texts

3. Applying the traits to their own work— first assessing it for strengths and weaknesses, then revising it as needed (See pages 156-157 in this guide for more information.)

Why should students be assessors?

Students who learn to be assessors also . . .

- learn to think like professional writers,

- take responsibility for their own revising, and

- make meaningful changes in their writing— instead of simply recopying a draft to make it look neater.

Role of Teachers and Students

Here is a quick summary of the kinds of activities teachers and students usually engage in while acting as assessors in the classroom.

Teachers

As assessors, teachers often engage in . . .

- roving conferences, roaming the classroom, observing students' work, and offering comments or questions that will help take students to next steps.

- one-on-one conferences, in which students are asked to come prepared with a question they need answered.

- informal comments—written or oral—in which the teacher offers a personal response or poses a reader's question.

- reading student work, using a general *teacher rating sheet* such as the one on page 179 in this guide, or an *assessment rubric* such as the ones in this guide (pages 181-186).

- tracking scores over time to calculate a final grade for a grading period.

Students

As assessors, students often engage in . . .

- reviewing scoring guides such as the checklist on page 24 in the handbook or the rubrics in this guide.

- using a *peer response sheet* such as the one on page 188 in this guide or the one on page 78 in the handbook.

- assessing and discussing written work that the teacher shares with the class.

- assessing their own work, using a scoring guide or rubric.

- compiling a portfolio and reflecting on the written work included.

Effective Assessment in the Classroom

> "Good assessment starts with a vision of success."
>
> —Rick Stiggins

Good assessment gives students a sense of how they are growing as writers. It indicates to teachers which students are finding success, as well as the specific kinds of help other students may need. To ensure that assessment is working in your classrooms, you should do the following things:

▪ Make sure ALL students know the criteria you will use to assess their writing. If you are going to use a rating sheet or rubric, provide them with copies.

▪ Give copies of rubrics or checklists to parents, too, so they can help their children know what is expected of them.

▪ Make sure your instruction and assessment match. You cannot teach one thing and assess students on another—if you expect them to be successful.

▪ Involve students regularly in assessing . . .
  ✔ published work from a variety of sources,
  ✔ your work (share your writing—even if it's in unfinished draft form), and
  ✔ their own work.

▪ Don't grade *everything* students write, or you'll be overwhelmed with stacks and stacks of papers to assess. Instead, you should encourage students to write *often*; then choose a few pieces to grade.

▪ Respond to the content *first*. Then look at the conventions. Correctness is important, but if you comment on spelling and mechanics before content, the message to the student is, "I don't care as much about what you say as I do about whether you spell everything correctly."

▪ Encourage students to save rough drafts and to collect pieces of work regularly in a portfolio. This type of collection gives students a broad picture of how they are progressing as writers.

▪ Ask students if they mind having comments written directly on their work. For some students, comments on sticky notes may seem less obtrusive.

Conducting Conferences

Conduct conferences to maintain an open line of communication with student writers at all points during the development of a piece of writing. Here are three common practices that you can employ to communicate with student writers during a writing project:

- **Desk-Side Conferences** occur when you stop at a student's desk to ask questions and make responses. Questions should be open-ended. This gives the writer "space" to talk and clarify his or her own thinking about the writing.

- **Scheduled Conferences** give you and a student a chance to meet in a more structured setting. In such a conference, a student may have a specific problem or need to discuss or simply want you to assess his or her progress on a particular piece of writing.

Special Note: A typical conference should last from 3 to 5 minutes. Always try to praise one thing, ask an appropriate question, and offer one or two suggestions.

- **Small-Group Conferences** give three to five students who are at the same stage of the writing process or are experiencing the same problem a chance to meet with you. The goal of such conferences is twofold: first, to help students improve their writing and, second, to help them develop as evaluators of writing.

Formative vs. Summative Assessment

Formative assessment is ongoing and is often not linked to a letter grade or score. It may be as simple as a brief one-on-one conference or an informal review of the beginning of a student's draft to suggest possible next steps. **Summative assessment,** on the other hand, is a summing up of a student's performance, and is generally reflected in a grade. Formative assessments usually occur in the form of a comment—oral or written. Summative assessments take the form of . . .

✔ a letter grade,
✔ total points earned,
✔ a percentage score, or
✔ some combination of these.

Responding to Student Writing

Responding to Nongraded Writing

(Formative)

- React noncritically with positive, supportive language.
- Use marginal dialogue. Resist writing on or over the student's writing.
- Respond whenever possible in the form of questions. Nurture curiosity through your inquiries.
- Encourage risk taking.

Evaluating Graded Writing

(Summative)

- Ask students to submit prewriting and rough drafts with their final drafts.
- Scan final drafts once, focusing on the writing as a whole.
- Reread them, this time assessing them for their adherence to previously established criteria.
- Make marginal notations, if necessary, as you read the drafts a second time.
- Scan the writing a third and final time. Note the feedback you have given.
- Complete your rating sheet or rubric, and, if necessary, write a summary comment.

Approaches for Assessing Writing

The most common forms of direct writing assessment (summative) are listed below.

Analytical assessment identifies the features, or traits, that characterize effective writing, and defines them along a continuum of performance from *incomplete* (the first or lowest level) through *fair* (the middle level) to *excellent* (the highest level). Many analytical scales run from a low of 1 point to a high of 5 or 6 points. This form of assessment tells students exactly where their strengths and weaknesses lie: "Your writing has strong ideas but needs work on voice," or "Your writing has powerful voice but lacks accuracy."

Holistic assessment focuses on a piece of writing as a whole. In this sense, it is much like letter grading. Holistic assessors often use a checklist of traits to remind themselves of the kinds of characteristics they're looking for; this is called focused holistic assessment. The assessors do not, however, score traits separately, so student writers do not know where they were most or least successful in their work.

Mode-specific assessment is similar to analytic assessment except that the rating scales or scoring guides (rubrics) are designed specifically for particular modes of writing, such as narrative, expository, persuasive, and so on. This kind of assessment works best in a structured curriculum where students will be assigned particular forms and subjects for writing—rather than choosing their own writing topics. (See pages 181-186 in this guide for sample rubrics.)

Portfolio assessment gives students a chance to showcase their best writing or to document their growth as writers over time. In assembling a portfolio, students generally choose which pieces of writing they will complete and which ones they will include in their portfolios. (See page 189 in this guide for more information; also see pages 31-36 in the handbook.)

Teacher Rating Sheet

IDEAS

Fuzzy and disjointed   Clear and focused
General, sketchy   Rich in detail

     1   **2**   **3**   **4**   **5**

ORGANIZATION

No real lead, just dives in   Great lead!
Confusing order   Logical organization
Ideas not connected   Clear transitions
Just stops—no conclusion   Powerful ending

     1   **2**   **3**   **4**   **5**

VOICE

Inappropriate voice   Right voice for audience and
   for audience and purpose   purpose
Sounds bored by topic   Enthusiastic about topic
Feels distant, disconnected   Holds reader's attention

     1   **2**   **3**   **4**   **5**

WORD CHOICE

Overused, tired words   Ear-catching phrases
Modifier overload!   Strong verbs, clear nouns
Meaning lost in unclear   Well-chosen modifiers
   phrasing   Meaning very clear

     1   **2**   **3**   **4**   **5**

SMOOTH SENTENCES

Hard to read   Easy to read aloud
Bumpy—or strung out   Smooth, fluent
Overlong sentences   Crisp, short sentences in
   add to confusion   technical writing

     1   **2**   **3**   **4**   **5**

CONVENTIONS

Numerous, distracting errors   Editorial correctness
Careless mistakes   Attention to detail
Ineffective layout   Effective layout

     1   **2**   **3**   **4**   **5**

Assessment Rubrics

The following six pages include rubrics to assess these modes of writing: *narrative, expository, descriptive, persuasive, story,* and *research.* Use these rubrics as indicated below:

Narrative Writing

Use this rubric with forms of autobiographical and biographical writing that recall specific events. (See page 181.)

Expository Writing

Use this rubric with informational writing, including expository essays, summaries, basic reports and feature articles, workplace writing, etc. (See page 182.)

Descriptive Writing

Use this rubric with descriptive essays, observation reports, etc. (See page 183.)

Persuasive Writing

Use this rubric with persuasive essays, book reviews, editorials, etc. (See page 184.)

Story Writing

Use this rubric with short stories, fables, myths, tall tales, etc. (See page 185.)

Research Writing

Use this rubric with extended classroom reports, personal research reports, research papers, etc. (See page 186.)

Using Rubrics to Assess Writing

Before using these rubrics, you should read through the following list of important points. (You should also read through pages 176-179 in this guide.)

- Each rubric lists the six traits of effective writing as explained in the handbook, pages 19-24, and as used to assess writing on many state writing-assessment tests.

- Specific descriptors listed under each trait help you assess the writing for that trait.
- A piece of writing doesn't necessarily have to exhibit all of the descriptors under each trait to be effective.
- Each rubric is based on a 5-point scale. (A score of 5 means that the writing addresses a particular trait in a masterful way. A score of 3 means that the writing is average or competent in its development of a trait, and so on.)
- The rubrics can be used to assess works in progress and final drafts.
- Students should know beforehand how their writing will be assessed. (They should also understand the traits of effective writing.)
- You can change each rubric as needed to meet the needs of the students and/or the writing being assessed.

Using Rubrics as a Teaching Tool

Have students evaluate the effectiveness of published or student writing using a rubric as a basic guide. (You can use excerpts or complete pieces for these evaluating sessions.) At first, you may want students to focus on one specific trait (such as *organization*) during these sessions. Later on, you can ask them to evaluate a piece of writing for all of the traits. Have students compare and discuss their evaluations at the end of each session.

Note: As students gain more experience with the traits of effective writing, they will come to better understand and appreciate the importance of the traits.

ASSESSMENT RUBRIC

Narrative Writing

____ **STIMULATING IDEAS**

The writing . . .

- focuses on a specific experience or event.
- presents a clear and engaging picture of the action and people involved.
- contains specific details to develop the key elements.
- makes readers want to know what happens next.

____ **LOGICAL ORGANIZATION**

- forms a meaningful whole, jumping right into the thick of the action and ending shortly after the most important moment.
- presents details in an effective, coherent manner.

____ **ENGAGING VOICE**

- speaks in an engaging way that keeps readers wanting to hear more.
- shows that the writer really cares about the subject.

____ **ORIGINAL WORD CHOICE**

- contains specific, colorful words.
- presents an appropriate level of language (not too formal or too informal).

____ **SMOOTH-READING SENTENCES**

- flows smoothly from sentence to sentence.
- shows variety in sentence beginnings and lengths.

____ **CORRECT, ACCURATE COPY**

- follows the basic rules of grammar, spelling, and punctuation.

Scoring Guide

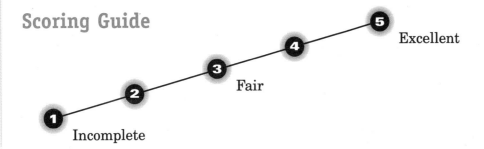

(Add any summary comments on the back of this sheet or at the bottom of the student paper.)

ASSESSMENT RUBRIC

Expository Writing

_____ **STIMULATING IDEAS**

The writing . . .

- focuses on a specific informational subject clearly expressed in a thesis statement or topic sentence.
- contains specific details and examples to support the thesis.
- thoroughly informs readers.

_____ **LOGICAL ORGANIZATION**

- includes a clear beginning, strong development, and an effective ending.
- presents ideas in an organized manner.
- uses transitions to link sentences and paragraphs in a logical way.

_____ **ENGAGING VOICE**

- speaks in a knowledgeable and/or enthusiastic way.
- shows that the writer is truly interested in the subject.

_____ **ORIGINAL WORD CHOICE**

- explains or defines any unfamiliar terms.
- contains specific nouns and action verbs.

_____ **SMOOTH-READING SENTENCES**

- flows smoothly from one idea to the next.
- shows variation in sentence structure and length.

_____ **CORRECT, ACCURATE COPY**

- follows the basic rules of grammar, spelling, and punctuation.

Scoring Guide

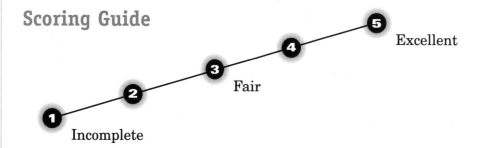

5 — Excellent
4
3 — Fair
2
1 — Incomplete

(Add any summary comments on the back of this sheet or at the bottom of the student paper.)

ASSESSMENT RUBRIC

Descriptive Writing

_____ **STIMULATING IDEAS**

The writing . . .

- showcases a specific person, place, object, or event.
- presents an effective picture of the subject.
- uses specific sensory details to enrich the description.
- holds readers' attention from start to finish.

_____ **LOGICAL ORGANIZATION**

- forms a meaningful whole, leaving readers with a clear impression of the subject.
- presents details in an effective manner (perhaps spatially).

_____ **ENGAGING VOICE**

- speaks in a sincere and/or an engaging way.
- shows that the writer really cares about the subject.

_____ **ORIGINAL WORD CHOICE**

- includes specific nouns and action verbs.
- uses colorful modifiers (but doesn't overwhelm readers).

_____ **SMOOTH-READING SENTENCES**

- flows smoothly from one idea to the next.
- shows variation that makes reading pleasurable and easy.

_____ **CORRECT, ACCURATE COPY**

- follows the basic rules of grammar, spelling, and punctuation.

Scoring Guide

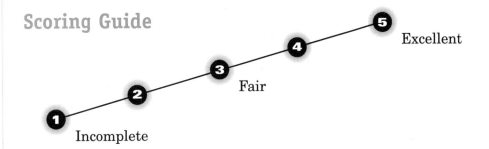

(Add any summary comments on the back of this sheet or at the bottom of the student paper.)

ASSESSMENT RUBRIC

Persuasive Writing

_____ **STIMULATING IDEAS**

The writing . . .

- focuses on a statement of opinion about a timely subject.
- contains specific facts, details, and examples to support the thesis.
- maintains a clear, consistent stand from start to finish.

_____ **LOGICAL ORGANIZATION**

- includes a clear beginning, strong support, and a convincing conclusion.
- presents ideas in an organized manner (perhaps offering the strongest point first or last).
- presents reasonable and logical arguments.

_____ **ENGAGING VOICE**

- speaks in a convincing and knowledgeable way.
- shows that the writer feels strongly about his or her position.

_____ **ORIGINAL WORD CHOICE**

- explains or defines any unfamiliar terms.
- uses language that shows a thorough understanding of the subject.

_____ **SMOOTH-READING SENTENCES**

- flows smoothly from one idea to the next.
- displays varied sentence beginnings and lengths.

_____ **CORRECT, ACCURATE COPY**

- follows the basic rules of grammar, spelling, and punctuation.

Scoring Guide

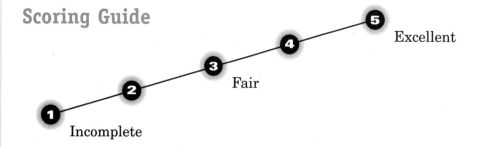

5 Excellent

4

3 Fair

2

1 Incomplete

(Add any summary comments on the back of this sheet or at the bottom of the student paper.)

ASSESSMENT RUBRIC

Story Writing

_____ **STIMULATING IDEAS**

The writing . . .
- effectively develops the plot, characterization, and setting.
- brings the story alive with specific details.
- uses a range of narrative strategies (dialogue, suspense, etc.).

_____ **LOGICAL ORGANIZATION**
- effectively moves from the exposition and rising action to the resolution.
- progresses in a story-like way. (What needs to be explained is explained; the characters' words and actions do the rest.)

_____ **ENGAGING VOICE**
- employs an appropriate and/or an engaging voice for the narrator and the other characters.
- maintains a consistent voice for each character.

_____ **ORIGINAL WORD CHOICE**
- contains specific and colorful words.
- develops dialogue with a level of language appropriate to each character.

_____ **SMOOTH-READING SENTENCES**
- flows smoothly from one idea to the next.

_____ **CORRECT, ACCURATE COPY**
- follows the basic rules of grammar, spelling, and punctuation.

Scoring Guide

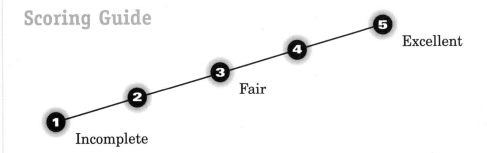

(Add any summary comments on the back of this sheet or at the bottom of the student paper.)

ASSESSMENT RUBRIC

Research Writing

_____ **STIMULATING IDEAS**

The writing . . .

- focuses on an interesting aspect of a specific subject that is expressed in a thesis statement.
- effectively supports the thesis.
- thoroughly informs readers.
- gives credit, when necessary, for ideas from other sources.

_____ **LOGICAL ORGANIZATION**

- includes a clearly developed beginning, middle, and ending.
- presents supporting information in an organized manner (perhaps one main idea per paragraph).

_____ **ENGAGING VOICE**

- speaks in a sincere and knowledgeable way.
- shows that the writer is truly interested in the subject.

_____ **ORIGINAL WORD CHOICE**

- explains or defines any unfamiliar terms.
- employs an appropriate level of language.

_____ **SMOOTH-READING SENTENCES**

- flows smoothly from one idea to the next.

_____ **CORRECT, ACCURATE COPY**

- adheres to the rules of grammar, spelling, and punctuation.
- follows the appropriate format for research papers (including correct documentation).

Scoring Guide

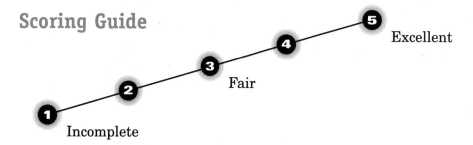

(Add any summary comments on the back of this sheet or at the bottom of the student paper.)

Peer Assessment

Young writers learn to write by writing. No one questions that. But their ability to improve as writers increases significantly if they read a lot. Any writer would tell your students that it is essential they become avid readers if they want to learn the craft of writing.

They would also tell your students to become part of a writing community. Writers need to talk about writing with other writers. They also need to know that someone just like them—a writer writing—is available when they need help. That's why it's important that your student writers share their work throughout the process of writing. They need to feel that they are among writing colleagues—all committed to helping each other improve as writers.

A Community of Writers

The reason some teachers find the workshop approach to writing so effective is that it naturally creates a feeling of comradeship among the writers in the classroom. (See pages 154-155 in this guide for more information.)

The exchange of ideas among fellow writers is especially important once they have produced early drafts of their work. Writers generally get so close to their writing, so to speak, that they can't always evaluate it objectively themselves. They need their fellow writers, their peers, to ask questions, make suggestions, and offer encouragement. (Use the following minilesson as a possible starting point for group assessing.)

Peer Editing Minilesson

Provide a writing sample from a previous year for students to evaluate using the peer response sheet on page 188 in this guide.

Then discuss the strengths and weaknesses of the paper as a class after the students have finished their individual evaluations. During this discussion, make sure to tell the students how you would assess the paper and your reasons for doing so.

Types of Evaluating

There generally are three types of assessment that can go on in a peer conference. There can be a **peer-revising session** in which two or more student writers share ideas about a piece of writing in progress. There can be a **peer-editing session** in which two student writers help each other with editing a revised draft. (See the guidelines listed below for editing sessions. Also refer your students to the "Editing and Proofreading Checklist," handbook page 83.) And then there are **peer-assessment conferences** in which fellow writers actually rate the finished pieces of writing.

Special Note: Peer assessment does not replace teacher assessment. Obviously, teachers will want to help their student writers as much as they can during the writing process. And they will want to assess the students' final products as well.

Editing Conference Guidelines

In an editing conference, a peer-editor should . . .

1. sit next to the author so that both students can see the piece of writing.

2. read the piece of writing back to the author exactly as it is written (mistakes and all).

3. allow the author to stop the reading at any time in order to edit his or her piece.

4. use a highlighting marker to point out other problems after the author has completed his or her corrections.

5. sign his or her name in the upper left-hand corner of the author's first page so that the teacher will know who helped edit the piece.

Special Note: Few peer editors are skilled enough to catch all of the mistakes in a piece of writing. Peer editors *plus* a teacher or a parent should always edit each piece of writing that will be assessed.

Peer Response Sheet

Strengths

I noticed . . .

_____ clear and easy-to-follow information.

_____ plenty of specific details.

_____ an attention-getting opening that made me want to read more.

_____ a strong voice that

* felt right for the topic, audience, and purpose,

* sounded like you.

_____ smooth-reading sentences.

_____ an effective closing, ending things at a good spot.

Problems

I did not notice . . .

_____ a clear main idea.

_____ enough supporting details.

_____ an easy-to-follow pattern of organization.

_____ an effective and/or appropriate voice.

_____ a clearly-stated closing.

_____ These words confused me:

1. _____

2. _____

_____ These sentences confused me: (Give the first few words of each one.)

1. _____

_____

2. _____

_____

_____ This is a question I have:

Using Writing Portfolios

"Portfolios have become each student's story of where they are as readers and writers."

—Linda Rief

More and more, language arts teachers are making portfolios an important part of their writing programs. Will portfolios work for you? Will they help you and your students assess their writing? Read on and find out.

What is a writing portfolio?

A writing portfolio is a limited collection of a student's writing for evaluation. A portfolio is different from the traditional writing folder. A writing folder (also known as a working folder) contains all of a student's work; a portfolio contains only selected pieces.

There are two basic types of portfolios to create. A *showcase portfolio* is usually presented for evaluation at the end of a grading period. As the name implies, it should contain a selection of a student's best work. A *growth portfolio* notes the way in which a writer is changing and growing. This type of portfolio is usually collected regularly—say, once a month—over a long period of time. (See pages 31-36 in the handbook for more information.)

Why should I ask students to compile writing portfolios?

Having students compile a portfolio makes the whole process of writing more meaningful to them. They will more willingly put forth their best efforts as they work on various writing projects, knowing that they are accountable for producing a certain number of finished pieces for publication. They will more thoughtfully approach writing as an involved and recursive process of drafting, sharing, and rewriting, knowing that this process leads to more effective writing. And they will more responsibly craft finished pieces (for showcase portfolios), since their final evaluation will depend on the finished products they include in their portfolios.

How many pieces of writing should be included in a portfolio?

Although you and your students will best be able to decide this, we advise that students compile at least three to five pieces of writing in a showcase portfolio each quarter. (The number of pieces in a growth portfolio may vary from month to month.) All of the drafts should be included for each piece. Students should also be required to include a reflective writing or self-critique sheet that assesses their writing progress.

When do portfolios work best?

Students need plenty of class time to work on writing if they are going to produce effective portfolios. If they are used right, portfolios turn beginning writers into practicing writers. And practicing writers need regularly scheduled blocks of time to "practice" their craft, to think, talk, and explore options in their writing over and over again. Portfolios are tailor-made for language arts classrooms that operate as writing workshops.

How can I help my students with their portfolio writing?

Allow students to explore topics of genuine interest to them. Also allow them to write for many different purposes and audiences and in many different forms.

In addition, expect students to evaluate their own writing and the writing of their peers as it develops—and help them to do so. Also provide them with sound guidance when they need help with a writing problem.

How do I grade a portfolio?

Base each grade or assessment on goals you and your students establish beforehand and on what is achieved as evidenced in the portfolio. Many teachers develop a critique sheet for assessment based on the goals established by the class.

What About Grammar?

In the late 1980s, researchers George Hillocks, Jr., and Michael W. Smith completed a thorough study of the teaching of grammar. The purpose of their study was to determine the effectiveness of grammar instruction in school curriculums. Their research indicates that the study of grammar has no real impact on writing quality (except for the implementation of the types of activities listed on this page).

But Hillocks and Smith do point out that students need some basic understanding of grammar and mechanics to produce accurate final drafts of papers: "We assume that to proofread with any care, some knowledge of grammar must be necessary." But they go on to say that no one knows for sure what that body of knowledge is and how it is acquired.

Until such knowledge is determined, the researchers suggest that what will help student writers the most is a handy reference or guide to the rules of grammar and usage (such as the "Proofreader's Guide" in the *Write Source 2000* handbook).

Promoting Meaningful Grammar Instruction

The following types of activities or procedures will help students gain a better understanding of grammar and mechanics:

- Link grammar work as much as possible to the students' own writing.
- Make editing of the students' writing an important part of classroom work. They should also have practice editing and proofreading cooperatively.
- Use minilessons for grammar instruction rather than hour-long grammar activities. (See pages 250-260 in this guide for sample minilessons.)
- Make grammar instruction fun as well as instructive. For example, develop grammar games and contests. (See the following page for two ideas.)

- Immerse students in all aspects of language learning: reading, writing, speaking, listening, and thinking. Educator James Moffett says the standard dialect is "most effectively mastered through imitating speech."
- Make sure your students understand why proper attention to standard English is important. Have experts (writers, editors, attorneys, etc.) share their thoughts on the importance of accuracy, consistency, and appropriateness in communications.
- Also make sure that your students understand what is meant by the study of grammar—the eight parts of speech, usage, agreement, and so on.
- Don't overwhelm students with too much grammar too often. Find out which skills give your students the most problems and focus your instruction accordingly.

Approaches to Use

Sentence combining—Use the students' own writing as much as possible. The rationale behind combining ideas and the proper punctuation for combining should be stressed.

Sentence expansion and revising—Give students practice adding and changing information in sentences that they have already created. Also have them expand and revise each other's writing.

Sentence transforming—Have students change sentences from one form to another (from passive to active, beginning a sentence in a different way, using a different form of a particular word, and so on).

Sentence imitation—Students should have practice imitating writing models. According to James Moffett, this activity is a great teacher of grammar because it exposes young writers to the many possibilities of English grammar beyond the basic forms. (See pages 132-133 in the handbook for guidelines and models.)

Daily Language Practice

It is possible to teach grammar using new and engaging activities. Middle-school students like these two methods:

MUG (Mechanics, Usage, Grammar) Shots

Time: 5-10 minutes. Sustained practice is the key to success.

Purpose: (1) To identify skills students are misusing. (2) To maintain skills.

Materials: Use sentences from student writing; ask students to write sentences full of errors and to contribute sentences that they are currently having trouble correcting.

Method: Write two of these sentences on the board at the beginning of the class period. Choose one of the following plans:

> **PLAN 1:** Each student copies the sentences and corrects them.

> **PLAN 2:** Students offer corrections orally.

It is most important that students attempt to explain the reason for each correction they offer. Classmates and the teacher may help them zero in on the exact reason. An atmosphere of discovery, cooperation, and investigation helps students risk making corrections.

Gramo (a game about the parts of speech)

Time: 10-15 minutes or longer if desired.

Purpose: (1) To teach the parts of speech. (2) To let students discover the complexity (and richness) of the English language.

Materials: You will have to make the following: Gramo cards and a teacher's master card. See samples on the next page.

Rules: Just like bingo.

1. Players each have a game card and tabs or markers.

2. The teacher has a master card and something to use for markers (bits of paper will do).

3. The teacher calls out a word ("G bug") and players mark on their cards. ("Bug" can be a noun, a verb, or an adjective.)

4. On a piece of scratch paper, students note which word was called and where they marked their card. For example, G-bug-N or G-bug-V.

5. When a player has filled a row, column, or diagonal with markers, he or she yells out "Gramo."

6. All players wait for the "Gramo" player to recite his or her answers. (Anyone who thinks they also have a winning card must say "Gramo" before the answers are read aloud.) There can be several winners in one game.

7. If there is a winner (or winners), all the players clear their cards, and a new game begins.

8. If there is no winner (maybe the student who yelled "Gramo" had an incorrect answer), the other players should not clear their cards, and that particular game continues until there is a winner.

9. Cards can be traded after a couple of games.

10. Rules can be extended. For example, someone could play two cards at one time.

11. Allow only two wins on one card; then the card must be traded. This keeps top players from monopolizing the game.

12. If a card has "noun" printed in two squares under the same letter ("noun" might be in two squares under the letter "G"), the player may put a marker on each square. This makes that card more valuable.

Giving points as a reward keeps students on task. You or a designated student can place a check after each student's name when he or she wins a round of "Gramo."

G R A M O

Noun	Noun	Noun	Noun	Noun
Verb	Verb	Verb	Verb	Verb
Adjective	Adjective	Adjective	Adjective	Adjective
Preposition	Preposition	Preposition	Preposition	Preposition
Proper Noun	Proper Noun	Proper Noun	Proper Noun	Proper Noun
Conjunction	Conjunction	Conjunction	Conjunction	Conjunction
Adverb	Adverb	Adverb	Adverb	Adverb
Pronoun	Pronoun	Pronoun	Pronoun	Pronoun

Sample Game Card

G R A M O

ADJ	PREP	ADJ	ADVERB	VERB
VERB	NOUN	ADVERB	PREP	PRONOUN
PRONOUN	ADVERB	FREE SPACE	PROPER NOUN	NOUN
CONJ	PROPER NOUN	CONJ	ADJ	ADVERB
NOUN	ADJ	ADVERB	VERB	PREP

Sample Game Card

G R A M O

		FREE SPACE		

Reading Strategies

The strategies on the following pages will help you promote personalized, active reading in your classroom.

Improving Critical Reading Skills

English educators Fran Claggett, Louann Reid, and Ruth Vinz, the consulting authors of the *Daybook of Critical Reading and Writing* series (Great Source, 1999), recommend that young readers approach texts (especially fiction) in the following five ways in order to improve their critical reading skills:

1 Interact with the Text

Readers interact with a text by highlighting important or startling lines, writing notes or questions in the margins, circling words that are puzzling, or noting their reactions while reading. (Of course, if readers don't own the text, they should make all of their notations in a notebook.) By interacting with a text, readers become much more attentive and engaged in their reading and, as a result, gain more from the experience. (See page 195 in this guide for an example.)

2 Make Connections with the Text

What is happening in a text takes on more significance for readers if they make personal connections with it. The most obvious way for readers to connect with a text is to ask themselves (and try to answer) the following types of questions:

- *Have I faced a situation similar to the one faced by the main character?*
- *Have I known similar characters?*
- *Have I encountered similar problems?*
- *Would I have reacted in the same way?*
- *Do I have the same beliefs as _____?*
- *Have I read or heard about similar events?*

3 Shift Perspectives

Young readers typically think about a text in one way as they read. In other words, they take everything at face value. But if readers step back and ask themselves "what if" questions, a text often opens up in new ways for them. Here are some sample questions that can help readers see a text in new ways:

- *What if a different character told the story?*
- *What if this story took place in a different time or place?*
- *What if the main character held different beliefs?*

4 Study the Style and Craft of a Text

Writers deliberate very carefully about word choice, character development, plot development, and so on. Good critical readers constantly ask themselves questions about the writer's style and craft: *Why did the writer use that word? Why is this character introduced? Why did the story end here? Why weren't more details included about _____?* By thinking about a writer's choices, readers can better understand what the writer is trying to express.

5 Focus on a Writer's Life and Work

A writer's life often affects how he or she views the world, so gaining background information about a writer may help readers understand a text more fully. In addition, a writer's beliefs and interests become clearer by reading more than one of his or her titles.

Focusing on Nonfiction

The *think-and-learn strategy* that follows will help readers improve their understanding of nonfiction texts.

Think BEFORE reading . . .

- Readers should ask themselves what they already know about the topic.

Think DURING reading . . .

- In a notebook they should write out questions, definitions, and important things they need to remember.

Think AFTER reading . . .

- Readers should tell themselves (or someone else) what they learned.
- They should write a summary of their reading.

(See pages 307-322 in the handbook for more about reading nonfiction.)

Interacting with a Text

The sample page below comes from the *Daybook of Critical Reading and Writing* series (Great Source, 1999), and it shows a reader interacting with a text. (In this series, students are able to make notations in their books.)

One
Becoming an Active Reader

Active readers get involved in what they read. One of the simplest ways to become involved—to make the selection "your own"—is to mark up the page with questions, reactions, and ideas. Circle words that seem interesting or strange. Underline sentences that might be meaningful and write "Wow!" in the margin. Highlight important information. Draw boxes around phrases that are confusing and mark the sections with a "Huh?" As you read this piece by Mildred D. Taylor, notice how one active reader became involved in the selection.

Response Notes

Like Mildred Taylor?

huh?

Taylor's background

slavery

wow!

sounds like my father

"Author's Note" from *Roll of Thunder, Hear My Cry*
by Mildred D. Taylor

My father was a master storyteller. He could tell a fine old story that made me hold my sides with rolling laughter and sent happy tears down my cheeks, or a story of stark reality that made me shiver and be grateful for my own warm, secure surroundings. He could tell stories of beauty and grace, stories of gentle dreams, and paint them as vividly as any picture with splashes of character and dialogue. His memory detailed every event of ten or forty years or more before, just as if it had happened yesterday.

By the fireside in our northern home or in the South where I was born, I learned a history not then written in books but one passed from generation to generation on the steps of moonlit porches and beside dying fires in one-room houses, a history of great-grandparents and of slavery and of the days following slavery; of those who lived still not free, yet who would not let their spirits be enslaved. From my father the storyteller I learned to respect the past, to respect my own heritage and myself. From my father the man I learned even more, for he was endowed with a special grace that made him tower above other men. He was warm and steadfast, a man whose principles would not bend, and he had within him a rare strength that sustained not only my sister and me and all the family but all those who sought his advice and leaned upon his wisdom.

He was a complex person, yet he taught me many simple things, things important for a child to know: how to ride a horse and how to skate; how to blow soap bubbles and how to tie a kite knot that met the challenge of the March winds; how to bathe a huge faithful mongrel dog named Tiny. In time, he taught me the complex things too. He taught me of myself, of life. He taught me of hopes and dreams. And he taught me the love of words. Without his teachings, without his words, my words would not have been.

10

Insights into Critical Reading

Listed below are the types of insights that critical readers gain over time through their many reading experiences. Sharing these insights with students may help them become more insightful and skillful readers themselves.

Short Fiction

- Studying the characters helps readers connect with a story.
- Point of view—the vantage point from which a story is told—helps to determine how much readers will learn about each character.
- Knowing the basic structure of a plot leads to a more thoughtful analysis of a story.
- The description of the setting contributes to the tone or mood in a story.
- Connecting a story's theme to their own lives helps readers find deeper meaning in a story.

Poetry

- Analyzing the layout adds to an overall appreciation of a poem.
- Studying the sensory details in a poem leads to a better understanding of the poet's message or purpose.
- Exploring figures of speech deepens readers' insights into a poem.
- Studying the rhymes and/or rhythms in a poem helps readers appreciate its "music."
- Responding personally to a poem leads to better understanding.
- Noting the sound patterns—*alliteration, repetition,* etc.—in a poem gives readers insights into its tone or mood.

Nonfiction

- Employing a reading strategy (such as think and read) connects readers more thoughtfully to a text. (See "Focusing on Nonfiction" on page 194 in this guide.)
- Sorting out the main ideas and supporting details is the basis for understanding nonfiction texts.

- Making generalizations based on the reading leads to better understanding.
- Considering causes and effects helps readers connect ideas as they read.

Persuasive Writing

- Knowing the basic structure of an argument (see pages 121-122 in the handbook) leads to a more thoughtful analysis of persuasive texts.
- Identifying the writer's viewpoint is the starting point for analyzing and understanding a persuasive piece.
- Knowing that persuasive writers may use loaded words and stories that appeal to the emotions helps readers judge the quality of an author's argument.

Authors

- Writers draw on experiences and relationships in their own lives to create believable characters and situations in their stories.
- Writers of historical fiction blend events that happened in history with fictional details to make history come alive.
- Writers tackle tough issues to show that there are lessons to be learned from difficult situations.
- Writers use exaggeration to entertain and add humor and to give insights into the characters and their actions.

Themes

- Readers must always ask themselves "What is the writer trying to say to me?" while reading. They will know the theme when they can answer that question.
- Readers should look for additional themes beyond the primary one. These secondary themes can add to their understanding and appreciation of a text.

Keeping a Reader-Response Journal

Young active readers have strong feelings and ideas about their reading that they need to express. One way for them to do this is to keep a journal while they read. Then, whenever they need to react in some way to their reading, they can explore these feelings in their journals.

You might direct them to write a certain number of entries (at least four or five) for each book. You might also suggest that they write at least one entry after the opening chapter, at least three entries during their reading, and one entry after finishing the book. Middle-school students can easily write entries of a half page or longer in their journals if they are reading books of their own choosing.

Getting Them Started

If some of your students find it difficult to make anything but cursory remarks about their reading, encourage them to write entries non-stop. Uninterrupted writing (5-10 minutes per entry) naturally produces a free flow of ideas and helps students get the feel for exploring their thoughts and feelings.

Guiding Feedback

Young readers will appreciate your reaction to their journal entries, during the reading as well as after the reading. This is especially important if they need something clarified during their reading and writing—something that can't wait until the book is completed. This exchange of ideas enhances the reading process.

Providing Time to Share

Time should be set aside whenever possible for class discussions. During one discussion, your students might share favorite journal entries with the class or their reading group. During another discussion, they might raise certain questions about their reading. (This is especially effective if you have many students who have read the same book.) At another time, students might review their books (but without giving away the entire plot).

Response Journals Questions

Use these questions to help your students write in their reading journals. This list is not meant to cover every issue that might concern your students as they write, and it should be used only when they need a starting point for a journal entry.

1. What were your feelings after reading the opening chapter(s) of this book? After reading half of the book? After finishing it?

2. Did this book make you laugh? Cry? Cringe? Smile? Cheer? Explain.

3. What connections are there between the book and your own life? Explain.

4. What are the best parts of this book? Why? What are the worst parts of this book? Why?

5. What is the author saying about life and living through this book? Explain.

6. What parts of the book seem most believable? Why? What parts seem unbelievable?

7. Do you like the ending of the book? Why or why not? Do you think there is more to tell? What do you think might happen next?

8. What do you feel is the most important word in the book? The most important passage? The most important element (an event, a character, a feeling, a place, a decision)? Why is it important?

9. In what ways are you like any of the characters? Explain

10. In what ways do any of the characters remind you of people you know?

11. What character would you like to be in this book? Why? What personality traits of this character would you like to acquire?

12. What would you and one of the characters talk about in your first conversation? Begin the conversation.

13. What makes you wonder in this book? What confuses you in this book?

14. What came as a surprise in the book? Why?

15. Has this book helped you in any way?

Reading for Pleasure

"Reading is a special opportunity
[for students] to engage the
emotions and thoughts foremost
in their minds."

—David Bleich

Experiencing Literature

We must give students an opportunity to read for pleasure. We must let them lose themselves in a book or other pieces of writing without asking for a response or conducting an evaluation.

We must give them time . . . time to discover all the worlds and feelings and people who live between the covers of books. We must give them time and space to experience reading like Emily Dickinson did . . . "If I read a book and it makes my whole body so cold that no fire can ever warm me, I know that is poetry. If I feel physically as if the top of my head were taken off, I know that is poetry. These are the only ways I know it. Is there any other way?"

When we set aside class time for pleasure reading, we should model for them the pleasure of reading. This is not a time to correct papers or catch up on paperwork from the front office.

Reading for pleasure means we reduce the rules to the bare minimum. We allow students to abandon a book or read two or three books simultaneously. And, we allow them to share their thoughts and feelings about their reading. (See page 197 in this guide for more.)

The following four rules should be all that is required for pleasure reading to work in your classroom:

1. Have a book in hand when it is time for pleasure reading to begin.
2. Read for the entire time.
3. Do not complete homework.
4. Do not talk or disturb others.

Pleasure Reading in Action

Here are three effective, pleasurable reading activities for you and your students to try.

Many people still love to hear a book read. Once upon a time it was traditional for teachers to read to students for 10 minutes in the morning and after "noon hour," and, believe it or not, they still do. When you read to your students, you are showing them how to give voice to characters, how to let feelings flow, how to interpret a book. When you read aloud to your students, you are giving them something to share together. Sharing a book is a pleasurable way for teachers and students to really get to know each other.

Brown bag reading is also pleasurable. What is it? Give each student a brown bag. They write their name and a subject of keen interest on the outside of the bag. Each student announces his or her subject to the class and then waits to see what will appear in the bag. That is, he or she waits to see what a classmate or the teacher slips into the bag. It may be merely a quotation or a note telling him or her where to find a magazine article on this subject. It may be a book or an article clipped from a newspaper. It may be a piece of writing by a student who has the same interest and wishes to share some thoughts or a classroom report from another year. Periodically you can have a "reading for pleasure" session where students can discover what is in their "reading bags."

Chew! is another effective activity. What is "Chew!"? It is a very peaceful and pleasurable way to spend a lunch hour. Students arrive with both a lunch to eat and a book to read.

We all know reading is a pleasure. Let's be sure our students discover reading for pleasure, too . . . that they discover again or possibly for the first time that reading makes them wonder and sniffle and sigh.

Making Literature Connections

The next eight pages list important, high-interest titles that middle-school teachers may want to use when planning units for different sections or chapters in the handbook.

THE PROCESS OF WRITING

*A Book Takes Root:
The Making of a Picture Book*
Michael Kehoe

*Desktop Publishing:
The Art of Communication*
John Madama

*Edit Yourself: A Manual for Everyone
Who Works with Words*
Bruce Ross-Larson

*Grammatically Correct: The Writer's
Essential Guide to Punctuation,
Spelling, Style, Usage and Grammar*
Anne Stilman

Hey World, Here I Am!
Jean Little

The Librarian Who Measured the Earth
Kathryn Lasky

Nitty-Gritty Grammar
Judith P. Josephson and Edith H. Fine

What Do Authors Do?
Eileen Christelow

*Where Do You Get Your Ideas?
Helping Young Writers Begin*
Sandy Asher

Wild Words and How to Tame Them
Sandy Asher

JOURNAL WRITING

*The Amazing and Death-Defying
Diary of Eugene Dingman*
Paul Zindel

Anne Frank: The Diary of a Young Girl
Anne Frank

Anni's Diary of France
Anni Axworthy

Catherine, Called Birdy
Karen Cushman

Coast to Coast With Alice
Patricia Rusch Hyatt

The Court of the Stone Children
Eleanor Cameron

*A Gathering of Days: A New England
Girl's Journey, 1830-1832*
Joan W. Blos

A Hand Full of Stars
Rafik Schami

*Louisa May Alcott:
Author, Nurse, Suffragette*
Carol Greene

Nothing But the Truth
Avi

An Owl in the House: A Naturalist's Diary
Heinrich Bernd

*Pedro's Journal: A Voyage with
Christopher Columbus*
Pam Conrad

Running Girl: The Diary of Ebonee Rose
Sharon Bell Mathis

A Snake-Lover's Diary
Barbara Brenner

*Snowbound: The Tragic Story
of the Donner Party*
David Lavender

Zlata's Diary: A Child's Life in Sarajevo
Zlata Filipoviâc

WRITING FRIENDLY LETTERS

Anastasia at This Address
Lois Lowry

Beethoven Lives Upstairs
Barbara Nichol

Dear Dad, Love Laurie
Susan Beth Pfeffer

Dear Dr. Bell . . . Your Friend, Helen Keller
Judith St. George

Dear Levi: Letters from the Overland Trail
Elvira Woodruff

Dear Mr. Henshaw
Beverly Cleary

*Dear Mrs. Parks: A Dialogue with
Today's Youth*
Rosa Parks

Everyday Letters Ready to Go!
Cheryl McLean

*Letters from a Slave Girl:
The Story of Harriet Jacobs*
Mary E. Lyons

Letters from Rifka
Karen Hesse

*Messages in the Mailbox:
How to Write a Letter*
Loreen Leedy

*Sincerely Yours: How to Write
Great Letters*
Elizabeth James and Carol Barkin

Stringbean's Trip to the Shining Sea
Vera B. Williams and Jennifer
Williams

AUTOBIOGRAPHICAL WRITING

The Abracadabra Kid: A Writer's Life
Sid Fleischman

*Do People Grow on Trees?
Genealogy for Kids
and Other Beginners*
Ira Wolfman

The Gift of the Girl Who Couldn't Hear
Susan Shreve

A Girl from Yamhill: A Memoir
Beverly Cleary

*The Great Ancestor Hunt: The Fun of
Finding Out Who You Are*
Lila Perl

Homesick: My Own Story
Jean Fritz

I Am a Star: Child of the Holocaust
Inge Auerbacher

I Am Rosa Parks
Rosa Parks

Looking Back: A Photographic Memoir
Lois Lowry

The Moon and I
Betsy Byars

My Brother, My Sister, and I
Yoko Kawashima Watkins

My Life in Dog Years
Gary Paulsen

So Far from the Bamboo Grove
Yoko Kawashima Watkins

Steal Away
Jennifer Armstrong

*Voices from the Field:
Children of Migrant Farmworkers
Tell Their Stories*
(Interviews)
S. Beth Atkin

[BIOGRAPHICAL WRITING]

Bill Cosby: Actor and Comedian
(People to Know Series)
Michael A. Schuman

A Boy Called Slow:
The True Story of Sitting Bull
Joseph Bruchac

Cleopatra
Diane Stanley

Daniel Boone
Laurie Lawlor

Explorers and Traders
Claire Craig

Fiddler to the World:
The Inspiring Life of Itzhak Perlman
Carol H. Behrman

Frances Hodgson Burnett:
Beyond the Secret Garden
Angelica S. Carpenter and
Jean Shirley

Grandma Moses: Painter
of Rural America
Zibby O'Neal

I'm Nobody! Who Are You?
The Story of Emily Dickinson
Edna Barth

Lives of the Athletes: Thrills, Spills
(And What the Neighbors Thought)
Kathleen Krull

Lives of the Musicians: Good Times, Bad
Times (And What the Neighbors
Thought)
Kathleen Krull

Lives of the Writers: Comedies, Tragedies
(And What the Neighbors Thought)
Kathleen Krull

Pablo Casals: Cellist of Conscience
(People of Distinction Series)
Jim Hargrove

Richard Wright and the Library Card
William Miller

Robert E. Peary and the Fight
for the North Pole
Madelyn K. Anderson and
Mandela Anderson

Sacajawea
Judith St. George

Sojourner Truth
(Junior World Biographies)
Norman Macht

Walt Disney: A Biography
Barbara Ford

[WRITING NEWS STORIES]

Darnell Rock Reporting
Walter Dean Myers

Dateline: Troy
Paul Fleischman

Extra! Extra!: The Who, What, Where,
When, and Why of Newspapers
Linda Granfield

A Hand Full of Stars
Rafik Schami

How to Do Leaflets, Newsletters
and Newspapers
Nancy Brigham et al.

Read All About It! Great Read-Aloud
Stories, Poems, and Newspaper Pieces
for Preteens and Teens
Jim Trelease

Twelve-Year-Old Vows Revenge After
Being Dumped by Extraterrestrial
on First Date
Stephen Roos

[W R I T I N G   S T O R I E S]

The Giver
Lois Lowry

If I Forget, You Remember
Carol Lynch Williams

Love and Death at the Mall: Teaching Writing for the Literate Young
Richard Peck

On My Honor
Marion Dane Bauer

Saying Goodbye
Marie G. Lee

Taming the Star Runner
S. E. Hinton

The 38 Most Common Fiction Writing Mistakes (And How to Avoid Them)
Jack M. Bickham

The True Confessions of Charlotte Doyle
Avi

What Do Authors Do?
Eileen Christelow

What's Your Story? A Young Person's Guide to Writing Fiction
Marion Dane Bauer

[W R I T I N G   P O E T R Y]

Beast Feast
Douglas Florian

Creatures of Earth, Sea, and Sky
Georgia Heard

Falling Up: Poems and Drawings
Shel Silverstein

Festivals
Myra Cohn Livingston

A Fire in My Hands: A Book of Poems
Gary Soto

Gathering the Sun: An ABC in Spanish and English
Alma Flor Ada et al.

How to Read and Write Poems
Margaret Ryan

Jazmin's Notebook
Nikki Grimes

Joyful Noise: Poems for Two Voices
Paul Fleischman

Let's Do a Poem: Introducing Poetry to Children
Nancy Larrick

The Music of What Happens: Poems That Tell Stories
Selected by Paul B. Janeczko

Pass the Poetry, Please!
Lee Bennett Hopkins

Poem-Making: Ways to Begin Writing Poetry
Myra Cohn Livingston

The Random House Book of Poetry for Children
Jack Prelutsky

Slam Dunk: Basketball Poems
Selected by Lillian Morrison

Small Talk: A Book of Short Poems
Selected by Lee Bennett Hopkins

Speaking of Poets: Interviews with Poets Who Write for Children and Young Adults
Jeffrey S. Copeland

Under the Sunday Tree
Eloise Greenfield

WRITING OBSERVATION REPORTS

Astronomy
Philip Steele

*Birds of North America:
A Guide to Field Identification*
Chandler Robbins et al.

The City Kid's Field Guide
Ethan Herberman

Exploring the Titanic
Robert D. Ballard

My Side of the Mountain
Jean Craighead George

*Notes from Little Lakes: The Story
of a Family and Fifteen Acres*
Mel Ellis

*Out of the Ark: Stories
from World's Religions*
Anita Guneri

Social Smarts: Manners for Today's Kids
Elizabeth James and Carol Barkin

The Thirteen Moons (Series)
Jean Craighead George

*What's the Difference? A Guide to
Some Familiar Animal Look-Alikes*
Elizabeth A. Lacey

Who Belongs Here? An American Story
Margy B. Knight

*The Wild and Exciting
World of Skateboarding*
Bill Gutman

Wild World (Series)
Jim Flegg et al.

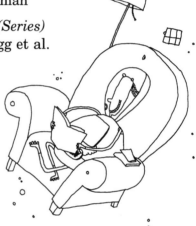

WRITING PERSONAL
RESEARCH REPORTS

*Everything You Need to Know
About Peer Pressure*
Robyn M. Feller

*The Kid's Guide to Service Projects: Over
500 Service Projects for Young People
Who Want to Make a Difference*
Barbara A. Lewis

*Know Your Hometown History:
Projects and Activities*
Abigail Jungrels

*Lives Turned Upside Down: Homeless
Children in Their Own Words and
Photographs*
Jim Hubbard

Overcoming Disability
Brian Ward

The Pressure to Take Drugs
Judith Condon

Under Our Skin: Kids Talk About Race
Debbie H. Birdseye and Tom Birdseye

We Remember the Holocaust
David A. Adler

*Where Do You Get Your Ideas?
Helping Young Writers Begin*
Sandy Asher

[WRITING RESEARCH PAPERS]

The Big Book for Our Planet
Edited by Ann Durrell et al.

Desktop Publishing:
The Art of Communication
John Madama

How to Write a Good School Report
Elizabeth James and Carol Barkin

Online Kids: A Young Surfer's
Guide to Cyberspace
Preston Gralla

10,000 Ideas for Term Papers,
Projects, Reports and Speeches
Kathryn Lamm

Writing: A Fact and Fun Book
Amanda Lewis

Writing with Style
Sue Young

[WORKPLACE WRITING]

Better Than a Lemonade $tand!
Small Business Ideas for Kids
(*Kids Books by Kids*)
Daryl Bernstein

Boys at Work
Gary Soto

Careers for Bookworms and
Other Literary Types
Marjorie Eberts and Margaret Gisler

Circle of Gold
Candy Dawson Boyd

The Complete Handbook
of Model Business Letters
Jack Griffin

Everyday Letters Ready to Go!
Cheryl McLean

How to Do Leaflets, Newsletters &
Newspapers
Nancy Brigham et al.

The Kids' Money Book
Neale S. Godfrey

Midstream Changes: People Who Started
Over and Made It Work
Nathan Aaseng

Not for a Billion Gazillion Dollars
Paula Danziger

Producing a First-Class Newsletter
Barbara A. Fanson

Really No Big Deal
Margaret Bechard

The Totally Awesome Business Book for
Kids: With Twenty Super Businesses
You Can Start Right Now!
Adriane G. Berg and Arthur Berg
Bochner

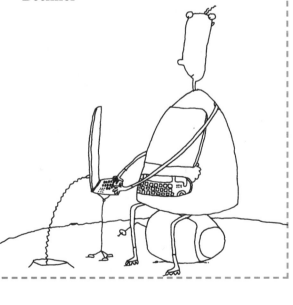

THE TOOLS OF LEARNING

Classic Brainteasers
Martin Gardner

Computer Graphics—How It Works, What It Does
Larry Kettlekamp

Computers Simplified (3-D *Visual Series*)
Ruth Maran

Creating Web Pages Simplified
(3-D *Visual Series*)
Ruth Maran and Paul Whitehead

Everything You Need to Know About American History Homework
Anne Zeman and Kate Kelly

Everything You Need to Know About Geography Homework
Anne Zeman and Kate Kelly

Everything You Need to Know About Math Homework
Anne Zeman and Kate Kelly

Everything You Need to Know About Science Homework
Anne Zeman and Kate Kelly

Great Scenes and Monologues for Children
Edited by Craig Slaight and Jack Sharrar

How to Be School Smart: Secrets of Successful Schoolwork
Elizabeth James and Carol Barkin

Internet and the World Wide Web Simplified (3-D *Visual Series*)
Ruth Maran and Paul Whitehead

Kids Do the Web
Cynthia Overbeck Bix et al.

Speaking Up, Speaking Out: A Kid's Guide to Making Speeches, Oral Reports, and Conversation
Steven Otfinoski

Stories in My Pocket: Tales Kids Can Tell
Martha Hamilton and Mitch Weiss

Student Resource Guide to the Internet
Cynthia B. Leshin

A Student's Guide to the Internet
Elizabeth L. Marshall

Surviving Homework: Tips from Teens
Amy Nathan

10,000 Ideas for Term Papers, Projects, Reports and Speeches
Kathryn Lamm

Think Positive: Cope with Stress
Catherine Reef

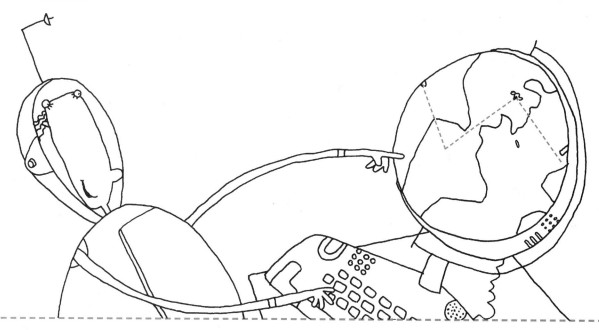

STUDENT ALMANAC

America's Top 10 Curiosities
Jenny E. Tesar

*Animal Athletes: Olympians of
the Wild World*
Cynthia O. Bix and Diana Landau

Animal Atlas
Falvio Cerfolli

Coast to Coast
Betsy Byars

*The Complete Handbook of Science Fair
Projects*
Julianne B. Bochinski

*Computers
(Inventors and Inventions Series)*
David Wright

Cool Math
Christy Maganzini

*Exploring the Sky: 100 Projects for
Beginning Astronomers*
Richard Moeschl

*The Great Voyager Adventure: A Guided
Tour Through the Solar System*
Alan Harris and Paul Weissman

How Math Works
Carol Vorderman

*It Happened in America: True Stories from
the Fifty States*
Lila Perl

Journey to the Planets
Patricia Lauber

Languages of the World
Scott Morris

North American Indian Sign Language
Karen Liptak

The On-Line Spaceman and Other Cases
Seymour Simon

Physics Lab in a Hardware Store
Robert Friedhoffer

Physics Lab in a Housewares Store
Robert Friedhoffer

*The Planet Hunters:
The Search for Other Worlds*
Dennis B. Fradin

*Roman Numerals I to MM: Numerabilia
Romanana Uno Ad Duo Mila*
Arthur Geisert

Shh! We're Writing the Constitution
Jean Fritz

Sign Language Talk
Laura Greene and Eva B. Dicker

The White House
Leonard Everett Fisher

*Who Talks Funny? A Book About
Languages for Kids*
Brenda S. Cox

*Why Do You Speak As You Do?
A Guide to World Languages*
Kay Cooper

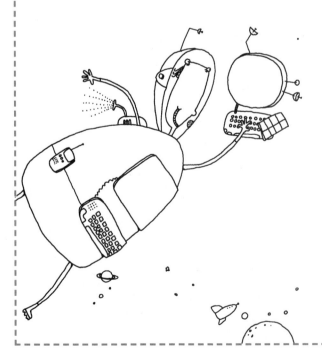

Thinking and Learning Strategies

The thinking and learning strategies on the following pages cover important areas often included in a complete language program.

Writing to Learn

> "I hear and I forget; I see and I remember; I write and I understand."
>
> —Chinese Proverb

Q. What exactly is "writing to learn"?

A. Writing to learn is a method of learning that helps students get more out of their course material. It is thinking on paper—thinking to discover connections, describe processes, express emerging understandings, raise questions, and find answers. It is a method that students can use in all subjects at all ages.

Q. What is the purpose of writing to learn?

A. The main purpose is better thinking and learning. (Better writing is a by-product.) This is why writing to learn is not just for English teachers.

Q. What makes writing to learn work?

A. Writing is uniquely suited to foster abstract thinking. The linearity of writing—one word after another—leads to more coherent and sustained thought than simply thinking or speaking. Also, when writing is used, all students can respond, including those who are reluctant to answer out loud.

Q. What are the advantages of writing to learn for students?

A. Writing to learn provides students with a way of learning, not just a set of facts. It forces students to personalize learning so that they understand better and remember longer. It also encourages higher-level thinking skills.

Q. What are the advantages for teachers?

A. Teachers using writing to learn will see learning, thinking, and writing improve among their students. They will also notice improved communication, rapport, and motivation as students become more independent and more actively involved in the learning process. Also, teachers will come to rely less and less on "writing to show learning," which needs to be graded.

Q. How do you implement a writing-to-learn program?

A. First of all, there is no one "program" for writing to learn. Teachers can begin with pages 366-368 in *Write Source 2000*. After discussing these pages, both students and teachers should have a good idea of what writing to learn is all about.

Then the teacher must select, from the wide variety of activities available, those that best suit the needs of his or her students. Once an activity is selected, it is very important that students understand they are "writing to learn," not "writing to show learning." If they understand that they are not writing simply to please their teacher, but to personalize and better understand information, you are on your way.

Q. Which writing-to-learn activities are good to begin with?

A. Admit slips, stop 'n' write, and exit slips are excellent activities to begin a writing-to-learn program, although there are any number of effective activities that teachers can use. (See pages 164-165 in this guide for a list of writing-to-learn activities.)

Collaborative Learning

Collaborative learning is a powerful class-room strategy for both teachers and students. Collaborative learning means essentially "to work together," but this strategy is infused with new knowledge about group dynamics from the areas of communication and psychology.

Obviously, you already know a lot about cooperative learning. You have been or are a member of many groups—families, sport teams, community groups, faculty committees, and so forth. Sometimes when we look at these groups, we tend to remember how ineffective they can be. In fact, we may have a large body of knowledge about what NOT to do. This is okay. If nothing else, it is an incentive to discover what TO DO.

So what should a teacher who wants to use collaborative learning do?

First, we suggest that you experiment with collaborative learning before deciding if this class-room strategy is for you and your students. We provide three strategies you can use for this experimentation. The group skills you will want to work with are described in *Write Source 2000* (pages 369-372).

While you are experimenting, keep these points in mind:

1. Collaborative learning allows teachers to move away from the front of the room and rely less on lecturing.
2. Collaborative learning provides students with one of the most powerful ways to learn—verbalization.
3. Collaborative learning gives students more ownership of their learning and therefore motivates them to become better students.

Three Strategies That Work

The three strategies you can use for experimentation follow:

1 Tell/Retell Groups

Application: Any reading-to-learn activity
Recommended group size: 2
Group skills to emphasize: "Skills for Listening" (page 370), and "Skills for Observing" (page 371)

STEP 1: One member reads a portion of the assigned material; the second member becomes an "active listener."

STEP 2: The second member tells what she or he heard; the first member then becomes the "active listener." They decide together what the essential information is. (It's okay for them to look back at the reading material.)

STEP 3: Reverse roles and read the next portion.

2 Smart Groups

Application: Any reading-to-learn activity
Recommended group size: 2
Group skills to emphasize: "Skills for Cooperating" (page 371), and "Skills for Clarifying" (page 371)

STEP 1: Both students read assigned material. While reading, they put a faint check mark beside each paragraph they understand and a question mark beside any sentence, word, or paragraph they do not completely understand.

STEP 2: At each question mark, team members ask for help. If they both have questions, they try together to make sense of the material. If they both agree to seek outside help, they may consult another team or the teacher. If time allows, they may share what they remember about the passages they both understand.

3 **Up with Your Head Groups**

Application: Checking comprehension and reviewing

Recommended group size: 4-5

Group skills to emphasize: "Skills for Responding" (page 372)

STEP 1: Ask each student to number off within each group.

STEP 2: The teacher or a panel of students asks a question about the material that has been read.

STEP 3: Each group "puts their heads together" to make sure every member in their group knows an/the answer. When the question is "open" (one without a "correct" answer), the group reaches a consensus of opinion.

STEP 4: The questioner calls a number (1, 2, 3, 4, 5), and students with the corresponding number raise their hands to respond. When the question requires a specific answer, only one student need reply; but when the question is "open," a member from each group may reply.

What's the Next Step?

You will probably have many questions after experimenting. Questions such as these are common: "What is the teacher doing while students work?" "How do I assess student work?" "What happens when one group finishes before others?" "What is the best way to form groups?" "Are there more ways to use cooperative learning?" "How can I use cooperative learning in reading workshops / in writing workshops / to build vocabulary?"

Many sources of information about collaborative learning are available. Ask other teachers, your curriculum director, and your department head to help you locate these sources.

Group Skills You Already Know

1. Moving desks quietly

2. Staying in your own space

3. Sitting so all members of a team can see everyone's face

4. Taking turns

5. Calling classmates by their name

6. Using #3 voices
   (A #1 voice would be a whisper; a #10 voice would be a yell.)

Teaching Thinking

For those of you who are ready to make your classrooms more "thinking oriented," we feel Arthur L. Costa offers the best advice in *Developing Minds.* He suggests teachers teach for thinking, about thinking, and of thinking.

Teaching for Thinking

How can you create a thinking climate in your classroom? Read on and find out.

■ Personalize the learning in your classroom. Students will approach learning more thoughtfully when the subject matter means something to them personally. Common sense (plus plenty of studies) tells us students won't become thoughtfully involved in work that is not personally relevant.

■ Promote activities that have been considered fillers: stories, poems, posters, letters, recipes, riddles, debates, discussions, etc. These are the types of activities that get students actively thinking and learning.

■ Engage your students in projects. Have them produce a class newspaper. Have them write and produce a play or a news show. Have them develop instructional manuals for skateboarding or bike repairing.

■ Involve students in collaborative learning. Collaboration is at the heart of learning outside of school. We learn how to ride, fish, bake, fix, etc., with the help of friends and family members.

■ Encourage open, active learning in your classroom. Give students every opportunity to explore, take risks, and make mistakes in your classroom. Ask them open-ended questions. Initiate role-playing activities, dramatic scenarios, discussions, and debates. Pose problems, search for alternatives, test hypotheses, and, generally, challenge your students to think and act for themselves.

Teaching About Thinking

Experts believe it's important that teachers help students think about their own thinking (metacognition). Here are some things you can do to help students metacogitate.

■ Explore with students how the brain works. Discuss left-brain thinking versus right-brain thinking.

■ Select biographies of famous thinkers to share with your students.

■ Discuss creative thinking, logical thinking, the connection between thinking and writing, the characteristics of effective thinkers, etc. (See the thinking section in *Write Source 2000,* pages 283-299, for help with this.)

■ Help students think about their own learning. Have them estimate how long an assignment will take and what materials they will need to complete the assignment. Have them keep track of their progress on an extended project in a personal journal and so on.

■ Remind students that it's all right to make mistakes, to get stuck, to reach dead ends. Help them learn from these experiences.

■ Urge students to connect what they have already learned to new information. Also take every opportunity to connect what they are learning to their personal lives.

> "Believe all students can think, not just the gifted ones. Let your students know that thinking is a goal. Create the right climate and model it."
>
> —Arthur L. Costa

Teaching of Thinking

A third component in a thinking classroom includes direct instruction of thinking skills. Here's how to work thinking skills into your curriculum.

- Review a taxonomy of thinking skills (such as the one on page 290 in the handbook), and select a limited number to emphasize throughout the year—perhaps one comprehension skill *(summarizing),* one analyzing skill *(classifying),* one synthesizing skill *(predicting),* and one evaluating skill *(persuading).*

- Produce your own activities for instruction or use commercially produced thinking materials. (See the sample problem-solving scenario below.)

- A thinking-skill lesson plan should follow this general format: Introduce the skill. *(Find out what the students already know about it.)* Demonstrate the skill. *(Get your students actively involved.)* Have your students try this skill in an activity. *(Give them an opportunity to work in pairs.)* Follow up with a discussion of the activity. That is, have students reflect on the thinking they have done.

- Develop specific thinking activities that complement the thinking section in *Write Source 2000.* You might . . .

  - give your students opportunities to think and write creatively. (See "Offbeat Questions, page 55.)

  - provide your students with a number of opportunities to focus on specific levels of thinking in writing assignments. (See pages 283-290.)

  - give students opportunities to think logically. (See pages 291-296.)

  - have students identify and work through a problem to solve or a difficult concept to understand. (See "Asking Questions," page 296.)

  - have students refer to the thinking and writing chart (page 299) regularly for writing assignments.

Problem-Solving Scenario
INVENTING
Are You Game?

For twenty years Mr. Sporto and his gym classes have batted, blocked, and kicked with gusto. But twenty years is a long time, and Mr. Sporto is losing some of his enthusiasm. What he needs is a new game, a game that will renew the competitive fire in his eyes.

- **Create a new game or sport for Mr. Sporto, and if it helps him forget football and baseball for a while, he just might use it next semester.** (Work in groups, if your teacher allows it.)

Building Vocabulary

We know there is a strong connection between a student's vocabulary and her or his reading ability. The same is true for a student's ability to listen, speak, and write. In fact, we now recognize that each person actually has four vocabularies, one each for reading, listening, speaking, and writing (listed here from largest to smallest). Although there is much overlap, students will always be able to recognize more words than they can produce. This is important to keep in mind as you develop a program of vocabulary development for your students.

Vocabulary development must also occur across the curriculum. Students must read, hear, speak, and write with the words they are attempting to learn in their classes. Anything less, and the words will not become part of their permanent "producing" vocabulary.

Existing studies tell us two things: (1) giving students lists of vocabulary words with little or no context is not an efficient way to teach vocabulary, and (2) students must be actively involved with the words they are attempting to learn.

> "Colors fade, temples crumble, empires fall, but wise words endure."
>
> —Edward Thorndike

Vocabulary-Building Strategies

The strategies that follow take all of our opening points into consideration:

Previewing in Context
1. Select five or six words from a chapter or selection students are about to read.
2. Tell students to open their books to the page and paragraph in which each word is located. Have them find the word, read it in context, and figure out the meaning.
3. Ask students to write down what they think each word means.
4. Discuss possible meanings and arrive at the correct definition in this context.

Studying Context Clues
1. Students should read the context clues section of their *Write Source 2000* handbook. (See page 324.)
2. Students should practice identifying the types of context clues as they use the previewing and self-collection techniques.

Self-Collecting
1. Students should set aside a portion of their class journals or notebooks to collect personal vocabulary words.
2. They may collect new and interesting words from any source, preferably outside of school.
3. Students should analyze each word with the help of a dictionary or glossary and perhaps a thesaurus.
4. Students may want to write journal entries that contain these new words.

Vocabulary

word	definition	usage
platonic	a relationship	They had a platonic
	without romance	relationship.

Studying Prefixes, Suffixes, and Roots

1. Students should learn the most common prefixes, suffixes, and roots.

2. Students can be assigned three or four word parts each week for the entire year (see lists for each level on page 215 of this guide).

3. Students can be given a number of strategies for learning these word parts:

   - Assign students one word part a day (every day except Monday, perhaps). As you are taking roll, students can write out the word part, definition, a sample word, and a sentence using this word. Then have them exchange and correct papers.

   - Ask students to brainstorm for word associations that will help them remember the meaning of each word part.

   - Challenge students to combine the word parts they have studied into as many words as possible (perhaps in 5 minute's time, or as an assignment for the next day). Special cards can also be used for this purpose:

Word Card

de		ion
re	flex flect	or
in		ible

   - Require students to create "new" words, not in the dictionary, using the word parts they have learned. To qualify, a new word should be one that makes sense and might actually be used if it were known to a large number of people.

   - Invite students to share a "new" word and challenge the others to guess what it means and to write a sentence (or two or three) in which they use this word.

   - Direct students to start a special section in their notebooks for word parts they come across in their other classes.

Other Forms of Word Study

1. **Special groups:** Students can be introduced to special groups of words found in computer language, music, advertising, politics, and so on.

2. **Word play:** A certain amount of "word play" is essential to vocabulary growth. Any type of word game will work so long as it is appropriate for the level of the students.

3. **Word-a-day:** At the beginning of the class period, a word is printed on the board (a word that a student can use in his or her reading, listening, writing, and speaking vocabularies). As students enter the classroom, they immediately grab a dictionary and look up the word. As a class, students discuss the meaning and agree on a definition and a part of speech. They then use the word in a sentence, showing that they know what the word means and how to use it correctly.

   Each student jots down this information in a notebook. Each page is divided by a line drawn vertically at a point about one-third the width of the page. On the left side of this line, the word is written. On the right side of the line, the part of speech, definition, and sentence are written. This allows the student to cover the definitions by simply folding the paper.

   A written quiz can be given each Friday, covering the five words from the recent week and five words from any past weeks. The student must write the word in a sentence, proving again that he or she knows what the word means and how to use it.

Studying Word Parts

The following lists of word parts can be used as the basis of a vocabulary program for levels 6, 7, and 8. (All of these word parts are defined in the handbook on pages 329-339.)

LEVEL 6

Prefixes:

anti, bi, circum (circ), deca, di, ex (e), hemi (demi, semi), hex, il (ir, in, im), in (im), intro, mono, multi, non, penta, post, pre, quad, quint, re, self, sub, super (supr), tri, un, uni

Suffixes:

able (ible), an (ian), ar (er, or), cide, cule (ling), en, ese, ful, ion (sion, tion), ist, ity (ty), ize, less, ology, ward

Roots:

anni (annu, enni), aster (astr), aud, auto (aut), bibl, bio, breve, chrom, chron, cide, cise, cit, clud (clus, claus), corp, crat, cred, cycl (cyclo), dem, dent (dont), derm, dic (dict), domin, dorm, duc (duct), erg, fin, fix, flex (flect), form, fort (forc), fract (frag), geo, graph, here (hes), hydr (hydro, hydra), ject, join (junct), jur (jus), juven, lic (licit), magn, mand, mania, meter, micro, migra, multi (multus), numer, omni, ortho, ped (pod), phon, pop, port, prehend, punct, reg (recti), rupt, sci, scrib (script), serv, spec (spect), sphere, tele, tempo, terra, therm, tract (tra), typ, uni, vid (vis), zo

LEVEL 7

Prefixes:

ambi (amphi), bene (bon), by, co (con, col, cor, com), contra (counter), dia, dis, eu, extra, fore, homo, inter, mis, ob (of, op, oc), para, per, peri, poly, pro, se, syn (sym, sys, syl), trans (tra), ultra, under, vice

Suffixes:

ance (ancy), ate, cian, ish, ism, ive, ly, ment, ness, some, tude

Roots:

ag (agi, ig), anthrop, arch, aug (auc), cap (cept), capit (capt), carn, cause (cuse, cus), civ, clam (claim), cord (cor, card), cosm, cred, cresc (cret, crease, cru), dura, dynam, equi, fac (fact, fic), fer, fid (feder), gam, gen, gest, grad (gress), grat, grav, hab (habit), hum (human), hypn, jud (judi, judic), leg, lit (liter), log (logo, ology), luc (lum), man, mar (mari, mer), medi, mega, mem, mit (miss), mob (mot, mov), mon, mori (mort, mors), nov, onym, oper, pac, pan, pater (patr), path (pathy), pend (pens), phil, photo, poli, portion, prim (prime), psych, put, salv (salu), sat (satis), scope, sen, sent (sens), sign (signi), sist (sta, stit, stet), solus, solv (solu), spir, spond (spons), strict, stru (struct), tact (tang, tag), test, tort (tors), vac, vert (vers), vict (vinc), voc

LEVEL 8

Prefixes:

a (an), ab (abs, a), acro, ante, be, cata, cerebro, de, dys, epi, hyper, hypo, infra, intra, macro, mal, meta, miso, neo, oct, paleo, pseudo, retro, sex (sest)

Suffixes:

asis (esis, osis), cy, dom, ee, ence (ency), ice, ile, ite

Roots:

acer (acid, acri), acu, ali (allo, alter), altus, am (amor), belli, calor, caus (caut), cognosc (gnosi), cur (curs), cura, doc, don, dox, end (endo), fall (fals), fila (fili), flu (fluc, fluv), fum, gastro, germ, gloss (glot), glu (glo), greg, helio, hema (hemo), hetero, homo, ignis, later, liver (liber), loc (loco), loqu (locut), lude, matri (mater), morph, nat, neur, nom, nomen (nomin), nounce (nunci), nox (noc), pedo, pel (puls), phobia, plac (plais), plenus, pneuma (pneumon), pon (pos), proto, que (qui), ri (ridi), rog (roga), sacr (secr), sangui, sed (sess, sid), sequ (secu), simil (simul), somnus, soph, sume (sump), ten (tin, tain), tend (tens), tom, tox, trib, tui (tut), turbo, ven (vent), viv, vol, volcan (vulcan), vor

Improving Student Spelling

> "For better or worse, spelling places third in the American public's priorities for curriculum emphasis. Writing places eighth. In short, spelling is more important than what it is used for . . . writing."
>
> —Donald Graves

How should spelling be addressed in today's language arts classrooms if, in fact, the public gives it such a high priority? That question and more are explored in this discussion. What you'll find first is a list of instructional do's as reflected in the current research on spelling.

Spelling Practices That Work

- Devoting approximately 10 minutes per day to direct instruction
- Presenting and studying words in short lists
- Drawing words from one of the master lists of high-frequency words
- Employing the pretest-study-test method of instruction
- Asking students to correct their own pretests
- Providing students with a strategy to learn how to spell new words
- Linking spelling instruction, whenever possible, to the students' own writing

Spelling and Writing

There is really only one hard-and-fast rule to remember: Do not let students become overly concerned about the correctness of their spelling during the drafting stages of the writing process. They should, however, be made to realize that before a piece of writing can be considered ready for publication, it must be as free of careless errors as possible.

Meeting Students' Needs

How can you help students improve their spelling skills as they work on their writing? First, you can ask them to circle which words are spelled incorrectly in their work before they ready a draft for publication. If a student needs more direction, you can write at the top of the paper, "There are four words misspelled," and let the student attempt to find the four words.

Next, teach your students the systems they can use to correct a misspelling. These should include using a poor speller's dictionary, compiling a personal dictionary of frequently misspelled words, utilizing computer spell checkers, and having access to the classroom spelling expert.

Why Spelling?

You may hear from middle-school students, "Why do I have to learn to spell when I can use a computer spell checker?" The truth of the matter is that there is still a very good reason for learning to spell, especially the words a writer uses again and again. A writer who can spell can put the words behind him or her and focus on more important matters like exploring and shaping ideas. In addition, no spell checker is foolproof. You still must check for errors after using this computer feature.

Weekly Lists

Weekly spelling words for levels 6, 7, and 8 are provided on the next six pages. These words come from the commonly misspelled words listed in the *Write Source 2000* handbook (pages 412-418). The "Weekly Spelling Words" can serve as starting points for planning spelling units. Ten words are provided for each week. Add more words from one of the published high-frequency lists or from content units you are studying. (See page 223 in this section for more spelling ideas.)

Weekly Spelling Words: Level 6

1 (Nouns)
barber
carpenter
cousin
family
governor
neighbor
people
soldier
visitor
women

2 (School Words)
arithmetic
chorus
coach
discuss
history
honor
journal
professor
quarter
sentence

3 (Compound Words)
afternoon
anybody
anyhow
anyone
blackboard
breakfast
cardboard
classmate
cupboard
worthwhile

4 (One-Syllable Words)
aid
ghost
guess
laugh
length
pure
raise
tired
view
voice

5 (Two-Syllable Words)
fashion
feature
legal
maintain
obey
occur
often
suppose
until
useful

6 (Three-Syllable Words)
accomplish
appearance
approval
continue
determine
disapprove
elephant
establish
generous
hospital

7 (Consonant Blends)
bridge
brought
cranky
crumble
friend
grease
grudge
sprinkle
stomach
strength

8 (*er* Endings)
altogether
another
catcher
either
father
loser
pitcher
prisoner
remember
together

9 (Adjectives)
attractive
careless
eligible
enormous
excellent
famous
formal
lovely
planned
primitive

10 (Food Words)
banana
catsup
cracker
dessert
loaves
piece
pumpkin
salad
sandwich
vegetable

11 (Short $\breve{a}$ Sound)
adapt
basket
began
canal
candle
can't
handle
package
pasture
perhaps

12 (Soft *c* or *g* Sound)
accident
angel
bandage
certain
decided
edge
except
gentle
innocence
original

13 (Nouns)
address
alarm
color
employment
gadget
kitchen
label
magazine
material
weather

14 (Two-Syllable Words)
again
assume
attach
because
become
belong
custom
dual
escape
expect

15 (Three-Syllable Words)
imagine
importance
improvement
monument
opinion
paragraph
personal
probably
specific
supplement

16 (Long $\bar{i}$ Sound)
admire
alive
appetite
diamond
divide
divine
lightning
likely
quiet
tries

Weekly Spelling Words: Level 6

17 (Money Words)
allowance
amount
budget
dollar
fifty
forty
fourth
mortgage
nineteen
paid

18 (Double Consonants)
bottle
bubble
cabbage
cannon
carrot
college
commit
connect
current
disappoint

19 (*ing* Endings)
baking
being
coming
having
hopping
living
making
shining
using
writing

20 (*tion/sion* Endings)
attention
condition
constitution
division
edition
imitation
invitation
occasion
omission
vacation

21 (Time Words)
always
annual
August
daily
diary
February
minute
season
Tuesday
Wednesday

22 (*ou* Words)
about
account
around
couldn't
counter
court
enough
mountain
route
touch

23 (Silent Letters)
afraid
arctic
bright
climb
depot
design
frighten
knew
scene
science

24 (Four-Syllable Words)
celebration
emergency
independent
interested
investigate
legislature
preferable
repetition
respectfully
ridiculous

25 (Journey Words)
above
across
baggage
desert
forth
forward
immigrant
journey
toward
welcome

26 (Double Consonants)
grammar
hammer
happen
innocent
message
mirror
misspell
stopped
success
yellow

27 (Consonant Blends)
asleep
between
complain
control
enclose
explain
instead
precise
scream
tried

28 (Consonant Digraphs)
challenge
chief
children
thankful
theater
thief
though
whale
where
whole

29 (Three-Syllable Words)
adventure
argument
beginning
compromise
dangerous
decorate
discover
entertain
maximum
natural

30 (*y* Endings)
angry
bury
busy
company
country
guilty
noisy
really
safety
very

31 (Soft *c* or *g* Sound)
average
concert
danger
entrance
exercise
genius
imaginary
medicine
receive
since

32 (Four-Syllable Words)
automobile
comparison
environment
identical
industrial
inflammable
intelligence
participate
preparation
temperature

Weekly Spelling Words: Level 7

1 (School Words)
absent
attendance
classroom
dictionary
geography
language
library
principal
university
writing

2 (One-Syllable Words)
bounce
crawl
eight
loose
lose
meant
phase
their
there
whose

3 (Two-Syllable Words)
alarm
alike
basis
collar
defense
doesn't
hoping
jealous
measure
review

4 (Adjectives)
anxious
careful
different
exhausted
fiery
infinite
peculiar
pleasant
possible
terrible

5 (Verbs)
announce
attack
believe
convince
describe
disappear
distribute
irrigate
omitted
wander

6 (Adverbs)
aboard
already
certainly
coolly
extremely
formerly
hastily
occasionally
quite
unfortunately

7 (People Words)
architect
assassin
athlete
burglar
captain
champion
director
guard
sheriff
treasurer

8 (Health Words)
accidental
ache
ambulance
conference
cough
doctor
muscle
operate
physician
protein

9 (Nouns)
breath
brother
column
freight
grief
pleasure
principle
souvenir
statute
strength

10 (Three-Syllable Words)
animal
catalog
hesitate
interview
minimum
opposite
permanent
recommend
sensible
several

11 (Four/Five Syllables)
advertising
appropriate
associate
controversy
dissatisfied
independence
machinery
miserable
particular
satisfactory

12 (Soft *c* or *g* Sound)
ceiling
damage
deceive
evidence
forcible
instance
mileage
procedure
violence
wreckage

13 (Double Consonants)
according
appeal
arrange
bottom
button
cannot
immense
occurred
parallel
possess

14 (Time Words)
after
afterward
ancient
becoming
before
calendar
century
holiday
temporary
tomorrow

15 (Two-Syllable Words)
anger
arouse
before
conscious
despair
fulfill
issue
losing
moisture
vacuum

16 (Three-Syllable Words)
appliance
equipment
illustrate
liable
molecule
paradise
recognize
Saturday
separate
vehicle

Weekly Spelling Words: Level 7

17 (Long ē Sound)
apiece
behave
concrete
eager
handkerchief
neither
previous
realize
relieve
succeed

18 (Adjectives)
awful
commercial
cozy
curious
desirable
essential
favorite
fortunate
horrible
immortal

19 (Nouns)
basement
biscuit
blanket
bucket
building
chimney
laundry
scissors
screen
surprise

20 (Adverbs)
almost
apparently
completely
entirely
finally
generally
hurriedly
practically
surely
usually

21 (Consonant Digraphs)
anything
approach
choice
clothing
emphasize
enough
further
throughout
which
width

22 (Three-Syllable Words)
accurate
agreement
arrival
attitude
commitment
expression
happiness
obstacle
summarize
usable

23 (Four/Five Syllables)
anticipate
available
community
illiterate
impossible
interesting
participant
representative
ridiculous
voluntary

24 (People Words)
author
candidate
character
conductor
customer
guide
individual
musician
niece
playwright

25 (Silent Letters)
among
column
crumb
dough
gnaw
knock
listen
sleigh
straight
tongue

26 (Outdoor Words)
acre
airy
alley
breeze
canyon
caterpillar
climate
cocoon
fountain
squirrel

27 (*tion* Endings)
addition
competition
corporation
definition
exhibition
initiation
installation
intention
perspiration
pronunciation

28 (*y* Endings)
accompany
beauty
casualty
country
dairy
electricity
grocery
jewelry
ninety
secretary

29 (Soft *c* or *g* Sound)
concerning
courage
encourage
exceed
legible
marriage
presence
privilege
religious
sincere

30 (Finance Words)
abundance
balance
bankrupt
benefit
bought
expensive
federal
manual
mathematics
valuable

31 (Three-Syllable Words)
adjustment
anyway
assistance
comedy
courtesy
discussion
envelope
familiar
nuclear
persistent

32 (Mixed List)
answer
buckle
coverage
dining
duplicate
embarrass
handsome
ladies
lecture
written

Weekly Spelling Words: Level 8

1 (Food Words)
cafeteria
canister
casserole
chocolate
cocoa
coffee
liquid
recipe
restaurant
spaghetti

2 (Nouns: Places)
apartment
avenue
cemetery
closet
dormitory
gymnasium
island
laboratory
prairie
vicinity

3 (Nouns: People)
accomplice
audience
cashier
creditor
employee
guardian
lieutenant
mayor
personnel
volunteer

4 (Adjectives)
adequate
artificial
dependent
elaborate
extinct
genuine
impatient
influential
likable
naive

5 (Verbs)
accelerate
apologize
attempt
breathe
canceled
conceive
cooperate
envelop
harass
interrupt

6 (Nouns: Things)
aluminum
balloon
bicycle
canoe
carriage
diploma
ellipse
ghetto
nickel
salary

7 (Adverbs)
anywhere
definitely
especially
exceptionally
financially
immediately
indefinitely
naturally
ordinarily
wholly

8 (Two-Syllable Words)
against
belief
buoyant
deserve
equipped
offense
persuade
quotient
schedule
welfare

9 (One-Syllable Words)
cried
dealt
fierce
gauge
hoarse
hymn
reign
seize
squeeze
weigh

10 (Three-Syllable Words)
actual
beautiful
changeable
criticize
existence
foliage
medium
paralyze
reservoir
tragedy

11 (Language Words)
abbreviate
communicate
correspond
imaginative
knowledge
literature
parentheses
rhyme
studying
syllable

12 (y Endings)
anniversary
authority
battery
boundary
capacity
curiosity
difficulty
extraordinary
juicy
majority

13 (Challenge Words)
all right
colonel
conscience
counterfeit
forfeit
leisure
miscellaneous
mischievous
received
weird

14 (Nouns: People)
amateur
beggar
citizen
daughter
engineer
lawyer
league
official
villain
women

15 (Nouns: Things)
angle
barrel
bruise
carburetor
cylinder
disease
faucet
missile
pamphlet
tariff

16 (Adjectives)
agreeable
awkward
disagreeable
enthusiastic
fertile
illegible
inferior
initial
lovable
similar

Weekly Spelling Words: Level 8

17 (Double Consonants)
accustomed
appreciate
brilliant
bulletin
difference
exaggerate
necessary
opportunity
questionnaire
sufficient

18 (Soft *c* Sound)
absence
census
confidence
delicious
guidance
insurance
license
noticeable
obedience
patience

19 (Two-Syllable Words)
bargain
beneath
condemn
devise
headache
partial
pronounce
rhythm
volume
whether

20 (Three-Syllable Words)
alcohol
antarctic
diaphragm
disastrous
furthermore
guarantee
hydraulic
interfere
resistance
unconscious

21 (Four-Syllable Words)
anxiety
catastrophe
declaration
equivalent
experience
fundamental
incredible
magnificent
negotiate
variety

22 (Government Words)
amendment
article
attorney
ballot
bureau
committee
conservative
government
politician
statute

23 (*ion* Endings)
application
association
civilization
commission
complexion
concession
decision
description
graduation
precision

24 (Silent Letters)
aisle
autumn
bough
doubt
eighth
fatigue
foreign
height
pneumonia
unique

25 (Soft *c* or *g* Sound)
annoyance
certificate
circumstance
device
discipline
efficiency
facilities
fragile
nuisance
pronounce

26 (Consonant Blends)
blizzard
brief
grateful
gruesome
plateau
precede
proceed
prominent
skiing
statue

27 (Adjectives)
appropriate
athletic
colossal
divisible
haphazard
miniature
perpendicular
unnecessary
various
visible

28 (*ly/ment* Endings)
absolutely
achievement
advertisement
appointment
assignment
competitively
development
judgment
tournament
truly

29 (Three-Syllable Words)
analyze
behavior
committed
distinguish
fascinate
loneliness
opponent
prejudice
souvenir
typical

30 (Silent Letters)
although
campaign
hemorrhage
knuckles
psychology
receipt
scenery
subtle
technique
thorough

31 (*ous* Endings)
anonymous
continuous
courageous
courteous
hazardous
humorous
monotonous
mysterious
outrageous
previous

32 (Mixed List)
business
career
congratulate
deteriorate
economy
hygiene
interpret
manufacture
symptom
therefore

Additional Spelling Activities

Consider the ideas and activities listed on this page when planning weekly spelling units.

Pretest

Select 20-25 words from the master list in the handbook (pages 412-418) to use as a pretest at the beginning of the year. Students who have mastered these words may not need weekly spelling practice. (You may also want to implement a posttest at the end of the year.)

High-Frequency Words

Words from one of the many published high-frequency lists (words student writers use again and again) could be incorporated into the weekly spelling lists or midweek spelling minilessons. (You might create sentences containing these high-frequency words for brief dictation sessions.)

Commonly Mixed Pairs

Refer to the list of commonly mixed pairs in the handbook (pages 419-433) for additional words to incorporate into the weekly spelling lists or into midweek spelling minilessons. (Some of these words are in the master spelling list.)

Minilessons

Check the minilessons in this guide related to spelling, or create your own. These activities could be used as spelling practice activities.

Systematic Practice

As students practice spelling words, they should be encouraged to employ a basic spelling strategy (examine, pronounce, cover, and write) and repeat this process to ensure mastery.

Board Work

Display two or three of the most challenging words from the spelling list on the board during a class period. Announce that the words will be erased at the end of the period, and the students will be expected to spell them correctly on a slip of paper before dismissal.

Regular Writing

Encourage (or require) students to use words from their weekly spelling lists in journal writings, in regular writing assignments, and in other writing-related activities.

Prefix and Suffix Work

Students could be provided with a limited number of prefixes and suffixes and then asked to create as many new words as possible, adding these affixes to selected words in the weekly spelling lists.

Word Searches

Students could be asked to look for words from their weekly spelling lists in the books, periodicals, and newspapers that they read in class and on their own.

Specialized Spelling

Students could be asked to list (and spell correctly) words related to areas of interest like baseball, astronomy, fashions, and so on. (Students may enjoy creating their own specialized dictionaries.)

Quarterly Assessment

Select words from the weekly spelling lists for an end-of-the-quarter assessment test. (Words that are misspelled by many of the students should be worked with again during the next quarter.)

"When children write early, their experiments with sounds and symbols produce spellings that may not be entirely correct, but research shows that if these children continue to have ample opportunity to write, they gradually increase their spelling power."

—Donald Graves

Professional Titles for Language Arts Teachers

We highly recommend the following titles on writing, reading, and teaching for middle-school language arts teachers. All titles are Heinemann-Boynton/Cook publications, unless otherwise indicated.

Active Voice: A Writing Program Across the Curriculum
James Moffett

According to many writing experts, this book offers the best sequence of compositions available in print. The forms of writing cataloged in *Write Source 2000* reflect Moffett's approach to writing.

Creating Writers: Linking Writing Assessment and Instruction
Vickie Spandel and Richard J. Stiggins

Teachers who are concerned about writing standards, state writing assessment tests, and assessing writing should read this book. Special emphasis is given to the traits of good writing and the revising process. (Available through Addison Wesley Longman.)

A Fresh Look at Writing
Donald H. Graves

In *A Fresh Look at Writing,* Donald Graves expands on many of his earlier approaches to writing. He addresses portfolios, record keeping, instructional methods, and examines a wide range of writing including fiction, poetry, and nonfiction.

In the Middle (Second Edition)
Nancie Atwell

Teacher and researcher Nancie Atwell details her successful middle-school writing and reading workshops. *In the Middle* contains a clear discussion of workshop procedures, practical advice, techniques for conferring with writers and readers, and many examples of student writing.

Literacy at the Crossroads
Regie Routman

Regie Routman teaches in the Shaker Heights, Ohio, City School District. Her latest book, *Literacy at the Crossroads,* addresses the "back to basics" movement. The book clarifies issues, offers suggestions, and provides insight concerning the current state of reading and writing instruction.

The Online Classroom: Teaching with the Internet
Eileen Giuffre Cotton

This book makes it easy for teachers to use the Internet. The first half of the book tells how to use the Internet; the second half gives lessons to use in the classroom. (Available through Eric Clearinghouse—Reading and Communication Skills.)

Seeking Diversity
Linda Rief

Linda Rief, an eighth-grade teacher in Durham, New Hampshire, presents an enlightening and stimulating look at her classroom where "the intellectual and emotional needs of her students are the crux of her curriculum." Students and the teacher alike thrive in Ms. Rief's classroom. This book is must reading for all teachers in the middle grades and beyond.

Student-Centered Language Arts and Reading, K-13: A Handbook for Teachers
James Moffett and Betty Jane Wagner

This valuable resource covers all aspects of the language arts, including talking and listening, performing, reading, writing, word play, and assessment. This one book covers almost everything that a language arts teachers needs to know when planning a curriculum. (Available through Houghton-Mifflin Company.)

Minilessons

The following pages contain more than 150 minilessons that you and your students can use with the *Write Source 2000* handbook. These minilessons cover all the important skills, strategies, and topics addressed in the handbook.

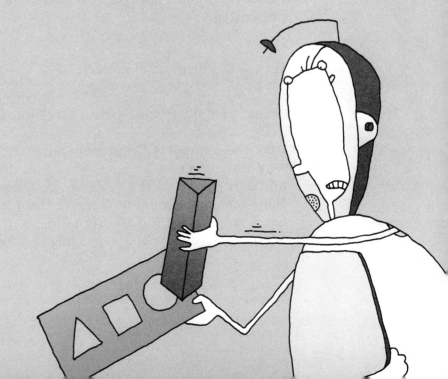

The Process of Writing

Here's help. . . . . Understanding Writing

- ■ **STUDY** "The Writing Process in Action" (HB 6-7).
  DIVIDE a piece of paper into two columns.
  At the top of the left column, **WRITE** the step in the writing process that you enjoy the most.
  At the top of the right column, **WRITE** the step that is hardest for you.
  In the left column, **LIST** five things you like about this step.
  In the right column, **LIST** chapters, pages, or sections in your handbook that might help you with the step that is hardest for you.
  DISCUSS your lists as a class.

Quote me on that. . . . . Understanding Writing

- ■ **READ** "Thinking Aloud About the Process" (HB 8).
  THINK UP three quotations of your own that might help other students with the writing process.
  WRITE your quotations and **SHARE** them with the class.

Long Ago and Far Away . . . . One Writer's Process

- ■ **REVIEW** Brian Krygsman's process of prewriting (HB 10-11).
  Then **STUDY** the following quotation: "Thorough prewriting makes the rest of the writing process go more smoothly."
  EXPLAIN in a brief paragraph how this quotation applies to Brian's prewriting.

Take it to heart. . . . . One Writer's Process

- ■ **READ** the first draft that Brian Krygsman wrote about medieval castles (HB 12-13).
  STUDY the comments Brian made after writing his first draft (HB 14-15).
  APPLY the comments to one of your own drafts. **ASK** yourself: Is there any part that is off the subject? Do I need to add an example? Are there ideas that could be clearer? Do I need to be more specific? **MAKE** notes on your writing as Brian did.
  Then **REVISE** your writing according to your notes.

What a voice! . . . . Traits of Effective Writing

- **STUDY** "Engaging Voice" (HB 22).
  THINK of one of your first "best" friends.
  Then **WRITE** a paragraph, sharing one experience about this person.
  USE your best personal voice.
  SHARE your finished product with a classmate.

The Right Stuff . . . . Traits of Effective Writing

- **REVIEW** "Original Word Choice" (HB 22) and "Using Strong, Colorful Words" (HB 135-136).
  READ the short paragraph below.
  Then **REWRITE** the paragraph and **REPLACE** some or all of the underlined words with more colorful, specific words and phrases. Make the paragraph as interesting and specific as you can.

  > The boy walked down the road. He was excited. The fair was in town, and he knew he would have fun. There were fun games, exciting rides, and strange animals at the fair. There was also food that tasted great. There were lots of people to watch, too.

All Dressed Up . . . . Writing with a Computer

- **CHOOSE** a lengthy essay or report that you have written. If it is not already saved on your computer, **ENTER** it.
  FORMAT your writing with a title and headings, page numbers, and any other special features, using "Designing Your Writing" as a guide (HB 27-29).
  WORK ON your design until it is just the way you like it. Then **PRINT OUT** your document.

Keyboard Fluent . . . . Writing with a Computer

- **STUDY** "Using a Word-Processing Program" (HB 30).
  Then **TRY OUT** the different commands and symbols that appear on the monitor when you start up the word-processing program on your computer.
  REFER to the program manual, or **ASK** someone for help if you're not sure how everything works.

Only the Best . . . . Developing a Portfolio

■ Do this minilesson near the end of the quarter or the semester.
   READ "A Showcase Portfolio" (HB 33).
   Then **LOOK** through your writing. In your class notebook, **LIST** at least three pieces that you would include in a showcase portfolio.
   WRITE a few sentences about each piece, telling why you chose it, what the piece says about you as a writer, what skills it shows off, and so on.

My, how I've grown. . . . . Developing a Portfolio

■ Do this minilesson near the end of the quarter or the semester.
   READ "A Growth Portfolio" (HB 33).
   COMPARE one or two pieces of writing that you completed earlier in the year to your most recent pieces.
   LIST ways your writing has improved, or at least changed. What new skills have I learned about? What new forms of writing have I learned? What do I still need to work on?

Learning the Ropes . . . . Publishing Your Writing

■ **READ** "Places to Publish" (HB 41).
   CHOOSE a contest or magazine to which you would like to submit your work.
   WRITE a letter requesting the writers' guidelines for the contest or magazine. In your letter, also ask how you can get a sample copy of the magazine or contest publication.
   REFER to 'Writing Business Letters " for help (HB 241-250).

Take it on-line. . . . . Publishing Your Writing

■ **READ** "Publishing On-Line" (HB 42).
   VISIT the Write Source Web site (**thewritesource.com**), and visit two of the sites that are listed that publish student writing.
   READ samples of published writing if they are included. Then **SUBMIT** a favorite piece of your writing for publication.

The end becomes the beginning..... Choosing a Subject

■ Do this minilesson with a classmate.
   READ "Sentence Completion" (HB 49).
   CHOOSE one open-ended sentence to complete in many different ways (at least 10).
   ALTERNATE responses with your partner, working from each other's ideas.
   CHECK one sentence that would make a good writing topic.

At the Starting Line .... Choosing a Subject

■ **REVIEW** "Sample Subjects" (HB 51).
   CREATE a cluster (HB 48) using one of the sample subjects as the nucleus word. **ADD** at least six details to your diagram.
   SCAN your cluster for a word or an idea that appeals to you.
   WRITE freely for 5 to 8 minutes exploring this idea.

Make a list. .... Gathering Details

■ One way to collect details for your writing is to make lists.
   THINK of a holiday that your family celebrates. This will be your subject. On a sheet of paper, **MAKE** two lists. One list will be all the things you already know about the subject. The other list will be all the questions you have about the subject. (How did this holiday get started?) The second list will tell you what you need to find out before you would begin writing about the subject.

Same and Different .... Gathering Details

■ **USE** a graphic organizer to gather your thoughts for writing.
   IMAGINE that you are going to write about how two places (two countries, two schools, etc.) are the same, and how they are different.
   GATHER details about your two subjects using a Venn diagram (HB 56).
   When you're finished, **FIND** a focus for your writing. For example, you may decide to stress one or two significant differences or similarities.

In Support . . . . Writing the First Draft

■ You will need an essay, a report, or some other longer piece of writing to complete this minilesson.
   READ "Types of Support" (HB 64).
   REVIEW your writing, noting the different types of support you used.
   As a class, **SHARE** different examples of support for discussion.

From Beginning to End . . . . Writing the First Draft

■ **SELECT** a writing sample in the handbook that you enjoy or find interesting.
   WRITE the following words—*Beginning, Middle,* and *Ending*—on a piece of paper, leaving space after each word to write two or three sentences.
   Then **ANALYZE** your sample, according to the effectiveness of the beginning, middle, and ending parts.
   MAKE your comments for each part on your paper.
   USE "Writing the First Draft" as a guide for your analysis (HB 63-66).

Hit the target. . . . . Revising Your Writing

■ **STUDY** "Five Keys to Good Revision" (HB 69) and pay special attention to "Picture your audience."
   LIST three different audiences for whom you might write.
   EXPLAIN the ways your writing would change for each audience.

Making Big Changes . . . . Revising Your Writing

■ You will need a first draft to complete this minilesson.
   As a class, **READ** and **DISCUSS** "A Link to the Traits" (HB 70-72).
   Then **REVIEW** and **REVISE** your first draft, focusing on the organization, ideas, and voice.
   SHARE the changes you've made with a classmate.

Any comments? . . . . Group Advising

■ Do this minilesson with two other students.
   STUDY "Making Helpful Responses" (HB 77).
   TURN to page 186 and read the sample story, "The Magic Coin."
   COMMENT on the story as if it had been written by a member of your group. Talk about what you like, what you think could be improved, what you have questions about, and so on.
   SUMMARIZE your responses in a brief paragraph.

In Response . . . . Group Advising

■ Do this minilesson with one or two other students, each with a piece of writing in progress.

    MAKE a copy of the response sheet (HB 78) on your own paper for each writer-reader in your group.

    TAKE TURNS reading and responding to each other's writing.

Afterward, **SHARE** your response sheets with the writers.

The Right Choice . . . . Editing and Proofreading

■ Do this minilesson with a partner, each with a revised piece of writing in hand.

Carefully, **STUDY** "Checking for Word Choice" (HB 82).

With your partner's help, **CHECK** your piece of writing for word choice.

    MAKE changes as needed.

Then **HELP** your partner check his or her writing in the same way.

Check it out! . . . . Editing and Proofreading

■ **FIND** a short piece of your writing that needs to be edited.

    USE "Editing and Proofreading Checklist" (HB 83) as a guide.

    MAKE your corrections, and **WRITE** a final copy.

Sentence Doctor . . . . Composing Sentences

■ Do this minilesson with a partner.

    STUDY "Sentence Fragment" (HB 86).

    WRITE six sentence fragments. Make sure that some of your fragments need a subject and some need a verb.

    TRADE fragments with your partner, and correct each other's work.

It's not definite. . . . . Composing Sentences

■ **READ** "Indefinite Pronouns" (HB 89).

    WRITE five sentences using these indefinite pronouns as the subjects: *each, everybody, all, any, none.* Make sure to use the correct verb form (singular or plural) to go with each subject.

    EXCHANGE your work with a partner, and **CHECK** the subject/verb agreement in each of your classmate's sentences.

Make it longer. Combining Sentences

- **SELECT** a piece of your writing to check for sentence smoothness.
  FIND some short sentences that could be combined into longer, smoother sentences.
  REWRITE your piece with these longer sentences.

Put them together. . . . . Combining Sentences

- Do this minilesson with a partner.
  STUDY "Combining with Key Words" (HB 94).
  WRITE five sets of "shorter sentences." Your sentences should follow the patterns of the sample sentences on page 94.
  TRADE sentences with your partner, and **COMBINE** each other's sentences.

Building Blocks . . . . Building Paragraphs

- **REVIEW** the parts of a paragraph (HB 99).
  PICK a topic that you know a lot about.
  WRITE a topic sentence for a paragraph about the topic following the formula in the handbook.
  LIST three or four details that support or explain your topic sentence. These details should make your topic clear and interesting.
  TURN each detail into a sentence for the body of your paragraph.
  Then **FORM** a closing sentence about your topic.

Match the topic to the type. . . . . Building Paragraphs

- **STUDY** the different types of paragraphs (HB 100-103).
  THINK OF one topic that you could write about for each kind of paragraph: *descriptive, narrative, expository,* and *persuasive.*
  WRITE a topic sentence for each paragraph.

For Starters . . . . Expository Essays

- **READ** "Starter Sentences" (HB 112).
   WRITE one starter sentence that follows each pattern given on page 112: *problem and solution, cause and effect, comparison and contrast,* and *before and after.* For ideas, think about things you have heard in the news and things that have happened in your school.
   As a class, **DISCUSS** some of your sentences.

Charting Your Course . . . . Expository Essays

- **READ** "Sample Expository Essay" (HB 108-109), and **STUDY** the line diagram (HB 110).
   Then **CREATE** your own line diagram in response to the following writing prompt:
   What four books would you recommend to all of your classmates?
   (Consider using the diagram as a starting point for an essay.)

I object! . . . . Persuasive Essays

- **READ** the sample persuasive essay (HB 116-117).
   In your class notebook, **LIST** three surprising or convincing details that the writer included.
   Also **LIST** any details that don't seem quite so convincing.
   DISCUSS your ideas with a classmate.

Keep on schooling? . . . . Persuasive Essays

- Do this minilesson with a classmate.
   STUDY the following opinion statement:
   Year-round schooling offers the best opportunities for students.
   LIST three important points in support of this opinion.
   Also **LIST** one or two important points against it.
   SHARE your ideas with a classmate.

Modeling a Master . . . . Writing with Style

■ **READ** "Modeling the Masters" (HB 132-133).
   FIND a short passage in one of your favorite books.
   WRITE your own passage modeled after the professional passage.

The Real You . . . . Writing with Style

■ **WRITE** freely about one of the worst days that you've experienced. (Write as if you were talking to a group of your classmates.)
   EXCHANGE your writing with a partner, and **UNDERLINE** or **CHECK** parts that sound natural in each other's work.
   SHARE particularly effective "natural writing" with the entire class.

Great Technique . . . . Writing Techniques and Terms

■ **REVIEW** "Writing Techniques" (HB 138-140).
   CHOOSE five writing techniques that are new to you.
   WRITE an example for each technique.
   Then **SHARE** your examples in a small group or with the class. See if others can identify the technique you were using.

Seeing is believing. . . . . . . Writing Techniques and Terms

■ **REVIEW** "Writing Terms" (HB 141-143).
   SELECT one term to illustrate. (You and your classmates should try to choose different terms.)
   USE the "brainstorming" illustration (HB 141) as a guide.
   SHARE your finished work with your classmates.

The Forms of Writing

The Time Machine . . . . Journal Writing

■ **READ** the description of a diary (HB 148).
WRITE a diary entry about yesterday or today. Do this before you read the next sentence in this minilesson!
Now . . . **IMAGINE** that you are your parents' age. Read the diary entry you just wrote.
Then **WRITE** a short paragraph telling your reactions to reading about yourself when you were a middle-school student.

Dear Diary . . . . Journal Writing

■ **READ** the description of a reader response journal (HB 148).
Then **READ** the sample phase biography, "My Grandpa's Story" (HB 166). Write a journal entry telling your feelings and reactions to this story.

Did you hear the one about . . . ? . . . . . . Friendly Letters

■ **REVIEW** the prewriting guidelines for a friendly letter (HB 152).
THINK of a friend or relative you would like to write to.
LIST the main ideas you want to include. Make sure to include a funny story or a joke!

You've got real mail! . . . . Friendly Letters

■ E-mail is faster, but letters still have some advantages. For one thing, it's fun to get letters in the mail. Also, letters are more personal, especially if they're handwritten. And you can include things in a letter, like a comic strip you cut out of the newspaper or a bookmark you made.
THINK of five people who would like to get a letter from you. (If you need help, ask your parents for ideas.)
For each person, **LIST** one thing you would want to tell him or her in a letter, and one thing you could include with the letter.

I'll never forget . . . 1 . . . . Autobiographical Writing

■ **READ** the prewriting guidelines (HB 155).
  Then **READ** the sample personal narrative, "Splash Mountain" (HB 154).
  THINK of an event in your life that was important or memorable. It should
    be a very short event (15 minutes or less).
  MAKE a "quick list" of facts and feelings about the event.

I'll never forget . . . 2 . . . . Autobiographical Writing

■ Do this minilesson as a follow-up to "I'll never forget . . . 1."
  READ "Knowing Where to Begin" (HB 157).
  LOOK over the quick list you made in the last minilesson.
  CHOOSE the fact or feeling you could use to begin a narrative.
  TURN the fact or feeling into a beginning sentence.

Subject Gathering . . . . Biographical Writing

■ **STUDY** the "Gathering Details" chart (HB 163).
  LIST four potential subjects for biographical stories. One subject should be
    very well known to you; the next one should be somewhat known to you;
    the third should be little known to you; and the fourth, a famous person.
  Then **IDENTIFY** one or two sources of information next to each subject.

Who's who in my life? . . . . Biographical Writing

■ **READ** "Writing Tips" (HB 165).
  THINK of a person you know well and would like to write about.
  WRITE four sentences you could include in a biography of that person: one
    sentence that tells why you chose this person to write about, one sentence
    that gives physical details, one sentence that tells the person's thoughts
    or feelings about something, and one sentence of background information.

Give me the facts. . . . . Writing News Stories

■ To do this minilesson, you'll need a copy of your school newspaper or the local
  news section of a newspaper.
    On a sheet of paper, **DRAW** three 5 W's charts (HB 170).
    READ three articles on the front page of the newspaper.
    For each article, **FILL IN** one of your 5 W's charts, listing the important facts.

Just give the news. .... Writing News Stories

■ To do this minilesson, you'll need a copy of your school newspaper or the local news section of a newspaper.

READ the most important news story (It is probably at or near the top of the first page and has a big headline.)

On a sheet of paper, **WRITE** the headings *Timeliness, Importance, Local Angle,* and *Human Interest.* Leave a few lines between the headings.

After each heading, **WRITE** a sentence or two telling how the news story measures up. Tell how timely it is, and what details in the story tell you this. Tell how important it is, and what details tell you this. And so on.

Great Plot, Mr. Dickens .... Writing About Literature

■ **REVIEW** "Finding an Idea" (HB 176).

THINK of your favorite novel or short story.

CHOOSE one of the four elements of literature from page 176.

WRITE a paragraph about that element in the story you chose. Use the points listed on page 176 as guidelines.

(If you don't know a story well enough to do this from memory, read a short story and then write about it.)

Just Like in Real Life .... Writing About Literature

■ **READ** "Responding in a Journal" (HB 180).

THINK of a character in a novel or short story who was like you in some way, or who had an experience similar to one of your own.

EXPLORE the connection between the character and you in a journal entry.

Create a Frankenstein. .... Writing Stories

■ **READ** "Create a Character" under "Prewriting" (HB 188).

CREATE a main character for a story by combining traits from three different people. One person should be a friend of yours. The second person should be someone from history. The third person should be a celebrity, such as a movie star or an athlete.

WRITE down the three people's names. Under each name, list at least five details about that person's appearance, personality, behavior, talents, problems, and so on.

Then **PICK** any combination of details to create your character.

LIST all the traits you will give your character.

Finally, based on his or her traits, **GIVE** your character a name.

It's a fight! . . . . Writing Stories

■ **READ** "Form a Conflict" under "Prewriting" (HB 188).
  WRITE down the titles of three novels and/or short stories you have read
    and remember well. (You may include movies, too.)
  Next to each title, **WRITE** a sentence telling the main conflict in the story.
    Be specific. (For example, the conflict in the short story "Amigo Brothers"
    by Piri Thomas is between two friends who must fight each other in an
    important boxing match.)
  Use these ideas to help you form a conflict for a story of your own.

Toot your horn. . . . . Writing Poetry

■ **THINK** of a musical instrument.
  LIST at least 20 words related to the instrument—words about what it
    looks like, what it sounds like, and so on.
  USE these words in a free-verse poem about the instrument. Use at least
    one example of onomatopoeia.
  Here's where to find help: Check out the sample free-verse poem (HB 200),
    the definition of free verse (HB 205), and the definition of onomatopoeia
    (HB 203).

A Snake-Shaped Poem . . . . Writing Poetry

■ **READ** the definition of concrete poetry (HB 206).
  WRITE a concrete poem about a snake or other animal.

What's the sense of it? . . . . . Writing Observation Reports

■ **REVIEW** "Gathering Details" (HB 211).
  MAKE a Five Senses Organizer on a sheet of paper.
  THINK of your favorite holiday.
  FILL in the organizer with the sights, sounds, smells, tastes, and textures
    that are part of your favorite holiday.

Look at that! . . . . Writing Observation Reports

- **OBSERVE** a person or an animal for 10 minutes. (If you're observing a person, get permission first.)
  TAKE NOTES about everything the person or animal does.
  As soon as 10 minutes is up, **REVIEW** your notes.
  TURN them into complete sentences using lots of specific, active verbs to describe the actions you observed.

It's about buffalo. . . . . Writing Summaries

- **STUDY** the "Writing Guidelines" and "Sample Summary" (HB 214-215).
  READ "The Return of the Buffalo" (HB 28-29).
  WRITE a summary of the excerpt from that research paper.

In Your Own Words . . . . Writing Summaries

- **STUDY** "Paraphrasing" (HB 216).
  READ the sample paragraph about John Sutter (HB 285).
  WRITE a paraphrase of the paragraph.
  Afterward, **REVISE** it, following the guidelines on page 216.

Ten Wonders of Your World . . . . Writing Personal Research Reports

- **REVIEW** "Prewriting—Choosing a Subject" (HB 220).
  MAKE a list of 10 "I wonder" questions.
  PUT a check next to the questions that interest you the most.

Go to your corner. . . . . Writing Personal Research Reports

- Do this minilesson as a follow-up to "Ten Wonders of Your World."
  STUDY "Organize with a Grid" (HB 221).
  DRAW a grid on a sheet of paper. Include the numbers 1 through 4 and the headings *What I Knew, What I Wanted to Know, What I Found Out,* and *What I Learned.*
  CHOOSE one of the "I wonder" questions you wrote.
  FILL IN parts 1 and 2 of your grid using your "I wonder" question as your topic.
  If you have time, do some research and fill in parts 3 and 4 of your grid.

Why is this here? . . . . Writing Research Papers

- **READ** "Questions to Consider" (HB 227).
  COPY the four questions on a sheet of paper. Leave several lines between questions.
  READ the sample research paper, "*Mir* Flies on for the Next Generation" (HB 233-234).
  After each question you copied, **LIST** some details from the research paper that answer the question. For example, after "Who am I writing for?" you might list your classmates or even Captain Kirk. These details were probably included because the author knew readers would be familiar with *Star Trek*. After "What do they want to know?" you might write that life on *Mir* isn't glamorous.

To Put It Another Way . . . . Writing Research Papers

- **READ** the sample research paper, "*Mir* Flies on for the Next Generation" (HB 233-234). Matt Korman wrote this paper for his classmates and teacher.
  IMAGINE that you are Matt and you are going to share your paper with your neighbor, an elderly man who immigrated to the United States from Russia. Your neighbor has never heard of Captain Kirk and the *USS Enterprise,* so you need to write a new beginning for your paper.
  WRITE a beginning paragraph that will be clear and interesting to your neighbor. You may use information that now comes later in the paper, or think of a completely new beginning.

Don't forget to say thanks. . . . Writing in the Workplace

- **REVIEW** "Traits of Good Workplace Writing" (HB 240).
  THINK of someone in your school who has been especially helpful to you.
  WRITE a thank-you letter or an e-mail message to that person.
  CHECK your writing for the traits listed on page 240.

Mission Accomplished . . . . Writing in the Workplace

- **REVIEW** "Traits of Good Workplace Writing" (HB 240).
  WRITE a brief summary report of a class project or field trip, or of a project you did on your own.
  ASK a classmate to review your summary for the traits.

Dear Sir .... Writing Business Letters

- **REVIEW** "Writing Business Letters" (HB 241-250). Pay special attention to "Sample Request Letter" (HB 248).
    - **CHOOSE** a government agency that you would like information about (the National Park Service, the FBI, NASA, the Coast Guard, etc.).
    - **WRITE** a letter requesting information about the agency. Be specific in the information you ask for.
    - **GET** the agency's address from an almanac or the Internet.
    - **ADDRESS** and **MAIL** your letter.
    - **SHARE** with the class the information you receive.

Satisfaction Guaranteed .... Writing Business Letters

- **REVIEW** "Writing Business Letters" (HB 241-250). Pay special attention to "Sample Letter Stating a Problem" (HB 249).
    - **THINK** of a product you bought that you were unhappy with.
    - **WRITE** a letter to the manufacturer of the product to express your complaint. Make sure to give all the important details: what the product is, when and where you bought it, what the problem is, and so on. Also, make sure to say what action you want the manufacturer to take. Do you want a replacement, a refund, a repair, or something else?
    - **GET** the address of the company from the packaging of the product or from the Internet.
    - **MAIL** your letter.

You need to know. ... Special Forms of Workplace Writing

- **REVIEW** "Writing Guidelines: Memos" and "Sample Memo" (HB 252-253).
    - **WRITE** a memo informing a secretary, a counselor, a custodian, a bus driver, or an aide about something he or she needs to know. This could be an important question or concern, a reminder, a thank-you, an update, and so on.
    - **REVIEW** your memo and then consider delivering it.

In a Minute .... Special Forms of Workplace Writing

- **REVIEW** "Writing Guidelines: Minutes" and "Sample Minutes" (HB 256-257).
    - **TAKE** notes on a conversation other people are having at home or at school. (Ask permission first!)
    - **WRITE** up your notes in the form of minutes.

The Tools of Learning

From the Horse's Mouth .... Types of Information

- **REVIEW** "Primary vs. Secondary Information Sources" and "Types of Primary Sources" (HB 262-263).
    IMAGINE that you want to do a research project on raising horses.
    LIST five sources that could provide information on your topic. Include at least one primary source. For secondary sources, list title and author. You may need to check your library or the Internet to locate sources.

List of Books .... Types of Information

- In your classroom or library, or at home, **FIND** a biography of someone you are interested in. Make sure the biography you choose has a bibliography. (Refer to handbook pages 230 and 281 for more about bibliographies.)
    STUDY the bibliography. **WRITE DOWN** six sources of information including, if possible, at least three primary sources.
    In a few sentences, **EXPLAIN** why primary sources are important to a biographer.

On the Web .... Using the Internet

- On the Internet, **KEY IN** the Write Source Web site at **thewritesource.com**.
    EXPLORE the site.
    Then **WRITE DOWN** three spots on the site that will be helpful to you.
    SHARE your findings with your classmates.

See Hunt .... Using the Internet

- **REVIEW** "Searching for Information" and "Word-Searching Guide" (HB 270-271).
    FIND two different search engines on the Internet. (You could search **www.yahoo.com** and **www.excite.com**, or any two search engines you choose.)
    Using both search engines, **LOOK** for information on a topic you are studying or are just interested in. Use the same keywords both times.
    WRITE DOWN the Internet address of the first site listed by each search engine. **VISIT** these two sites, and decide which one is more helpful.

It has to be here somewhere. . . . . Using the Library

- **REVIEW** "Searching for Information," "Using the Card Catalog," and "Using the Computer Catalog" (HB 274-276).

    THINK OF a career you are interested in.

    USE your library's catalog to find at least five books (or other sources) that would be helpful in researching the career you chose.

    For each source, **WRITE** down the title, the name of the author, and the call number.

    If you have time, **FIND** these sources and learn more about the career.

Hide and Seek . . . . Using the Library

- Do this minilesson with a partner.

    REVIEW "Finding Books" (HB 277).

    In your library, **FIND** five books, one each from five different classes of the Dewey decimal system.

    WRITE the title of each book and the author on an index card. (You'll have five separate index cards.)

    EXCHANGE cards with your partner.

    Using the card catalog, **LOOK UP** the books your partner wrote down, and **WRITE DOWN** their call numbers.

    FIND each book in the library.

A Matter of Chance . . . . Thinking and Writing

- **READ** the sample paragraph (HB 287).

    Then **MAKE** and **FILL IN** a Venn diagram to help you organize your thoughts about the subject of the writing. (See handbook page 313 for help.)

What next? . . . . Thinking and Writing

- **READ** the sample paragraph (HB 285).

    Then **WRITE** a diary entry as if you were John Sutter. Tell what you have decided to do now that the gold rush has forced you to leave your farm. Where will you go? How will you earn a living? Use what you know about Sutter to help you predict what he might do.

    Note: The paragraph gives you the information for area 3 in your diagram. You must decide for yourself what to include in areas 1 and 2.

In My Opinion .... Thinking Logically

- **STUDY** "Using Logic to Persuade" (HB 292-293).
    Then **WRITE** an opinion statement about a specific place plus at least two or three supporting facts.
    EXCHANGE your work with a partner, and **CHECK** the effectiveness of each other's opinion and supporting facts.

Let's get fuzzy. .... Thinking Logically

- Do this minilesson with a partner.
    READ "Avoiding Fuzzy Thinking" (HB 294-295).
    WRITE a new example for each kind of fuzzy thinking. Here's an example of a statement that jumps to a conclusion:
        Because cars sometimes run into each other, cars should be outlawed.
    SHARE your results.

Be creative. .... Thinking Better

- **READ** "Becoming a Better Thinker" (HB 298).
    For one day, **DO** everything differently from the way you normally do it. Start with the way you get out of bed in the morning. Find some new twist for different things you do during the day.
    At the end of the day (or the next morning), **WRITE** a journal entry telling your reactions to your experiences. Did you learn anything? Did you have more fun than usual?

Good move! .... Thinking Better

- **REVIEW** "Basic Writing and Thinking Moves" (HB 299).
    On a sheet of paper, **LIST** at least three "moves" (*observe, gather, question,* etc.) that you are good at.
    Then **LIST** at least three "moves" that you seldom use, or that are hard for you.
    ASK a classmate or friend to help you brainstorm ways to get better at the kinds of thinking that are hard for you. (Check your handbook's table of contents and index for more ideas.)

That's "chartable." . . . . Reading Charts

- Do this minilesson with a partner.
  REVIEW the opening page of "Reading Charts" (HB 301).
  LIST two ideas for charts concerning the students in your school. As a class, **EVALUATE** each group's ideas.

Line up. . . . . Reading Charts

- **STUDY** "Line Diagram" (HB 306).
  TURN to page 110 to see another example of a line diagram.
  Now **TURN** to the chapter "Building Paragraphs" (HB 97-106).
  Use the information in this chapter to help you **MAKE** a line diagram showing the four types of paragraphs. Include in your diagram one or two details about each type of paragraph.

Setting a Table . . . . Study-Reading Skills

- **REVIEW** the main idea/supporting details pattern of nonfiction (HB 310-311).
  READ "Sample Expository Paragraph" (HB 102).
  Then **FILL IN** a table organizer for the information in the sample paragraph. (Include just the essential or important details in your organizer.)

It's very hot there. . . . . Study-Reading Skills

- **STUDY** "KWL" (HB 321).
  MAKE a KWL chart on a sheet of paper.
  WRITE "The Sun" at the top of your chart; this will be your topic.
  FILL IN the "K" and "W" columns of your chart.
  READ the sample essay answer (HB 380).
  FILL IN the "L" column of your chart.

Keep griddle cakes off gridirons. . . . . Improving Your Vocabulary

- **REVIEW** "Checking a Dictionary" and "Model Dictionary Page" (HB 326-327).
  READ the definitions of all the entry words shown on the model dictionary page.
  WRITE a sentence using five of the entry words correctly. (Skip the two entry words that are people's names.)

Root got you stumped? . . . . . . Improving Your Vocabulary

- Do this minilesson with a partner.
  STUDY the roots that refer to "The Human Body" (HB 339).
  COPY five roots listed in the chart onto a sheet of paper.
  Next to each root, **WRITE** a word that is formed from it. (*Dentist* is formed from *dent*.)
  USE the dictionary if you need help. (Make sure you know the meaning of each word you list.)

Ups and Downs of Fiction . . . . . Understanding Literature

- **STUDY** "How Stories Develop" (HB 184-185).
  On a sheet of paper, **DRAW** a large plot line.
  CHOOSE a short piece of fiction that you like—a short story, fable, myth, etc.
  IDENTIFY the important points on your plot line. For example, write a sentence summarizing the exposition, a few sentences describing the rising action, and so on.

Book Talk . . . . Understanding Literature

- Do this minilesson in a group of three or four.
  READ "Discussing Literature: A Book Group" (HB 345).
  THINK of a short story or novel you have all read. (If you can't think of one, read "The Magic Coin" on handbook pages 186-187.)
  DISCUSS the story or novel, using the questions on page 345 as a guide.

Talk to me! . . . . Preparing a Speech

- **READ** "An Attention-Getting Beginning" (HB 350).
  READ the model speech, "Lord Aaron's Castle" (HB 353).
  Do you think Aaron chose the best information to begin his speech? Even if your answer is yes . . .
  WRITE a new beginning for the speech. Use information that appears in the speech, or something you know about castles. Make sure your beginning gets attention. (See handbook pages 10-11 for more information about castles.)

Performance Tips . . . . Preparing a Speech

■ **LIST** at least five things you should do when you give a speech.
Then **REFER** to the tips under "Give Your Speech" (HB 354).
ADD to your list as necessary after reviewing these tips. Use your list as a guide when you give your next speech.

I witness the news. . . . . Viewing Skills

■ **REVIEW** "Watching the News" (HB 356-357). Pay special attention to "Watch for Correctness."
WATCH a national or local news program on television.
As you watch, **TAKE NOTES.** Jot down a few main ideas highlighting the subject of two news stories. Then **WRITE** whether you think each story is *final* (meaning that all the facts are in) or *developing* (more facts will become available).
WATCH the same news program for the next few days, to see how the stories develop.

TV Time . . . . Viewing Skills

■ Do this minilesson with a partner.
REVIEW "Watching Commercials" (HB 360).
IMAGINE that you are in charge of creating a commercial to sell a new kind of candy bar.
CHOOSE one of the four types of commercials.
BRAINSTORM for an idea for your commercial.
WRITE a paragraph telling what would happen in your commercial.

Make a note of it. . . . . Classroom Skills

■ Do this minilesson with a partner.
STUDY "Taking Reading Notes" (HB 364).
SELECT one page from a social studies or science book that each of you will read and take notes on.
FOLLOW the handbook tips as closely as you can.
Afterward, **COMPARE** notes to see how each of you did.

Logging On .... Classroom Skills

- **REVIEW** the guidelines for keeping a learning log (HB 366).
  Then **RECORD** your reactions to one of your classes for a week: What did
    you do? What did you learn? What ideas do you have for tomorrow's
    assignment?
  At the end of the week, **EVALUATE** the log's usefulness.

What's the story? .... Group Skills

- Do this minilesson in a group of three or four.
  REVIEW "Skills for Listening" (HB 370).
    Have one group member **TELL** a funny or strange story about something
      that has happened to her or him.
    Then have the next group member **RETELL** the story from memory.
  REPEAT this until all members of the group have retold the story.
  DISCUSS how the story changed from one member to the next.

Everybody listen! .... Group Skills

- Suppose you are the secretary for your school's student council. Also suppose
  your group, like many groups, is having a hard time getting anything
  accomplished because everybody talks and nobody listens.
  STUDY the guidelines for group skills (HB 369-372).
    Quickly **REVIEW** the guidelines for writing summaries (HB 213-215).
    WRITE a summary of "Group Skills" to submit to your student council as a
      recommendation.

Ask me anything. .... Taking Tests

- **REVIEW** "Understand the Question" (HB 377).
    CHOOSE four of the key words, and **LIST** them on a sheet of paper.
    For each key word, **WRITE** an essay-test question related to a subject you
      are studying in your language class. **DISCUSS** the questions as a class.

Be prepared! . . . . Taking Tests

■ Do this minilesson with a partner a few days before a major test.
   TURN to "Preparing for a Test" and "Taking a Test" (HB 374).
   One of you **READ** "Preparing . . ." out loud while the partner listens. Then,
      SWITCH roles for "Taking a Test."
   As a class, **DISCUSS** all of the points covered in the reading.

Time is on my side. . . . . Planning Skills

■ **REVIEW** "Planning Your Time" (HB 383).
   Then **CREATE** a weekly planner in your class notebook and **FILL** it **IN** for
      one week.
   As a class, **DISCUSS** the results of your planning at the end of the week.

Make it easy on yourself. . . . . Planning Skills

■ **STUDY** "Completing Assignments" (HB 384).
   USE the guidelines to create your own personal study plan.

Proofreader's Guide

Here a Dot, There a Dot . . . . Periods

- **REVIEW** the four ways to use periods (HB 387).
  WRITE two sentences that each use periods in all four ways: at the end of a sentence, after an initial, after an abbreviation, and as a decimal.

Long List, Short Words . . . . Periods

- Do this minilesson with a partner.
  REVIEW the information on using periods after abbreviations (HB 387.3).
  LIST as many abbreviations as you can.
  FIND at least four different uses of abbreviations by skimming your textbooks.
  WRITE down each example, and **SHARE** them with the class.

Stop that snowboard. . . . . Commas

- **READ** about using commas to set off interruptions (HB 390.2).
  TURN to the sample expository paragraph, "Snowboarding" (HB 102).
  CHOOSE any four sentences in the paragraph, and **REWRITE** them, adding "interruptions." Your interruptions can say anything you like; just make sure to use commas correctly. For example, here is the first sentence of the paragraph with an added interruption:

  > "Snowboarding, *as you may know*, is one of the most popular and exciting winter sports in America."

The Old Comma-and-Conjunction Caper . . . . Commas

- **READ** about using commas between two independent clauses (HB 391.1).
  On a sheet of paper, **REWRITE** each pair of sentences below as one sentence. Use a comma and a coordinate conjunction (*and, but, or, for, nor, so, yet*) to combine the sentences.

  Sam has been waiting in the car. Linda is still inside getting ready.
  I eat a big breakfast. I always get hungry in the middle of the morning.
  It's almost completely dark. They're still trying to play baseball.
  Dad and Mom are still at work. I don't have anyone to help me.
  I could mow the lawn this afternoon. I could do it sometime tomorrow.

Get it together. . . . . Semicolons

■ **READ** about using a semicolon to join two independent clauses (HB 393.1).
Then **REWRITE** the following three compound sentences, using a semicolon
instead of a comma and conjunction to connect the two independent
clauses.

The Russian *Mir* space station is reality, and life there isn't glamorous.

The humid air makes molds grow, and the molds spoil the food.

The smell of gasoline hangs in the air, and food is served up freeze-dried.

I think; therefore, I am. . . . . Semicolons

■ **READ** about using semicolons with conjunctive adverbs (HB 393.3).
WRITE three sentences, each using a different conjunctive adverb. Make
sure to use semicolons (and commas) correctly in your sentences. Here is
one more example:

Many students do volunteer work; for example, Stuart visits a senior
residence.

Here's my question: Why?. . . . . Colons

■ **READ** about using a colon in a formal introduction (HB 394.2).
WRITE two sentences in which you formally introduce quotations from a
magazine or newspaper article. Make sure you use the colon correctly in
each sentence.

Sing, Dance, Howl at the Moon . . . . Colons

■ **READ** about using a colon to introduce a list (HB 394.5).
Then **WRITE** two sentences, introducing a list in each one. In your first
sentence, introduce three things that you like to do, and in your second
sentence, introduce three things you hate to do.
SHARE your sentences with a classmate.

What kind of question is that? .... Question Marks

- **READ** about using question marks (HB 398).
  WRITE two sentences that are direct questions, and two that are indirect questions. Make sure to use the correct end punctuation.

I wonder what she wrote. .... Question Marks

- Do this minilesson with a partner.
  READ about using question marks to show doubt (HB 398.3).
  Then **WRITE** two predictions in which you show doubt about the correctness of a fact or figure by using a question mark within parentheses.

"I disagree," I wrote. .... Quotation Marks

- **READ** about using quotation marks to set off direct quotations (HB 399.1).
  Then **TURN** to "The American Dream?" (HB 116-117).
  IMAGINE that you are reviewing Sally Dickerson's essay. You want to quote a few sentences from her essay.
  CHOOSE three sentences that seem especially important to quote.
  WRITE them on a sheet of paper, using quotation marks correctly.

  Example: Sally Dickerson wrote, "Because we are so attracted to the automobile, we too easily overlook its dangers."

"A Poem" .... Quotation Marks

- **READ** about using quotation marks to punctuate titles (HB 400.3).
  WRITE sentences containing the name of a song, a poem, a short story, a magazine article, and a book chapter. You may put more than one title in a sentence if you like. Make sure to punctuate the titles correctly.

Bird's-Eye View . . . . Capitalization

■ **REVIEW** "Capitalize Geographic Names" (HB 405.2).
  WRITE a brief paragraph about a flock of geese migrating from Canada to the Gulf of Mexico along the Central Flyway. (The Central Flyway is a wide band that runs north and south from western Canada to the western part of the Gulf of Mexico.) **MENTION** at least four or five of the provinces, states, cities, bodies of water, and other geographic landmarks the geese will fly over. For help, refer to the map on page 494 in your handbook. Your paragraph can be serious (telling facts about geese) or silly (for example, telling the geese's comments about the places they fly over).
Make sure to use capital letters correctly.

Capitalization 101 . . . . Capitalization

■ **STUDY** the "Capitalize/Do Not Capitalize" chart (HB 407).
  CLOSE your handbook.
  WRITE two sentences using each of the following words: *west, middle school, president,* and *earth.* In the first sentence, use the word in such a way that it needs to be capitalized. In the second sentence, use the word so that it doesn't need to be capitalized.

How many were there? . . . . Plurals

■ **REVIEW** the guidelines for "Plurals" (HB 408-409).
  CLOSE your handbook.
  On a sheet of paper, **WRITE** the plurals of these words:

  thief, country, spy, turkey, woman, deer, echo, fox, cupful

  OPEN your handbook to "Plurals" to check your work.

The chase is on. . . . . Plurals

■ **REVIEW** the guidelines for "Plurals" (HB 408-409).
  WRITE a paragraph about a dog chasing a cat through a neighborhood. In your paragraph, **USE** the plural forms of at least seven of these words.

  piano, sofa, tree, hedge, box, torch, bunny, patio, bucketful, leaf

Say it shorter. . . . . Abbreviations

- **STUDY** the guidelines for "Abbreviations" (HB 409).
  CLOSE your handbook.
  On a sheet of paper, **MAKE** three columns. **LABEL** the first column with *Abbreviations,* the second with *Acronyms,* and the third with *Initialisms.*
  Then **LIST** as many of each as you can within the time established by your teacher. (You can refer to any resource other than your handbook.)
  Afterward **SHARE** your work with your classmates to see who has the largest lists.

Where are we? . . . . Abbreviations

- **LOOK OVER** the "State Abbreviations" and "Address Abbreviations" (HB 247). Pay special attention to the postal abbreviations. Notice that they are in all capital letters and don't use periods.
  CLOSE your handbook.
    On a sheet of paper, **WRITE** the postal abbreviations for the following: Alabama, Alaska, Mississippi, Missouri, Nebraska, Nevada, Pennsylvania, Street, Road

  OPEN your handbook to page 247 and **CHECK** your work. **CORRECT** any errors you made.

You win! . . . . Numbers

- **REVIEW** the guidelines for "Numbers" (HB 410).
  WRITE an announcement for the newspaper indicating that you have just won the lottery. Include the following information: your name and age, your home address, the time you found out you won, the amount of money you won, and how much money you had before you won. Make sure to use numbers correctly.

Twenty 20-Page Stories . . . . Numbers

- **REVIEW** "Numerals in Compound Modifiers" (HB 410.6).
  WRITE three sentences like the example sentences in the handbook, using numbers before compound modifiers that also include numbers. (Your sentences could be about how many books you have read, stories you have written, and so on.) Use numbers correctly.

What's that spell? .... Spelling

■ **STUDY** "*i* before *e*" (HB 411.1). **MEMORIZE** the entire rule.
CLOSE your handbook.
On a sheet of paper, **WRITE** the words below. **REPLACE** each dash with
either *ie* or *ei*, whichever is correct. (All the words follow the rule!)
bel—ve, rec—ve, gr—f, fr—ght, dec—ve, fr—nd, rev—w, hyg—ne,
l—utenant, conc—t
OPEN your handbook to 411.1 to check your work against the rule and
examples. If you're still not sure about some words, look them up in a
dictionary.

Exception or Rule? .... Spelling

■ **STUDY** "Silent *e*," "Words Ending in *y*," and "Consonant Ending"
(HB 411.2 - 411.4).
CLOSE your handbook.
WRITE the "ing" form for the following words:
hurry, dribble, run, drive, tan, study, control, propose, play

How do you spell that? .... Using the Right Word

■ Do this minilesson with a partner.
OPEN your handbook to "Using the Right Word" (HB 419).
STUDY the pair "already, all ready" (HB 419.7).
Separately, you and your partner each **WRITE** one sentence using "already"
or "all ready."
READ your sentence to your partner, and have your partner **WRITE** down
"already" or "all ready," whichever is correct.
Then **LISTEN** as your partner reads his or her sentence, and you **WRITE**
down "already" or "all ready," whichever is used in the sentence.
CHECK each other's work.
DO the same for some of the following pairs of words:

accept, except (HB 419.2)	base, bass (HB 421.4)
affect, effect (HB 419.3)	brake, break (HB 422.2)
allowed, aloud (HB 419.4)	capital, capitol (HB 422.8)
altogether, all together (HB 420.1)	coarse, course (HB 423.4)

Go climb a rainbow. . . . . Sentences

■ **STUDY** "Parts of a Sentence" (HB 434.2 - 435.7)
   WRITE three simple sentences (HB 437.3) about one of your favorite relatives.
   In each sentence, **DRAW** a line between the complete subject and complete predicate, and **UNDERLINE** the simple subject and the simple predicate (verb).
   SHARE your work with a classmate, and **CHECK** each other's sentences for the correct markings.

Be direct. . . . . Sentences

■ **READ** "Direct Object" (HB 435.8).
   WRITE a sentence using each verb below followed by a direct object.
   Then **CIRCLE** each direct object.

   verbs: called, fried, washed, painted, built

   SHARE your work with a classmate. Make sure your partner's sentences do, in fact, each contain a direct object.

They're depending on you. . . . . Clauses

■ **STUDY** "Independent and Dependent Clauses" (HB 436.3).
   FIND three sentences anywhere in your handbook that contain independent and dependent clauses. **COPY** these sentences on a sheet of paper, and **UNDERLINE** the dependent clauses in each one.
   Then **WRITE** a sentence of your own that contains a dependent clause.

Three Phrases, Please . . . . Phrases

■ **REVIEW** "Clauses" and "Phrases" (HB 436.3 - 437.2).
   Then **LIST** the following groups of words on a piece of paper:

> if only I had known
> after we started lunch
> in the cafeteria
> under my bologna sandwich
> I found a dead fly
> at that point
> food didn't appeal to me

   IDENTIFY each word group as a clause or a phrase.
   COMPARE responses with a classmate.

That's simple. . . . . Types of Sentences

- **STUDY** "Types of Sentences" (HB 437.3 - 438.2).
   Then **WRITE** freely for 5 minutes about the hardest thing you have done.
   PUT a star (✱) in front of any simple sentences in your writing, a check (✔)
      in front of any compound sentences, a dot (•) in front of any complex
      sentences, and a plus (✚) in front of any compound-complex sentences.
   Only **MARK** the sentences you are sure of.
   SHARE your writing with a classmate; **CHECK** the accuracy of each
      other's markings.

You've got class. . . . . Kinds of Sentences

- **REVIEW** "Kinds of Sentences" (HB 438.3 - 438.6).
   WRITE one sentence of each kind. All your sentences should be about your
      class.
   SHARE your writing with a classmate.

Person, Place, and Thing . . . . Nouns

- **REVIEW** "Kinds of Nouns" (HB 439).
   LIST these nouns on a piece of paper:

      courage
      C. S. Lewis
      raisins
      honor
      Ford
      Islam

   IDENTIFY each noun as proper or common and concrete or abstract.
   ADD and **LABEL** four additional nouns.

Types of Gender . . . . Nouns

- Do this minilesson with a partner.
   REVIEW "Gender of Nouns" (HB 440.4).
   On a sheet of paper, **MAKE** four columns. **LABEL** them *Feminine,*
      Masculine, Neuter, and *Indefinite.*
   COPY the example words from your handbook under the correct headings.
   Then **ADD** as many more words to each column as you can within a period
      of time established by your teacher.
   When you finish, **COMPARE** your lists with those made by other students.

This is fun! . . . . Pronouns

- **STUDY** "Demonstrative Pronouns" (HB 444.3).

  LOOK at the list of demonstrative pronouns in the "Kinds of Pronouns" chart (445.2).

  WRITE four sentences, each one using a different demonstrative pronoun.

  Then **WRITE** one sentence using both *this* and *that,* and another sentence using both *these* and *those.*

And on Your Right . . . . Pronouns

- **REVIEW** the "Kinds of Pronouns" chart (HB 445.2).

  Now **SUPPOSE** you landed a job as a tour guide who has to show international visitors all the fascinating sights in your own bedroom. It's your first day of work, and you need to practice.

  WRITE down a first draft of your "talk."

  USE at least one relative, interrogative, demonstrative, intensive, and indefinite pronoun.

  TRADE papers with someone and challenge him or her to find an example of each different kind of pronoun.

Whodunit? . . . . Verbs

- **REVIEW** "Voice of Verbs" (HB 447.2 - 447.3).

  On a sheet of paper, **REWRITE** the sentences below, changing them from the active to the passive voice. The first one has been done for you.

ACTIVE	PASSIVE
I am eating the ice cream.	The ice cream is being eaten by me.
Larry is washing the car.	
Sasha is watering the flowers.	
Moondog is chewing Dad's shoe.	
Kylie is riding Mark's bike.	

  (In most cases, use active voice in your writing. It makes your writing sound more direct and forward moving.)

Munchies .... Verbs

■ **REVIEW** the sections on verb tenses (HB 448.1 - 448.6)—present, past, future, present perfect, past perfect, and future perfect.
THINK about the food you eat.
WRITE sentences about three days' worth of meals and snacks.
START your sentences with the following phrases and **USE** the appropriate verb tense:

> By yesterday noon,
> Yesterday,
> Since yesterday,
> Today,
> Tomorrow,
> Already by noon tomorrow

Describe it for me. .... Adjectives

■ **STUDY** "Adjective" (HB 451.4 - 452.5).
Then **READ** the descriptive paragraph "Rainbow Rock" (HB 100).
Afterward, **REVIEW** the following words that come from the paragraph:

huge	red	tricky	goat
rises	each	tiny	artificial
above	anybody	It	courage

On a sheet of paper, **WRITE DOWN** the words from the list that are adjectives.
Special Challenge: **IDENTIFY** the two compound adjectives in the paragraph.

Beyond Awesome, Different, and Cool .... Adjectives and Adverbs

■ **STUDY** the positive, comparative, and superlative forms of adjectives (HB 453.1 - 453.3) and adverbs (HB 454.1).
THINK of three different things to compare—*three roller coasters, three movies, three flavors of pizza,* etc.
SUPPOSE a friend describes the three things as "awesome, more awesome, and most awesome."
Not satisfied, you **WRITE** your own critique of the three.
USE the three degrees of adjectives and adverbs effectively in your critique.

Mega-Yikes! . . . . Interjections

- **READ** "Interjection" (HB 453).
  IMAGINE that you are in your house, talking on the phone and looking out the window. Suddenly, Bigfoot crashes into your backyard. He's about 12 feet tall. He's eating things that aren't edible, he's breaking things that aren't breakable, he's roaring like a hundred lions, and then . . . he notices you and heads straight toward you.
  Now **IMAGINE** that you are describing this to your friend, who is on the other end of the phone.
  WRITE down what you would be saying to your friend. **USE** lots of interjections.
  SHARE your writing with a classmate.

A Very Busy Place . . . . Prepositions

- **REVIEW** "Preposition" (HB 455).
  GET a large sheet of paper.
  DRAW a large picture of your school. Then **DRAW** someone or something **above** your school, leaning **against** your school, going **around** your school, **behind** your school, **inside** your school, **in front of** your school, **on top of** your school, **outside** your school, and going **through** your school.
  Then **LABEL** each person or thing you drew with the preposition it illustrates.

One or the Other . . . . Conjunctions

- **REVIEW** "Conjunction" (HB 456). Pay attention to "Correlative Conjunction" (HB 456.2 and 456.4).
  WRITE six sentences, each one using a different correlative conjunction.

Student Almanac

Ancient Messages . . . . Language

- Do this minilesson with a partner.
  REVIEW "How to Write in Cuneiform" (HB 460).
  Cuneiform writing was used in ancient times in the Middle East. Letters were made by using the tip of a reed to scratch lines into wet clay. The tip was cut into a triangle shape to make wedge-shaped marks.
  WRITE a short message in cuneiform using pen and paper.
  TRADE papers with your partner, and **TRANSLATE** each other's messages.

And they called it . . . . Language

- **REVIEW** "English from Around the World" (HB 461).

  LIST these words on a sheet of paper:

  chow mein, cola, espresso, lacrosse, noodle, sauerkraut, yogurt

  Next to each word, **WRITE** the language you think it came from. Use the sound and spelling of the word and what you know about the food or animal to help you guess.
  USE a dictionary to check your guesses. **CHECK** the history of the word in brackets [ ].

A Noise of Kindergartners . . . . Science

- Do this minilesson with a partner.
  REVIEW "Animal Facts" (HB 465). Pay special attention to the terms in the "Group" column. Many of them are very colorful, aren't they?
  MAKE UP some colorful, descriptive terms for groups of people (*sixth graders, kindergartners, teachers, aunts, uncles,* and so on).
  MAKE a chart showing the groups and the names you made up for them.
  SHARE your chart with your classmates.

Beam me up, Ruthenium. . . . . Science

- **REVIEW** "Periodic Table of the Elements" (HB 466).
  FIND five names of elements that would make good first or last names for characters in a science-fiction story. (You add the other part of the name.)
  WRITE one sentence using each character's full name. You might, for example, describe the character or tell something the character did.

Triangle Terms . . . . Mathematics

- **READ** the definition of a triangle (HB 479).
  START a glossary of triangle terms.
  INCLUDE the four kinds of triangles shown under "triangle."
  ADD at least three additional terms related to triangles.
  CONTINUE adding to your list throughout the year.

Do you speak math? . . . . Mathematics

- You're the statistician for your baseball team. And six team members want to know their batting average. (They can't figure it out themselves.)
  STUDY the batting performances below for the six players:

Bobo	3 for 10 (3/10)	Mark	7 for 14 (7/14)
Duke	5 for 12 (5/12)	Sam	1 for 4 (1/4)
Bub	6 for 11 (6/11)	TUG	2 for 4 (2/4)

  DETERMINE the batting average for each batter.
  CHECK your work using the "Decimal Equivalents . . ." chart in the handbook (HB 474).

Mostly Better . . . . Computers

- **READ** the first paragraph in the section "Computers" (HB 483).
  WRITE a paragraph about the advantages and disadvantages of computers compared to other writing tools.

A New Kind of Bomb . . . . Computers

- Many computer terms are just new uses for old words.
  OPEN your handbook to "Computer Terms" (HB 486).
  STUDY the following terms: *bomb, bookmark, desktop, flame, mouse.*
  WRITE one sentence about each term, explaining why you think it was adopted as a computer term. For example, why is "mouse" a good term for the device you use to move the cursor?

All Over the Map . . . . Geography

- **USE** "Index to World Maps" (HB 503) to help you **FIND** these countries on the maps: Belize, Finland, Haiti, Iraq.
  WRITE a sentence describing each country's location (its continent or region, bodies of water that border it, and so on).

You are here. . . . . Geography

- **STUDY** "Latitude and Longitude" (HB 492).
  On the United States Map (HB 495), **FIND** the latitude and longitude of your city. If your city is not shown, use the nearest big city. **MAKE** an estimate of the latitude and longitude based on the nearest lines.
  WRITE the coordinates as numbers and letters. (Example: 50° N, 104° W)

Movin' on Up . . . . Government

- **REVIEW** "U.S. Presidents and Vice Presidents" (HB 510-511).
  LIST all the vice presidents who later became president.
  DETERMINE whether or not being vice president is a good way to prepare for being president.

It's your responsibility. . . . . Government

- Do this minilesson with a partner.
  STUDY "Individual Rights and Responsibilities" (HB 509).
  DISCUSS "American citizens must . . . " Do you think any of these responsibilities should be changed? Should responsibilities be added?
  You and your partner each **WRITE** a few sentences explaining any changes you think should be made. Make sure to tell what your reasons are.

Invention of the Century . . . . History

- **OPEN** your handbook to "Historical Time Line" (HB 515-525).
  REVIEW the "Science and Inventions" portion of the time line.
  For each century, **CHOOSE** the one invention that you think is most important.
  WRITE a sentence about each invention you chose, telling why you think it is the most important one for that period.

Big News! . . . . History

- Do this minilesson in a group of three or four.
  LOOK at the end of the historical time line (HB 525).
  As a group, **THINK** of some recent events that are important enough to add to the time line.
  Try to **AGREE** on one event that is most important.
  SHARE the event with your classmates.

Minilesson Answer Key

Get it together. (page 252)

The Russian *Mir* space station is reality; life there isn't glamorous.

The humid air makes molds grow; molds spoil the food.

The smell of gasoline hangs in the air; food is served up freeze-dried.

How many were there? (page 253)

thieves, countries, spies, turkeys, women, deer, echoes, foxes, cupfuls

Where are we? (page 254)

Alabama	AL	Alaska	AK
Mississippi	MS	Missouri	MO
Nebraska	NE	Nevada	NV
Pennsylvania	PA	Street	ST
Road	RD		

What's that spell? (page 255)

believe, receive, grief, freight, deceive, friend, review, hygiene, lieutenant, conceit

Exception or Rule? (page 255)

hurrying, dribbling, running, driving, tanning, studying, controlling, proposing, playing

Three Phrases, Please (page 256)

if only I had known - clause
after we started lunch - clause
in the cafeteria - phrase
under my bologna sandwich - phrase
I found a dead fly - clause
at that point - phrase
food didn't appeal to me - clause

Person, Place, and Thing (page 257)

courage - common, abstract
C. S. Lewis - proper, concrete
raisins - common, concrete
honor - common, abstract
Ford - proper, concrete
Islam - proper, abstract
(student adds four more nouns)

Whodunit? (page 258)

The car is being washed by Larry.
The flowers are being watered by Sasha.
Dad's shoe is being chewed by Moondog.
Mark's bike is being ridden by Kylie.

Describe it for me. (page 259)

huge, red, each, tricky, tiny, artificial
Compound adjectives:
    man-made, rock-climbing

And they called it . . . (page 261)

chow mein - Chinese
cola - African
espresso - Italian
lacrosse - French Canadian
noodle - German
sauerkraut - German
yogurt - Turkish

Do you speak math? (page 262)

.3000, .4167, .5455, .5000, .2500, .5000

Movin' on Up (page 263)

John Adams	Theodore Roosevelt
Thomas Jefferson	Calvin Coolidge
Martin Van Buren	Harry S. Truman
John Tyler	Richard M. Nixon
Millard Fillmore	Lyndon B. Johnson
Andrew Johnson	Gerald R. Ford
Chester A. Arthur	George Bush

Index

Abbreviations, 254
Across-the-curriculum
  writing, 148, 160-173
Activities,
✱ Enrichment, 34
  Getting started, 8-16
  Minilessons, 225-264
✱ Start-Up, 34
Adjectives, 259
Admit slips, 164
Adverbs, 259
Advising, group, 53, 230-231
Almanac, student
  reference, 143-144, 261-263
Analytical assessment, 178
Application letter, 167
Arts, writing, 168
Assessing writing, 175-192
Assessment rubrics, 180-186
  Descriptive writing, 183
  Expository writing, 82
  Narrative writing, 81
  Persuasive writing, 184
  Research writing, 186
  Story writing, 185
Assignments, designing, 171-173
Autobiographical
  writing, 77, 236

Basic elements of writing, 57-66
Biographical writing, 79, 236
Bio-poems, 164
Book review, 83, 237
Books,
  Making literature
  connections, 199-206
Brainstorming, 164
Building paragraphs, 61, 232
Building vocabulary, 213-214,
  245-246
Business letters, 99, 167, 241

Capitalization, 253
Chapter notes, 31-144
Character sketch, 79, 236
Charts, reading, 117, 245
Choosing a subject, 45, 229
Class minutes, 164
Classroom skills, 129, 247-248
Clauses, 256
Closing paragraphs, 50
Clustering, 164
Collaborative learning, 209-210
Colons, 251
Combining sentences, 59, 232
Commas, 250
Complaint, letters of, 241
Completions, 164
Composing sentences, 57, 231
Computers, writing with, 39,
  227, 262
Conference guidelines, 177, 187
Conferences,
  Desk-side, 177
  Scheduled, 177
  Small-group, 177
Conjunctions, 260
Context, 213
Correct word, using, 255
Correcting spelling, 216
Correspondence, 164
Creative,
  Definitions, 164
  Writing, 20
Critical reading skills, 119, 194,
  196, 245
Cross-curricular writing,
  159-173

Daily language practice, 191
Daybooks *of Critical Reading*
  and Writing, 195
Desk-side conferences, 177
Dialogue writing, 164

Dialogues, imaginary, 164
Dictionary activities, 214
Documentary, 166
Drafting, 49, 230
Dramatic scenarios, 165

Editing,
  Conference guidelines, 177
  Peer, 187
Editing and proofreading, 55,
  231
Editorials, 81-82, 167
Elements of literature, 83, 123,
  237, 246
E-mail, 101, 167, 240
Essay tests, 133, 248
Essays,
  Expository, 63, 233
  Persuasive, 65, 233
Evaluating student writing,
  Assessment rubrics, 180-186
  Formative, 178
  Overview, 176
  Summative, 178
  Teacher rating sheet, 179
Evaluation, peer, 187-188
Exit slips, 165
Experiences, personal
  approach, 153-154
Expository essays, 63, 233

Feature article, 166, 167
Finding a focus, 47-48
First draft, writing, 49, 230
First thoughts, 165
Focused writings, 165
Formative assessment, 178
Framework, writing, 20
Friendly letters, 75, 235

✱ The start-up and enrichment activities are found after each set of chapter notes.